Terry Eagleton

transitions

General Editor: Julian Wolfreys

---

transitions Series
Series Standing Order ISBN 0–333–73684–6
(*outside North America only*)

You can receive future titles in this series as they are published by
placing a standing order. Please contact your bookseller or, in case of
difficulty, write to us at the address below with your name and address,
the title of the series and the ISBN quoted above.

Customer Services Department, Macmillan Distribution Ltd
Houndmills, Basingstoke, Hampshire RG21 6XS, England

---

transitions

Terry Eagleton

David Alderson

First published 2004 by
PALGRAVE MACMILLAN
Houndmills, Basingstoke, Hampshire RG21 6XS and
175 Fifth Avenue, New York, N.Y. 10010
Companies and representatives throughout the world

PALGRAVE MACMILLAN is the global academic imprint of the Palgrave Macmillan division of St. Martin's Press, LLC and of Palgrave Macmillan Ltd. Macmillan® is a registered trademark in the United States, United Kingdom and other countries. Palgrave is a registered trademark in the European Union and other countries.

ISBN 0–333–80127–X hardback
ISBN 0–333–80128–8 paperback

This book is printed on paper suitable for recycling and made from fully managed and sustained forest sources.

A catalogue record for this book is available from the British Library.
A catalog record for this book is available from the Library of Congress.

10   9   8   7   6   5   4   3   2   1
13 12 11 10 09 08 07 06 05 04

Printed in China

Contents

General Editor's Preface

Transitions: *transition* –, n. of action. 1. A passing or passage from one condition, action or (rarely) place, to another. 2. Passage in thought, speech, or writing, from one subject to another. 3. a. The passing from one note to another. b. The passing from one key to another, modulation. 4. The passage from an earlier to a later stage of development of formation ... change from an earlier style to a later; a style of intermediate or mixed character ... the historical passage of language from one well-defined stage to another.

The aim of *Transitions* is to explore passages, movements and the development of significant voices in critical thought, as these voices determine and are mediated by acts of literary and cultural interpretation. This series also seeks to examine the possiblities for reading, analysis and other critical engagements which the very idea of transition – such as the transition effected by the reception of a thinker's *oeuvre* and the heritage entailed – makes possible. The writers in this series unfold the movements and modulation of critical thinking over the last generation, from the first emergences of what is now recognized as literary thoery. They examine as well how the transitional nature of theoretical and critical thinking is still very much in operation, guaranteed by the hybridity and heterogeneity of the field of literary studies. The authors in the series share the common understanding that, now more than ever, critical thought is both in a state of transition and can best be defined by developing for the student reader an understanding of this protean quality. As this *tranche* of the series, dealing with particular critical voices, addresses, it is of great significance, if not urgency, that the texts of particular figures be reconsidered anew.

This series desires, then, to enable the reader to transform her/his own reading and writing transactions by comprehending past developments as well as the internal transitions worked through by particular literary and cultural critics, analysts, and philosophers. Each book in the series offers a guide to the poetics and politics of such thinkers, as well as interpretative paradigms, schools, bodies of thought, historical and cultural periods, and the genealogy of particular concepts, while transforming these, if not into tools or methodologies, then into conduits for directing and channelling thought. As well as transforming the critical past by interpreting it from the perspective of the present day, each study enacts transitional readings of critical voices and well-known literary texts, which are themselves conceivable as having been transitional and influential at the moments of their first appearance. The readings offered in these books seek, through close critical reading and theoretical engagement. to demonstrate certain possibilities in critical thinking to the student reader.

It is hoped that the student will find this series liberating because rigid methodologies are not being put into place. As all the dictionary definitions of the idea of transition above suggest, what is important is the action, the passage: of thought, of analysis, of critical response, such as are to be found, for example, in the texts of critics whose work has irrevocably transformed the critical landscape. Rather than seeking to help you locate yourself in relation to any particular school or discipline, this series aims to put you into action, as readers and writers, travellers between positions, where the movement between poles comes to be seen as of more importance than the locations themselves.

Julian Wolfreys

Acknowledgements

I would like to express my thanks to a number of people who, consciously or not, have provided me with various forms of help and support in the writing of this book, especially Howard Booth, Noel Castree, Laura Chrisman, Tony Crowley, Azzedine Haddour, Ken Hirschkop, Benita Parry, Laura Peters, Andrew McNeillie and Alan Sinfield. I am particularly grateful to Richard Kirkland for his scrupulous and insightful reading of Chapter 3. Stephen Regan read the whole manuscript for Palgrave Macmillan and made valuable suggestions on how it might be improved. Clearly none of these people can be held responsible for the book's contents.

This is also the appropriate place to register appreciation of a rather different kind to Jeff Moxham, who leant me a copy of *Literary Theory* back in 1984 and encouraged me both to pursue the study of literature and to recognise the ideological implications of such study.

Both the editors of this series, Julian Wolfreys and Anna Sandeman at Palgrave Macmillan, were extraordinarily patient in waiting for me to deliver the final manuscript. Michael Dunning and Matthew Frost provided many of the distractions which in part made that patience necessary so I guess that deserves acknowledgement too.

In the process of writing this book I changed institutions and so did Terry Eagleton, with the result that he ended up occupying an office only four doors down from me. I did finally get round to letting Terry know what I was up to, but, just for the record, I chose not to discuss the book with him in any detail. I am indebted to him, however, for letting me see draft copies of chapters of his forthcoming book, *After Theory*.

Finally, more formal acknowledgements and thanks are due: to A.P. Watt Ltd on behalf of Michael B. Yeats for permission to reprint extracts from W. B. Yeats's poetry in Chapter 3, and to the AHRB for generously funding a semester's sabbatical leave in which to complete this book under the Research Leave scheme.

Introduction

Thanks to the success of a certain book, it would be difficult to utter the words 'literary theory' without bringing Terry Eagleton's name to mind. That book – for some time now a bestseller – remains the one with which Eagleton has most frequently been linked. Its publication was nothing short of an event in the history of English Studies, so much so that there is a kind of inevitability about opening this account by referring to it. Yet the success of *Literary Theory* in many ways served to obscure Eagleton's achievements up to that point and has over shadowed subsequent work. First published in 1983, it was preceded by no fewer than nine other books, ranging from theological speculation on the significance of the body, to critical accounts of Shakespeare, modernism, the Brontës and Samuel Richardson, to (to my mind) the most rigorous theory of literary production to date and (already) a renunciation of that method in favour of a more eclectic, yet polemical, critical style. Since then, Eagleton has not only produced further critical accounts of literary and cultural theory, of both its history and recent developments, but has also written major works on the category of the aesthetic and the concept of tragedy, and has made telling interventions in the field of Irish Studies. This remarkable range and productivity has established him with little doubt as the foremost Marxist critic of recent times.

And yet, I feel the need to begin this book on the defensive, for a number of reasons. Partly because I am rather sceptical of the need for yet more accounts of literary theory and theorists which, in my experience, often have the effect of discouraging readers from getting to grips with the work being introduced to them. The implicit reasoning behind such texts is that the 'theory' being introduced is so formidably difficult as to require an introduction in the first place, and the effect tends rather to be a deferral of engagement than a hastening of it. The fact that there has not so far been such a book on Eagleton only partially set my mind at rest, since his writing is for the most part characterised by a lucidity the absence of which he has frequently criticised in others.

Those were not my only reservations, though, and one of the foremost in my mind had to do with the very existence of *Literary Theory* and other works by him, since a significant proportion of his output has been conceived as introductions – to Marxism, aesthetics, ideology, as well as literary theory – and there would therefore seem, on the face of it, something intellectually indefensible and perhaps personally embarrassing, even in these times of academic overproduction, to be writing an introduction to introductions. Moreover this aspect of his output has conditioned certain negative perceptions amongst other academics. In an extraordinary and at times absurd controversy conducted in the letters pages of the *London Review of Books* after Eagleton's highly critical review of Gayatri Spivak's *Critique of Postcolonial Reason*, Judith Butler protested 'Surely, neither the LRB nor Eagleton believes that theorists should confine themselves to writing introductory primers such as those he has chosen to provide' (Butler, 1999). Whilst technically registering that Eagleton has not merely written 'primers', the implicit slight is clear enough. Willy Maley, in an essay ostensibly intended to honour Eagleton's fiftieth birthday, effectively traduces his contribution to academic debate as a series of apparently vulgar Marxist witticisms.[1] The very absence of a book-length study of Eagleton to date – in contrast, say, to Paul de Man – may suggest that such perceptions are fairly widespread.

Such factors did influence my decision to take on the task, not merely because it seems to me that the depth and seriousness of Eagleton's work has been persistently misrepresented, but also because much of the commentary on him seems to me symptomatic of dismissive attitudes towards Marxism itself. The profoundly ideological message all too frequently disseminated these days is that Marxism is intellectually and historically *passé*. I return to a consideration of this in Chapter 2 especially, but it is a message which has also determined much of the content of this book, since my account of Eagleton stresses his primary affiliations with other Marxist intellectuals – not simply the 'Marxist canon', which in many accounts and for tendentious reasons, or simply because of ignorance, tend to peter out with Althusser – but with such figures as Aijaz Ahmad, Perry Anderson, David Harvey and Ellen Meiksins Wood (to name a few), figures who are lamentably – but alas not *un*accountably – neglected in theoretical debates in the supposedly interdisciplinary fields of literary and cultural studies. Reconnecting Eagleton with continuing debates on the left to which he has been an influential contributor and from which he has gained substantial critical resources allows us to see him less as the kind of Marxist maverick depicted by Maley than as someone steeped in a political and theoretical tradition which itself continues to engage resourcefully with the most pressing contemporary concerns. If one consequence of this book is that readers not only return to Eagleton's own writings, but go on to explore at least some of the wealth of Marxist analysis that has been produced over the last thirty years or so, that will be justification enough from my point of view for having written it.

Nonetheless, the misrepresentation of Eagleton noted above cannot simply be explained in terms of current attitudes towards Marxism; it also has to do with aspects of his output. Most straightforwardly, I think it has to do with his conscious decision to write for different audiences and with others' inability or unwillingness to distinguish between those writings. Works such as *Marxism and Literary Criticism, Ideology: An Introduction* and *The Illusions of Postmodernism*, whilst worthy of anyone's consideration, are more populist, whereas *Criticism and Ideology, Walter Benjamin, The Function of Criticism, The Ideology of the Aesthetic, Heathcliff and the Great Hunger* and *Sweet Violence*, say, are more innovative, make greater demands on the reader and represent more considered interventions. The distinction is not an absolute one, of course, but the greater part of this book focuses on the latter texts.

This said, it must be admitted that Eagleton's output is not conspicuous for innovative theoretical concepts which have been absorbed into the critical discourse of our times. It is difficult, for instance, to think of a particular term such as 'carnivalesque', 'habitus' or 'confession' which is as distinctively associated with him as those terms are with Bakhtin, Bourdieu and Foucault respectively. Geoff Wade writes that 'What does not permeate his work is an apprehendable, steadily developing "Eagleton's Theory of …" ' (Wade, 1994, 224). Again, Wade's point seems to me to misrepresent the case somewhat: there are certain themes which have consistently preoccupied Eagleton over the years, which I discuss below, and there are also major statements about those themes. Nonetheless the point that, at least after *Criticism and Ideology*, there is no attempt to elaborate a theoretical system is something that needs to be addressed, and there are at least two related points to be made about this. First, there are principled reasons for Eagleton's later reluctance to elaborate any such theoretical system, since there is a strong sense in his post-Althusserian

writings of the overvaluation of theory, a conviction that theory
cannot do the work of history, and that any theoretical elaboration
produced in circumstances detached from political struggle can only
represent an academicist assimilation of Marxism. Starting from
certain presuppositions which contradict these principles, then,
Wade fails to register the true value of Eagleton's writing, which in my
view lies precisely in its mode of engagement.

   The second point has to do with that mode of engagement,
distinguished principally by its dialectical spirit. If Eagleton refuses
to elaborate a theoretical system on principled grounds, his interventions in contemporary debates tend rather to point up the contradictions which propel those debates, to grasp the ideologically
determined positive and negative qualities of intellectual trends, and
to suggest what it might take for us to press beyond the contradictions
embodied in those trends, not merely at the level of ideas, but of social
relations. This accounts for key features of Eagleton's often polemical
style which have at different times and in different measures generated
confusion and resentment. It permits him in all sincerity to argue: that
Raymond Williams's position was 'a parody of the classic relation
between revolutionary intellectual and proletariat' (Eagleton, 1976,
35), whilst nonetheless concluding that 'no contribution could be
more vital than his' (Eagleton, 1976, 42) in the debate about Marxist
aesthetics; that Gayatri Spivak's arcane style represents 'the overcod-
ings of an academic coterie' but that she possesses 'a quite formidable
span of reference, which leaves most other cultural theorists looking
dismally parochial' (Eagleton, 2003, 160–1); or that Roy Foster's 'intellectual suavity ... conceals an extraordinary ideological naivety; and
this ... is a feature of the spuriously as well as admirably disinterested
[Anglo-Irish] tradition he inherits' (Eagleton, 2003, 231). That dialectical mode of engagement is, of course, one which extends to Eagleton's
consideration of more general trends within intellectual debate, and
permits him to grasp deconstruction, for instance, as both audaciously
radical, yet ultimately liberal reformist in its ideological bearings. Such
dialectical assessments emphatically do not constitute a kind of fence-
sitting – there is rarely any question of Eagleton occupying some
middle ground. Rather the force of each dialectical strand of argument
should be registered in full; neither should be read as tempering the
other, as if it were some display of characteristically English 'judicious-
ness'. In what follows, I have not attempted to downplay Eagleton's
polemicism, the value of which lies as much in the sense of urgency it

communicates as in its astuteness, though I hope to have avoided travestying such polemic as mere rant as some have not.

It is perhaps inevitable – a consequence that is of history rather than any personal limitations – that a Marxist critic in such times as these will adopt a mostly negative evaluative role in cultural debates. The transformation from the Marxist scientist of *Criticism and Ideology* to Benjaminian eclectic evident in Eagleton's later work was in part the consequence of a personal theoretical shift, but it was also no doubt conditioned by political defeats for the left which made the very idea of *constructive* socialist engagement less plausible. Yet, despite his reputation as a polemicist, it is not true simply to say that Eagleton's principal value resides wholly in asserting what tends to be repressed in current theoretical concerns. Throughout the period which has witnessed the hegemony of postmodern thought, Eagleton has not only critically engaged with such thought, but has maintained a fidelity to certain ideas formulated in his early career which have found, in the languages of deconstruction and psychoanalysis in particular, new formulations. These have to do with ethics and politics in their broadest senses, with nature, culture and ideology, the body, subjectivity and history. Rather than simply rehearse what by now are for many (at least on the left) familiar criticisms of postmodernism, I have spent a good deal of Chapter 2 emphasising these more positive contributions.

Finally, I should provide the reader with some orientations. I have attempted to take seriously the aims of this series to introduce students and general readers to a range of contemporary critical thought, and have consequently tried not to take too much for granted. This presents particular problems with a figure such as Eagleton whose style of argument is, as I have just stressed, very much one of engagement. This has frequently meant not only that I have needed to gloss Eagleton's own arguments but also those with which he is engaging. Naturally, some readers will find such accounts more helpful than others, and some will no doubt disagree with aspects of the accounts I have provided. Elsewhere, I have provided summaries of arguments which have been advanced by others on the left and on which Eagleton has drawn. These I take to be the necessary correctives to currently received wisdoms in literary and cultural studies about the analytical value of Marxism. They begin with an account of Marx's own arguments and their influence on Eagleton which, whatever its inadequacies, I hope will serve to make readers engage with its materialist method and revise their willingness to dismiss Marxism as 'metanar-rative'. As an introduction to Marxism, it dwells at least as much on outlining the logic and mystifications of the commodity as it does on epochal differences, since such an understanding of Marxism is important for the later discussion of postmodernism. This brief sum-mary of Marx's ideas is rendered progressively more complex over the course of Chapter 1 by an outline of some of Eagleton's major work from the 1970s. In an attempt to lend some added coherence to this chapter, I have also focused on a particular period of English social, political and literary history, that of the long nineteenth century, many of the concerns of which remain significant in cultural debates down to the present.

Moving into the 1980s, critique rather than theoretical elaboration became a more prominent element in Eagleton's output, though he also refused to cling safely to a 'pure' Marxism uncontaminated by contact with new currents of thought. Few other Marxists have been prepared to engage in quite such an inventive yet ultimately uncom-promising way with these currents. Some simply dismissed poststruc-turalist or postmodernist 'irrationalism'; others attempted to minimise Marxism's differences with poststructuralism; still others became postmarxists. Even now, it is still not entirely clear (at least to me) what the losses and gains of this engagement have been for Eagleton's thought, but what is more important than the fetishisation of an indi-vidual's 'career' is the effects of that work, and, in engaging with poststructuralism and postmodernism on and with its own terms, and thereby refusing to retreat into a language which was regrettably sim-ply becoming increasingly foreign to those other than the shrinking body of *New Left Review* readers, he has continued to remind students and others of the political implications and limitations of the discourse they articulate. Of course, such a strategy has its dangers too. There is always the risk of becoming too caught up not only in the terminology of the discourse but also in its habits of thought. Alternatively, in never matching up to the 'rigours' of that discourse because speaking from a position insufficiently inside it – yes, decon-struction also polices its borders – one's own work might end up look-ing to zealous practitioners like a pale imitation of that discourse or, worse, an uncomprehending perversion of it. Ideology powerfully determines the blindness of readers. I hope Chapter 2 serves to impress on readers the degree to which Eagleton's deconstructive practice is a knowing appropriation of it.

When Blackwells published *The Idea of Culture* in 2000, the lurid, almost gothic publicity declared 'Eagleton is back'. Hasta la vista baby. The fact that he'd been completing three volumes on Irish culture (one of them *for* Blackwells) is perhaps to English ways of thinking one way of going away for a bit; possibly even of being repressed. To some, his engagement with that eclectic and fraught 'discipline' called Irish Studies remains – and in light of subsequent work appears even more clearly to represent – something of a lacuna for him, but since it brought to the fore an aspect of his work that has been there in one way or another throughout, I have devoted a chapter to it. Doing so also provided a means of discussing postcolonialism, a field of study which both relates to a historical period and entails an extension of 'post-' theoretical concerns into an explicitly political field. (It also, in some ways, embodies a tension between these two definitions, since for some the postcolonial condition is said to precede decolonisation.) In Chapter 3 more than any other I have felt it necessary to provide some sense of the field, since its tensions and disputes are overdetermined by its interdisciplinarity as much as by any explicit ideological and political positions adopted within it. As with all of the chapters in the book, whilst it clearly privileges a particular perspective, I hope it provides a reasonably coherent sense of the general context in which Eagleton has launched his interventions.

One of the remits of this series, though, is to focus general critical theoretical concerns by discussing particular literary texts. Such discussions appear throughout this book in ways which some may encounter as interruptions. If they appear as such, they nonetheless hopefully serve as ways of making concrete its more abstract preoccupations. In each case, the reader will no doubt be struck by the care which I have taken to outline Eagleton's arguments. This is not simply out of a dutiful or even over-scrupulous sense of the need for such attentiveness, but because of the determinate complexity of the arguments themselves which have a habit of remorselessly pursuing dialectical contradictions through their every permutation. It is rare in Eagleton's work to encounter a linear argument such as lends itself to summary. More frequently, each paragraph announces a crucial qualification or presents the reader with an inversion of the logic of what has gone before. This has presented me with problems that I am far from confident I have overcome, particularly in the opening chapter's outline of *Criticism and Ideology*, but if I have erred on the side of a meticulous reproduction of Eagleton's arguments it is because I think that is

preferable to eliminating their complexities. The book ends – again in
conformity with the series' remit, but perhaps anticlimactically, given
the content of its various chapters – with a discussion of Oscar Wilde's
The Picture of Dorian Gray. I make no claims for this as an 'Eagletonian'
reading, but instead have considered certain critical appropriations of
Wilde, including Eagleton's, in ways which conveniently permit me to
recapitulate some of the concerns of the main chapters of this book
(Marxism, postmodernism, Irish culture), as well as to discuss one
example of Eagleton's 'creative' output, his play *St Oscar*. My discussion
of *Dorian Gray* also returns me to certain reflections on nineteenth-
century culture which were an important part of the opening chapter
and ultimately once again to tragedy and the body.

All of which means I have neglected elements of Eagleton's output in
conformity both with what I consider to be some of its most important
themes and with at least some of my own interests. This, then, should
not be mistaken for an intellectual biography. There is no extended discussion, for instance, of his involvement with the Catholic left, though
I do highlight the relevance of some of Eagleton's theological speculations, partly through his extraordinary reading of *The Merchant of
Venice*. Some will regret the privileging of engagements with certain
thinkers rather than others. Neither Habermas nor Bakhtin, for
instance, get much of a mention, and whilst I have indicated some ways
in which Walter Benjamin has exerted an influence on Eagleton, I have
not attempted any systematic account of that influence (partly because
I think that it is not, and could not be, systematic). My decisions in
these respects have been determined by political priorities, by a sense
that the crucial engagements are with intellectual forces within cultural
debate which are more or less dominant.

It should be possible to read each chapter discretely, but there are
also connections between them which I would want to stress. For this
reason, I hope readers will not simply raid it for the particular summary which is most important to them, since an awareness of
Eagleton's critique of postmodernism will illuminate what he has to
say about Irish Studies, and, of course, a half-way decent understanding of his Marxism is ultimately indispensable to any grasp of his work
at all. That, then, must be our starting point.

1 Marxism, Culture and English Studies

It is impossible to understand Terry Eagleton's work without some sense of the central tradition out of which it emerges, and this in itself is a complex phenomenon. Marxism is a tradition of thought which includes numerous interpretations, developments and modifications of the insights of Marx himself, some of which constitute necessary amendments to the inherent limitations of those insights whilst others result from attempts to be consistent to then in historically changed circumstances. Eagleton has drawn widely on this tradition and has contributed to it by demonstrating a degree of openness to contemporary theoretical and philosophical developments. For some Marxists, indeed, he is something of a heterodox figure. Donald Morton, for instance, rather sniffily refers to him as 'by no means a classical Marxist' (Morton, 2001, 36), a comment which would no doubt surprise those who think of him as a self-appointed keeper of the faith because he has maintained a degree of fidelity to key elements of classical Marxist theory, such as that of base and super-structure, which has distinguished him in the largely post-Marxist world of contemporary cultural and literary theory. Issues of fidelity and innovation are complex ones in Eagleton's writings, though. His major work of the 1970s, *Criticism and Ideology*, for instance, is a dialectical response to the writings of two very different figures, the English left intellectual, Raymond Williams, and the French Marxist Pierre Macherey, which some have claimed is rather too derivative of the latter but which, in fact, in its grasp of the limitations of both of these thinkers, ends up being both more insightful than either and more orthodox in its Marxism. Some sense of both Williams's and Macherey's work is therefore crucial to an understanding of Eagleton's project in that text which will be the principal focus of this chapter. But also necessary is some account of Marxism itself, not merely as a prelude to a discussion of that work, but also by way of introduction to the concerns of later chapters. The ideas of Marx have been rehearsed so many times, it might appear superfluous to do so again here,[1] but one of my other intentions is to provide an account which may act as a corrective to the conveniently travestied versions which form straw targets in so much contemporary cultural theory.

Marxism and history

> The present is … not identical with itself: there is that within it which points beyond it, as indeed the shape of every historical present is structured by its anticipation of a possible future. (Eagleton, 1991, 106)

Marxism is fundamentally a theory of history which should entail a commitment to social change; that is, a commitment to a socialist future in which the forces of production are not owned privately as they are in capitalist societies but under common ownership. Marxism is not therefore simply a moral imperative, an injunction that this is how things should be. In fact, Marx wrote very little about how societies might be organised in a post-capitalist future, even if various, mostly Stalinist or neo-Stalinist, political regimes have claimed a Marxist provenance. Rather it claims a scientific status, possessing much in common with other sciences such as economics and sociology, though being reducible to neither. It makes claims about how and why the majority of people are oppressed and what it is about capitalist societies that makes them vulnerable to change by precisely those people. Despite the popular representation of Marxists as dreamers and idealists therefore, Marxism defines itself against mere utopianism as a realist creed. Much of what follows does not initially deal with cultural, still less literary, matters, but since Marxism is the most interdisciplinary of sciences – not because it attempts to forge connections between things, but because it refuses the academic compartmentalisation of things in the first place – this outline is, in every sense, necessary.

Marx's theory of history might be summed up in one sentence: 'Men make their own history, but not of their own free will; not under circumstances they themselves have chosen but under the given and inherited circumstances with which they are directly confronted' (Marx, 1973, 146). The apparent banality of this statement is deceptive, since it might be understood to condense a number of key features of Marx's philosophy. First of all, it is a *materialist* statement, a claim that the activities of people – rather than, say, divine providence, fate or the necessary unfolding of ideas – are the driving force of history. Indeed, that word 'make' can be interpreted quite literally, since it is in the process of materially producing and reproducing our world – in the construction of the buildings we live and work in, the clothes we wear and the food we eat, as well as the tools and machines we use, the books we read, and so on – that history is made. If we are rational animals – a fact which, as Marx famously commented, distinguishes an architect from a bee – we are also *productive* animals, and it is the conjunction of these two aspects of our being – the way, that is, that each of these bears on the other – that is in many ways at the crux of Marxist analysis. Our condition as reflective and productive, rather than merely instinctual beings, constitutes indeed our species being and this is something we will return to, since it has important implications for our understanding of culture. We are also, though, social beings, and necessarily so, since it is in the material production and reproduction of our world that we enter into relationships with others – no one is truly self-sufficient – and hence form societies. However, these relationships are clearly not ones we negotiate for ourselves. Rather, we enter into an already existing set of relations bound up with this productive process. In our labours we work for others or we employ others; we may be self-employed, but even this possibility is made possible by particular social arrangements. It is for this specific reason that Marx claims we do not make history in circumstances of our own choosing.

But what is the relationship between making, or material production, and *history*? By history, Marx does not simply mean something like 'the past'. Rather, he is referring to a dynamic process, the impetus for which lies in changes occurring at the level of production, and more precisely in the conflicts generated there. For Marx, historical epochs are determined by certain dominant *forces and relations of production*. By the forces of production, he means the technology and labour which are involved in production, whilst relations of production are those human relations which characterise the productive process-under feudalism, for instance, between serf and lord, or, under capitalism, between boss and worker. It is crucial to note that the nature of these relations differ historically since that between lord and serf was part of a rigidly hierarchical structure requiring loyalty, obedience and the payment of tithes on the part of the serf in return for paternal protection from his lord, whereas that between boss and worker is a contract apparently 'freely' entered into, though for the vast majority of us, of course, there is no option but to accept the employment 'offered' to us. We are paid for this labour. Of course: another seemingly banal point, but one which also has the most profound implications (and it is one of the aims of Marxism to defamiliarise our relations to the world, to make us think again about those things we take for granted, possibly as being in some sense 'natural'). That capacity to work, our labour-power, is therefore our possession – for most people their most fundamental possession, that which is the basis of whatever wealth they might go on to acquire – and we (must) sell it. This is not true of all societies – those, for instance, in which your labour power is owed to others, in some sense an obligation to them. Labour power in capitalist societies is therefore a commodity, and just as other commodities compete with each other for our attention, so our own labour power competes with that of others who might do our job. It is also in the labour process that the secret of *the* distinctive feature of capitalism – its expansiveness – resides.

In the majority of cases, labour power is sold to produce commodities, and such commodities are also somewhat taken for granted by us in our daily lives. In doing so we fetishise these most paradoxical of creatures. The capitalist commodity may be real enough, but it is also an abstraction, since its *use value* – that quality for which we buy it in the first place – has been transformed into *exchange value*. That is, in the process of being bought and sold, it has been rendered the equivalent of something else. A certain kind of watch, for instance, might be worth the same as a fridge or two stepladders, it doesn't matter what – and the fact that it doesn't matter *is* what matters here, since from the perspective of exchange value everything is robbed of that particularity which resides in its use value. What mediates between these 'equivalent' items is money: we wouldn't pay for that watch by handing a fridge across the counter, or vice versa, and not only for practical reasons. Money becomes a necessity in societies in which the process of exchange has become so complex as to require some universally accepted standard of value (initially, this takes the form of a particular kind of commodity, such as gold). But in fulfilling a certain use value, in facilitating exchange, money also acquires a remarkable status as the very embodiment of value, the possession of which in greater and greater amounts confers greater and greater social power on the individual. Capital, though, is not a mere synonym for money. If we stash a wadge of fivers under the mattress we aren't acting like capitalists; we are simply hoarding. The capitalist, rather, typically invests money in the production of commodities in order to reap more money in the form of profit, and is therefore acting in accordance with the status which money has acquired as the embodiment of value.

Under the logic of exchange value, labour, too, by being rendered a commodity is rendered the equivalent of other commodities, including other forms of labour, but it differs from other commodities in this specific respect: it can be exploited as a watch or a stepladder can't. It is also the property of humans who generally dislike being exploited. Marx subscribes to a labour theory of value in which the (exchange) value of a commodity is determined by the necessary cost incurred by paying workers in order to satisfy their needs. Of course, there are other costs associated with production, such as that of machinery, but that machinery is also a commodity which has had labour invested in it, and was no doubt produced by other tools which themselves needed to be produced by workers, and so on right down to the point at which raw materials are extracted or fashioned from nature by other men and women. We might regard the commodity therefore as a kind of congealed labour, and this determines its value. (Value is related to but not identical to the price of a commodity, though for most of the three volumes of *Capital* Marx assumes commodities do indeed exchange at their value in money terms. Perhaps the relationship is best put by stating that whatever else determines the price of a commodity, it must at least realise its value.) What money therefore measures is the value of the labour which has gone into the production of a given commodity. When Marx claims that in the process of exchange commodities are fetishised what he means is that the social relations which are necessary to that process are masked in an exchange between things. When I buy a bag of sugar, I think merely about how much it costs, not (usually) about how it was produced, even though what I pay for it entails a measurement of that human cost. There is a paradox about this to which we will return later: the process of exchange is a tangible one, and in that sense real, but it is also a mystification in that it masks the real basis of the value of commodities. It is this process that for Marx endows commodities with an apparent life of their own, not least since they appear to be in competition with each other, just as the relative strength or weakness of a commodity is registered on the stock market.

But there is another, crucial dimension to the realisation of value in capitalist societies, and that is the process by which capitalism extracts *surplus value* in the production of that commodity. Surplus value is the difference between the value of the commodity and the cost of its production. The costs of production entail both constant and variable capital. Constant capital – for instance, machinery – is that which is simply calculated into the cost of the commodity, whereas variable capital refers specifically to labour costs as determined by market rates. A crucial norm which must be assumed in production, though, is the *socially necessary labour time* required to produce a certain commodity – that is, the normal amount of time it takes to produce a certain product in a society given such things as that society's stage of technological development. If a person is paid the market rate and produces at no faster than that of socially necessary labour time no surplus value is realised. Hence the task of the capitalist – the task, that is, which capitalism sets for her – is to lower the costs of production, always and necessarily in competition with other capitalists. If the costs of production are universally reduced the value of the commodity simply drops, and this, for complex reasons, is part of the reason why Marx claims there is an inherent tendency for the rate of profit to fall. That tendency may – though does not necessarily (Fine, 1989, 67–8) – generate crises in capitalism which, for this and other reasons, such as its tendency to overproduce commodities, is constitutionally prone to crises. At such moments, class conflicts inevitably become more acute, though the consequences of such conflicts are far from predictable.

A variety of means might be employed by capitalists to achieve competitive advantage, all of them at substantial human cost: an extension of the working day without an increase in wages or a reduction/freeze in wages for the same amount of work are the crudest and most obviously exploitative; straightforward injunctions to work faster under closer management surveillance might produce limited 'productivity gains' as well as greater stress and exhaustion in the individual worker; increased mechanisation of production results in lay-offs. In the modern world, an increasingly important means of realising surplus value is the location of factories in parts of the world where resistance to capitalism is weak and wages are consequently lower – often dramatically lower – than in much of the West. The fetishisation of commodities effectively undermines our grasp of such processes of exploitation, even though we may occasionally become aware of them, as, for instance, when a company is boycotted.

Hence Marx's sense that capitalism necessarily generates class conflict, a conflict between the two structural principles *necessary* to capitalism – capital and labour – regardless of the individual characters of those who are grouped together under those terms. The reformist vision of workers and capitalists existing peaceably (as Elizabeth Gaskell envisaged in the conclusion of her novel *North and South*, for instance) is improbable – and even strikes us intuitively as so – since it mistakes as personal disposition the systematic pressures on the capitalist to accumulate, and therefore to exploit. But in confronting the contradictions of capitalism and its class antagonisms we encounter highly complex matters, matters which determine Eagleton's particular mode of critique.

The conflicts generated by this struggle are likely to take various forms. Mostly, as in Trade Union disputes, these include struggles to maintain certain privileges, resist new forms of exploitation or increase wages, and only rarely connect with the larger political struggle to overturn the historically particular mode of social organisation we call capitalism. But what this account of capitalism neglects – fixated as it is, and as all properly socialist accounts should be, on exploitation – is the liberty which historically capitalism has delivered and which, at least for some, continues to deliver. Marx recognised that capitalism was thoroughly contradictory, which is to say that he grasped it historically in its *dialectical* form. He understood that it represented a form of progress even if he never underestimated the new forms of exploitation which it brought with it. Indeed, the bourgeoisie itself has played nothing less than a revolutionary role in overturning feudal or neo-feudal orders which set limits to the economic growth of those capitalist forces which were developing within them. The industrial revolution – so-called indeed because the profound changes it brought about were at the time considered comparable in extent with those wrought by the French Revolution – signalled capitalism's dominance in Britain and prompted Marx's and Engels' speculations in *The Communist Manifesto* of 1848:

> The bourgeoisie, where it has got the upper hand, has put an end to all feudal, patriarchal, idyllic relations. It has pitilessly torn asunder the motley ties that bound man to his 'natural superiors', and has left remaining no other nexus between man and man than naked self-interest, than callous 'cash payment'. It has drowned the most heavenly ecstasies of religious fervour, of chivalrous enthusiasm, of philistine sentimentalism, in the icy water of egotistical calculation. It has resolved personal worth into exchange value, and in place of the numberless indefeasible chartered freedoms, has set up that single unconscionable

> freedom – Free Trade. In one word, for exploitation, veiled by religious
> and political illusions, it has substituted naked, shameless, direct, brutal
> exploitation. (Marx, 1977, 223)

Marx's and Engels' admiration here is for the bourgeoisie's demystifi-
cation of an older order which sanctioned exploitation by appealing to
natural and divine hierarchies. Their grasp of this historical moment is
therefore to be distinguished from those other critiques of capitalism
which emerged around the same time, and which were more influential on the literary figures of the day, but which tended merely to
lament the passing of a paternalistic order. This does not mean that the
bourgeoisie is simply lauded for its achievements: the advantage of its
social dominance for Marx and Engels is that its exploitation of its
workforces is calculated, open and self-evident, making a revolutionary challenge to the bourgeoisie on the part of the working class
more likely. The implication here is that, whereas feudal societies were
legitimated by something which is not quite called *ideology* here,
the exploitative relations of bourgeois society are not so veiled, and
since the bourgeois social order is so nakedly exploitative its overthrow
is imminent. There is an optimism about this, obviously conditioned
by the radicalism of the times in which it was written – 1848, the year of
European revolution – which the later Marx necessarily had to modify:
capitalism, as we have seen, produces its own 'veil' in the form of
commodity fetishism, for instance. Indeed, the later Marx, and a great
deal of the Marxist tradition following him, has been devoted to
analysing the specific forms of ideology characteristic of a bourgeois
society which has proved more durable than Marx at first seemed to
envisage. We will return to the crucial concept of ideology below.

   We should not assume, either, that the bourgeoisie was admired by
Marx simply for the rather negative reason that it ushered in openly
exploitative relations. The radical bourgeoisie – the class which, for
instance, was at the forefront of campaigns for democracy in the late
eighteenth and early nineteenth centuries – claimed to stand for
freedom, and indeed freedom of a necessarily contradictory sort is an
integral part of the kind of exchange relations which capitalism
produces. The individual, in possession of her money, is free to
dispense with it as she wills, and indeed the process of exchange
implies an equality between those who are engaged in that process.
Certain principles of individuality, freedom and equality, then, are
determined by the material social relations of capitalism; they are not

simply ideas which the bourgeoisie just happened to advocate. In one sense, the autonomous human subject generated by and conceptualised under such conditions is a progressive figure, one who appears logically to demand the dignity of a democratic social order. For instance, even in what seem to us the bizarre hybrid social conditions of capitalism and 'communism' which exist in China today, the atomising, individualising properties of a capitalism which is encouraged by the state exist in considerable and increasing tension with that same authoritarian state control. If this early phase of capitalism as described by Marx generated a sense of the individual's autonomy and self-possession, a later one, as we will see in the following chapter, has tended to erode that sense of individual integrity, promoting a sense of the fragmentation of the subject.

This positive dimension of the bourgeois subject though, masks a negative one: the repression through commodity fetishism of a grasp of the social relations which render that individualism possible in the first place. Moreover, bourgeois principles of freedom are necessarily compromised by the bourgeois social order itself, which is therefore incapable of realising them fully. This is not least the case because it compels those individuals who are grouped together by capitalism as capitalists or workers to organise and defend their interests each against the other, to sacrifice, that is, that very individuality. As David Harvey explains,

> The working class must struggle to preserve and reproduce itself not only physically but also socially, morally and culturally. The capitalist class must necessarily inflict a violence on the working class in order to sustain accumulation, at the same time as it must also check its own excesses and resist those demands on the part of the working class that threaten accumulation. (Harvey, 1999, 34–5)

The realisation of a genuine socialism would represent a realisation of the full potential of those principles of liberty which capitalism claims to deliver, but the individualism it generated would be unrecognisable from our current understanding of that term, since it would be a socialised individualism which grasped the necessity of interdependence between individuals. Eagleton has consistently highlighted the progressive, yet necessarily limited features of bourgeois freedoms:

> The bourgeoisie may be an obstacle to freedom, justice and universal well being today, but in its heyday it was a revolutionary force which

overthrew its feudal antagonists, which bequeathed the very ideas of
justice and liberty to its socialist successors, and which developed the
forces of production to the point where socialism itself might become a
feasible project. ... A socialism which needs to develop the forces of production from the ground up, without the benefits of a capitalist class
which has accomplished this task for it, will tend to end up as that
authoritarian form of state power we know as Stalinism. And a socialism
which fails to inherit from the middle class a rich legacy of liberal freedoms and civic institutions will simply reinforce that autocracy.
(Eagleton, 1997, 42–3)

There is a further progressive feature of capitalism touched on here,
and that is the very expansiveness by which it is characterised, its constant revolutionising of the means of production in search of greater
'efficiency' and profit which, Eagleton suggests, makes socialism – at
least socialism of a desirable sort – possible. Socialism can only come
about when the productive forces of societies are sufficiently developed to produce goods in such abundance that people are liberated
from the drudgery of mere subsistence, but the socialist deployment of
those forces must be for the common good and for the full realisation
of use rather than exchange values. This is Eagleton's means of
accounting for the failure to achieve genuine socialism in the Soviet
Union and in other states where it was once said by some actually to
have existed. This sense of the contradictoriness of capitalism – its
simultaneously progressive and oppressive features – is something we
will return to in our later discussion of colonialism.

The significance of this genuine appreciation of the progressiveness
of bourgeois society is important in the critical interventions Eagleton
has been making in relation to cultural theory since the early 1980s.
At roughly that point, as we will see, Eagleton began a process of
engagement with philosophical and theoretical tendencies outside
Marxism which challenged Marxism's hegemony within literary and
cultural theory. His openness to those tendencies entailed a sense that
much of it represented a desire to press the logic of bourgeois freedom
to its limits without a commitment to the necessary means by which
those limits might be surpassed. The contradictions generated within
such theory were a consequence of its *idealising* tendencies.

This question of idealism requires some brief explanation. Just as
the feudal order had generated its own nemesis in the bourgeoisie
by placing limits on capitalist 'freedom', so Marx argued bourgeois
society created its own 'gravediggers' in the form of the systematically

exploited working class. This process – in which one social order generates from within itself its own negation – is dialectical, though the materialist nature of this dialectic distinguishes Marx's thought from that of his primary philosophical influence, Hegel, for whom the dialectical development of history was an unfolding of ideas, the process by which mind in its self-determinations came ultimately to grasp itself as *essentially* self-determining. Though Hegel was not uncritical of capitalism, bourgeois society represented for him the culmination of the principle of freedom. For Marx – as we have already begun to see – ideas are strictly secondary to and determined by the development of material conditions. This opposition between the idealism of Hegel and the materialism of Marx is crucial to the Marxist tradition. Idealism, in its various forms represents an attempt to resolve at the level of ideas conflicts which are ultimately social and can only finally be resolved at the level of the social. It is for this reason that Eagleton distrusts that overestimation of 'theory' and what it might achieve which is characteristic of much contemporary debate.

However, Marx's analysis of history is not simply a descriptive account of historical change – it does not simply supply us with a methodology for, say, the interpretation of literature; it also enjoins active participation in that change. This is a feature of Marx's thought from its early stages, as evinced by the famous – to some notorious – statement that 'philosophers have only *interpreted* the world, in various ways; the point however is to change it' (Marx, 1975, 423). This is precisely a rejection of philosophy's attempts to produce idealist resolutions to what Marxism grasps as social contradictions. As Eagleton has put it, 'Like many an anti-philosopher, Marx is trying here to shift the whole terrain on which the discourse is pitched, grasping philosophical puzzles as both symptomatic of a real historical subtext, and as a way of thrusting that subtext out of sight' (Eagleton, 1997, 15). This tells us something too about Eagleton's own way of arguing, something which is sometimes attacked for being vulgar-Marxist and which can, at its worst, be rather gestural: his habit of contrasting academic debates with popular experience, as when he points out in relation to current postmodern leftism that 'In a world of short-term contracts, just-in-time deliveries, ceaseless downsizings and remodellings, overnight shifts of fashion and capital investments, multiple careers and multipurpose production, such theorists seem to imagine, astonishingly, that the main enemy is the naturalised, static and unchanging' (Eagleton, 2003, x). It is precisely at such moments that Eagleton's dialectical temper asserts itself, foregrounding what is repressed in a given mode of thought.

The account of class relations provided here is, of course, overly schematic and in danger of being accused of abstraction from real historical processes, a kind of ready template which might be mapped onto those processes and which is always in danger of falsifying them. It is true that in some Marxist analyses this template is invoked too readily, but, whilst Marx focused on the capital/labour antagonism because he saw this as the crucially, though not solely, determining force for historical change in capitalist societies, his accounts of particular social formations were always alert to the greater complexity of class distinctions and relations, drawing our attention to the need for careful materialist analysis in any given society. In the best Marxist criticism, class relations are apprehended in all their complexity, making allowances for alliances, compromises and complicities, social phenomena which have been particularly important in the development of English history, and which we will return to when considering Eagleton's reading of *Wuthering Heights*.

Meanwhile, there is a term which has been invoked a number of times already in this discussion, one indispensable to Marxist analysis and especially to Eagleton's work, since it is the Marxist concept which connects material history with the processes of conceptualisation and valuation which inform cultural production and the study of it.

Ideology

According to Marx's materialist theory of history, 'It is not the consciousness of men that determines their being, but, on the contrary, their social being that determines their consciousness' (Marx, 1977, 389). In other words, our thoughts and perceptions – even many of our feelings and intuitions, since 'spontaneity' is no guarantee of uncontamination – are conditioned by the kind of society we inhabit and the place we occupy within that society; ultimately, for Marxism, by those forces and relations of production which give to any social formation its specific character. The words quoted from Marx here are taken from his classic but controversial 'base and superstructure' formulation which claims that the economic base – the forces and relations of production – determine an ideological superstructure comprising such things as philosophy, religion, even law and politics, which govern our consciousness of social relations. Clearly literature and culture also belong to this sphere. What Marx doesn't specify in this formulation is the nature of that determination; nor does his use of the term ideology here seem particularly negative, as it usually is in Marxist theory. These facts provide some sense of the complexity of the term, a complexity which has only intensified with various subsequent Marxist theorisations of it as these have been determined both by ambiguities, contradictions and limitations in Marx's own work and by attempts to reconcile Marxism with various philosophical trends. Since it is impossible to provide here a general overview of this history, I limit myself here to an account of Eagleton's use of the term. What makes this a difficult task is that there is no Eagletonian theory of ideology, as there is, for instance, an Althusserian one. There are actually good reasons for this, as we shall see, though there is also the potential in the refusal of such theorisation for the term to become unwieldy and unhelpfully expansive in its application.

First, we need to be clear about the significance of ideology for the Marxist tradition. Though it can refer to explicitly held political convictions such as liberalism, conservatism or socialism, this is not its most important meaning (at least, not for our purposes). Still less is it used to suggest that a particular body of beliefs is narrowly doctrinal and probably inhumane, a definition which tends to be invoked by liberals in order to denigrate Marxism itself. Eagleton defines ideology as, roughly, 'those modes of feeling, valuing, perceiving and believing which have some kind of relation to the maintenance and reproduction of social power' (Eagleton, 1983, 15). What this suggests is that ideology emerges out of a current state of affairs which it then – in the form of feelings, values, perceptions and so on – helps to perpetuate. In capitalist societies, that state of affairs would be capitalist social relations themselves. The important point is that ideology is not something imposed by some force external to those material conditions we inhabit, but is rather determined by them. Let us take as an example, the social Darwinism which developed in the nineteenth century. Social Darwinism extended the principle that evolution entailed 'the survival of the fittest' – not a phrase used by Darwin incidentally – to human societies in a way which naturalised the individualistic and competitive social relations characteristic of capitalism. A novel such as George Gissing's *New Grub Street*, for instance, is dominated by this ideological mode of perception, since it depicts the competitive relations between authors in the literary marketplace of the 1890s in terms of those authors' physical and mental aptitudes to succeed. Admittedly, it does contain a plea to ameliorate the conditions of those who are constitutionally unsuited to such conditions, but such special pleading effectively only serves further to naturalise the maladaptation of the unfit and insulates the dominant social relations from thoroughgoing critique: it is a reformist gesture. Social Darwinism, then, made the historically specific features of capitalism appear to be inevitable because grounded in natural processes and the constitutional 'fitness' of individuals to succeed or fail. Moreover, Social Darwinism is not some antiquated mode of thought: it retains its potency in our own entrepreneurial times, as when we hear, for instance, that businesses need to lay off workers in order to be 'leaner and fitter'.

Ideology, though, is not for the most part used to refer to a set of beliefs which are simply fictitious. As Eagleton comments, 'epistemology does not divide neatly down the middle between strict science and sheer illusion' (Eagleton, 1976, 71). Just to take one rather banal instance, we can imagine one of those factory workers who has been made redundant by that leaner and fitter company resignedly commenting 'Well, that's the way things are.' One couldn't really argue that this was a false statement. Indeed, in one sense, it would be harder to find a truer one. But it might nonetheless be regarded as ideological if it fatalistically suggested that things couldn't be any other way, though even that degree of fatalism might be said to reflect the strength of class politics at its particular moment of utterance. Moreover, not all false notions are on that count ideological. It is clearly factually wrong, though not necessarily ideological, to believe that Derby County is the best football team in England. However, in certain contexts such a belief might be considered ideological – if, for instance, it involved such a strong compensatory psychological investment as to make the individual supporter content with his rather bleak and ill-paid job rounding up supermarket trolleys.

But there is another sense in which ideology cannot be said simply to designate a set of false ideas, since, as we have already seen, in the later writings of Marx ideology is bound up with the phenomenal world itself, not least in the form of commodity fetishism. Here Eagleton brings out further the significance of Marx's insight into this feature of capitalism as it has been elaborated by the Marxist tradition. First,

> the real workings of society are … veiled and occluded: the social character of labour is concealed behind the circulation of commodities,

which are no longer recognisable as social products. Secondly... society is fragmented by this commodity logic: it is no longer easy to grasp it as a totality, given the atomising operations of the commodity, which transmutes the collective activity of social labour into relations between dead, discrete things. And by ceasing to appear as a totality, the capitalist order renders itself less vulnerable to political critique. Finally, the fact that social life is dominated by *inanimate* entities lends it a spurious air of naturalness and inevitability: society is no longer perceptible as a human construct, and therefore as humanly alterable. (Eagleton, 1981, 85)

We will consider in more detail that aspect of commodification which atomises our perception of any social totality in discussing postmodernism. Note, though, that we are here about as far from some conspiracy theory of ideology as we could possibly get: ideology is spontaneously generated by the processes of exchange through no calculation of anyone's; it is not something disseminated – consciously or otherwise – by a dominant social group in order to serve their own interests, though this does not mean that ideology does not take such a form on occasions.

The original definition of ideology that we started out with is a pretty broad one. So far, we have narrowly considered power relations in terms of class, leaving Marxism vulnerable to the objection that it is blind to those forms of oppression determined, for instance, by sex and race. One way in which Eagleton has attempted to rectify these forms of 'blindness' on the part of Marxism, is simply to extend the meaning of ideology to include those ideas and perceptions which contribute to forms of oppression not based, or not primarily based, on class. This extension is in one sense positive, since it recognises that, say, sexist or racist beliefs are bound up with certain structures of power, but the expansion of the term in this way nonetheless forces us to confront certain theoretical problems, since it is impossible to trace gender ideology, for instance, to material social relations. The persistence of gendered oppositions such as those between active and passive, rational and irrational across time and cultures is a remarkable fact, even though the precise social relations determined by those oppositions may have differed. Nonetheless, gender ideology has been transformed by material historical changes. The rigid separation between work and home which brought about the middle-class valuation of the feminised sphere of the home, for instance, was largely a consequence of the spatial organisation of the city in the nineteenth century, as suburban life grew at a distance from working life at a factory or office (Hall and Davidoff, 1987). We may best conceive of gender ideology, then, in terms of another aspect of the Marxist theorisation of ideology, that articulated by Marx's collaborator, Engels, though mostly now associated with Althusser: relative autonomy. In allowing for the relative autonomy of ideology from material social relations, one recognises that ideological traditions exert their own strong pressures on those relations but are nonetheless themselves also crucially affected by shifts in the forces and relations of production. The determination of superstructure by base, then, should not be thought of as a straightforward one-way process. This may begin to rectify certain theoretical problems, but the practical political issue for Marxism has been to accept that feminist politics – or those of race or sexuality – should not be thought of as in some sense 'secondary' because primarily 'ideological'. There is also, though, a need to think through feminist and other politics not reducible to class in relation to broader social relations and forms of ideology, since gender ideology, though it entails specific considerations, does not exist in some discrete realm untouched by other forces. Any feminism – or indeed, other social movement – which neglects other structural determinants of power is likely to end up in some way contributing to their reproduction, just as Marxism has previously failed to take seriously issues irreducible to class.

The broad definition of ideology provided by Eagleton may initially appear vulnerable to the charge of under-theorisation, and evidence to support this charge can be found in his introductory book on ideology. This provides a history of the concept, but one problem with his mode of evaluating the different definitions he reviews is that he tends to point out the inadequacy of theoretical versions by invoking particular instances of ideology for which they cannot account, thereby effectively appealing to some more or less intuitive or a priori understanding of the term. Eagleton partially acknowledges this in his conclusion when he states that 'it is doubtful that one can ascribe to ideology any *invariable* characteristics at all. We are dealing less with some essence of ideology than with an overlapping network of "family resemblances" between different styles of signification' (Eagleton, 1991, 222). The advantage of this apparently undertheorised, anti-essentialist account, though, is precisely that it refuses to specify in advance the forms that ideology will take. As we have seen at the outset of this section, Eagleton's understanding of ideology is a functional one – it is defined in terms of what it does, rather than the forms it takes, in terms of its effects rather than its precise modes of working. This enables us to grasp ideology, not merely as variable phenomena which may be present in a particular social formation as, say, both commodity fetishism and Social Darwinism may be said to be, but also as historically contingent in the forms it takes: postmodern irony, for instance, is a determinate ideological *sensibility* not reducible to an explicit set of beliefs, whereas the belief in a divinely ordained hierarchy is a largely obsolete ideological *creed*.

For the most part, then, Eagleton understands ideology as a force defined by the conservative work it performs and determined by the particular power relations it in turn helps to perpetuate, a force whose forms are therefore inevitably variable. It remains, though, a critical term in the way that the superficially related concept of 'discourse' is not: it suggests the inadequacy of particular modes of perception in relation to social relations, and therefore implies that a more adequate understanding of those social relations is not only possible but necessary in order to redress imbalances of power and outright exploitation. 'Discourse' is often invoked as if it carried similar implications – as when we talk sceptically about the validity of discourses of sexuality – but in refusing epistemological certainties and regarding sceptically the truth content of all discourses its critical force is less potent. The concept of ideology is an indispensable concept for a left which must be at least as confident in its own analyses of the world as those powerful forces it opposes.

Wuthering Heights

As we have just seen, Marxism is concerned primarily with matters other and more important than literature, and a Marxist critical practice is not something which emerges spontaneously from an understanding of Marxism, but rather requires elaboration. Consideration of *Myths of Power*, Eagleton's book on the Brontës, is a convenient way of demonstrating some of the problems faced by such a practice as well as one of Eagleton's early responses to those problems. Eagleton's most rigorous theoretical model is provided in *Criticism and Ideology*, which is discussed in detail below, but aspects of his thinking in that slightly later and more abstract and complex text are foreshadowed in *Myths of Power*. Rather than attempt a synopsis of *Myths of Power* as a whole, though, I want to focus principally on the account of *Wuthering*

Heights, partly because his reading of this text is remarkably alert to its dialectical structure, but also because in the final chapter of this book I consider Eagleton's re-reading of this novel as part of his engagement with Irish Studies.

Naturally, Eagleton insists on establishing the specific social relations which characterised the society in which the Brontës lived. In doing so, he challenges the dehistoricising influence of critics such as Lord David Cecil, whose 1934 account of Emily Brontë stressed her geographical isolation from historical change – in Yorkshire, we learn, 'life remained essentially as it had been in the days of Queen Elizabeth; a life as rugged and unchanging as the fells and storm-scarred moors and lonely valleys which were its setting' (Cecil, 1960, 149) – and a world view which was that of a mystic who believed that the relations between the forces of storm and calm were directed by a single, ultimately harmonious principle. (One still, just occasionally, gets this line trotted out in student essays.) It is not that Eagleton was the first to challenge such a perspective, but leftist discussions prior to *Myths of Power* tended merely to celebrate its passionate challenge to dominant Victorian social conditions and orthodoxies. For Arnold Kettle, for instance, Heathcliff's rebellion was specifically 'that of the worker physically and spiritually degraded by the conditions and relationships of … [his] society', even if he later adopts the exploitative traits of those who dominated him, and his relationship with Catherine gestures towards, even if it clearly does not realise, an unaliented existence (Kettle, 1967, 144). Raymond Williams, on the other hand, agreed with Cecil that there were affinities between the passion of the novel and the Romantic sensibility of Blake, but considered this as integral to the rebelliousness of the 1840s, since 'to give that kind of value to human longing and need, to that absolute love of the being of another is to clash as sharply with the emerging system, the emerging priorities, as in any assault on material poverty' (Williams, 1970, 61). Eagleton's grasp of the context of the novel, though, is considerably more complex than either of these earlier accounts. Kettle's Marxism is insufficiently materialist in its treatment of the class relations depicted in *Wuthering Heights,* opting as he does to see Heathcliff as representative of the proletariat in revolt against capitalists, and both Kettle and Williams attribute to the novel too straightforward a protest against the values of a capitalist society. Certainly Eagleton recognises that the Brontës lived through a period which witnessed 'some of the fiercest class struggles in English society. … Their childhood witnessed machine-breaking; their adolescence Reform agitation and riots against the New Poor Law; their adulthood saw the Plug strikes and Chartism, struggles against the Corn Laws and for the Ten Hours Bill' (Eagleton, 1975, 3). But he is equally keen to stress that the relations between landed and industrial bourgeois classes at the time when the Brontës wrote their novels were not purely conflictual, and were characterised in certain respects by mutual interest. Whilst the gentry and aristocracy were ideologically at loggerheads with the industrial bourgeoisie in some respects, they also invested in and profited from industrial projects, just as many wealthier industrialists aspired to join the ranks of the landed classes by buying up estates, though it also took time – normally a few generations – for the *nouveau riche* to be assimilated. (Moreover, this process of buying into the estates of the gentry was not new – we find it referred to in Jane Austen, for instance.) Hence, the picture Eagleton constructs is not one of outright challenge on the part of the bourgeoisie in relation to the landed classes, but that of a 'steady convergence of interests, inherited from centuries of rapprochement between the industrial bourgeoisie and a capitalist landowning class' (Eagleton, 1975, 7). Moreover, these dominant classes were, if anything, united in their opposition to that working class radicalism of the time – principally Chartism – which threatened both their interests.

We will see shortly the significance for the novels of this tense, but increasingly stable convergence of interests. First, we need to be clear about the nature of the relationship Eagleton traces between this history and the Brontës' novels, since it is in methodology as well as in contextual nuance that his reading departs from previous Marxist accounts. Eagleton is not interested in some form of literary critical empiricism, with proving that the novels contain direct or even oblique references to the turbulent events of these years. Rather he takes his cue from the Marxist sociologist of literature, Lucien Goldmann, in attempting to describe what Goldmann calls the 'categorial structure' of the works. We needn't detain ourselves with Goldmann's definition of 'categorial structure', not least since Eagleton's appropriation of it is a critical one, using it to refer to a structure of ideological thought determined by historical circumstances which in turn determines the form and content of the novels. This is immediately qualified, though, since Eagleton also stresses that each of the novels is distinct and is not simply reducible to that prior structure: literature has its own relatively autonomous formal traditions from which the author selects that material which apparently serves her purposes, a selection which is itself ideologically determined. Hence, the 'categorial structure' and the literary form selected have a reciprocally determining relation to each other. Eagleton is working with a complex model, then: fiction is at a second remove from history, since it is a literary production of an ideological structure determined by that history, a model of the relationship between ideology and literary text which will be further and more carefully elaborated in *Criticism and Ideology*.

The concept of categorial structure is most readily comprehensible in Eagleton's discussion of Charlotte Brontë's fiction. Unlike Emily, Charlotte produced more than one novel, so the underlying categorial structure can be perceived through a number of realisations of it. That structure is triadic, and is 'determined by a complex set of power-relations between a protagonist, a "Romantic-radical" and an autocratic conservative' (Eagleton, 1975, 74). The embodiment of these roles is complex, though, since they are not necessarily allotted straightforwardly to individual characters. Jane Eyre, for instance, is the eponymous protagonist but also exhibits both Romantic radical and conservative traits which vie for dominance in her just as the characters who more directly exhibit those qualities, Rochester and St John Rivers respectively, compete for her hand in marriage. The important point is that Charlotte's novels seek to achieve a rapprochement between the values manifest in these roles, something achieved most obviously in the dutiful but loving, selfless but voluntary care for Rochester which Jane performs at the end of the novel (when she returns to him, she does so symbolically by taking the place of a servant, signalling her willingness to serve him). This structural rapprochement relates to the historical, class rapprochement described by Eagleton, since the novels 'work towards a balance or fusion of blunt bourgeois rationality and flamboyant Romanticism, brash initiative and genteel cultivation, passionate rebellion and cautious conformity; and those interchanges embody a complex structure of convergence and antagonism between the landed and industrial sectors of the contemporary ruling class' (Eagleton, 1975, 4).

In Eagleton's view, it is precisely this process of convergence in Charlotte's novels that makes them inferior to Emily's novel. The superiority of *Wuthering Heights* is a consequence of its more uncompromising presentation of conflicts, something which marks it out as less dishonest and manipulative and therefore more objective in its working through of its material. This does not mean that the novel is less ideological than Charlotte's novels, but that Emily achieves a certain detachment from the conflicts she presents us with, something evident when we think of the characters of the novels: whereas Charlotte clearly shapes our responses to her divers characters, so that her designs on her readers are palpable – we know pretty much what to think of most of them – it is very difficult, and even beside the point, to come down decisively for or against Emily's. Moreover, though *Wuthering Heights* does end with the union of Hareton and Catherine, it nonetheless refuses to dilute the conflictual forces at work: unlike Jane Eyre and Rochester, who manage to resolve their differences, Heathcliff remains unassimilable to the end and, indeed, his death is necessary to the union which does eventually provide closure (though, as Eagleton also points out, the spirit of Heathcliff and Cathy – and their love, after all, is rendered *essentially* spiritual – appears to live on in the ghostly sightings of them by locals). Hence the *accommodation* between Romanticism and realism which Charlotte works hard to achieve is not permitted by Emily, and this refusal of compromise enables her to confront 'the tragic truth that the passion and society [*Wuthering Heights*] presents are not fundamentally reconcilable' (Eagleton, 1975, 100).

At the novel's core, in this respect, is the figure of Heathcliff. After all, he is the novel's problem figure: someone without origins and there-fore social place who mysteriously achieves wealth and a veneer of civility but whose excessive love for Catherine leads him to the grave and that other world which appears to be the only place capable of accommodating his love. It is he that presents Catherine with the dilemma that she is unable to resolve: she has to choose between him and Edgar Linton, an essentially social dilemma since it is a choice between wealth and impoverishment. Her solution is to attempt to choose both and, in the process, to divorce fulfilment from social existence by elevating – if that is the right word – her love for Heathcliff to the level of metaphysics whilst bowing to social pressures in marry-ing Linton, a 'solution' which kills both Catherine and Heathcliff, and doesn't exactly satisfy Linton.

But what does Heathcliff represent for Catherine? The answer to this is again bound up with his social position, since it is his lack of origins or determinate rank which make him significant in a close-knit com-munity in which familial belonging and class are paramount. Let us be clear, first of all, about the nature of the society, such as it is, which the novel presents to us. On the one hand, we have Thrushcross Grange, the residence of the wealthy landowning Lintons; on the other, we have Wuthering Heights itself, inhabited by the Earnshaws, representatives of the yeomanry, a class of independent farmers whose economic position was particularly precarious at this time – Eagleton records that many were either bought out by the gentry or moved off the land to throw in their lot with the industrial bourgeoisie (the first of these historical processes provides the novel with its resolution). The Lintons' position is further indicated by their cultured, even excessively refined, existence, whereas the lives of the Earnshaws are rather leaner, precluding much of a division between the different spheres of existence – work and leisure, labour and culture. In this context, Heathcliff's lack of determinate status both conditions others' responses to him in accordance with their own social positions – Hindley, who is to inherit the Heights, feels unsettled by his father's new favourite; Catherine, the daughter who will not inherit, loves him – and makes him a representative of the 'sheerly human' (Eagleton, 1975, 106). It is this last attribute which potentially makes him a representative of a kind of radical freedom: 'What Heathcliff offers Cathy is a non- or pre-social relationship, as the only authentic form of living in a world of exploitation and inequality, a world where one must refuse to measure oneself by the criteria of the class-structure and so must appear inevitably subversive' (Eagleton, 1975, 108). But though Heathcliff's position beyond, or 'outside', society – figured throughout in terms of a compact with nature in its most turbulent forms – may mark him out as a Romantic figure, he is not thereby romanticised, since the novel also makes it clear that such a position is only available to him through the neglect and maltreatment meted out to him by Hindley: again the potential that Heathcliff appears to represent is not socially realisable.

Once Catherine has chosen Edgar her relationship to Heathcliff becomes 'an elusive dream of absolute value' (Eagleton, 1975, 109), absolute because it has been detached from any possible realisation of it, from actual lived relations. Hence, the love of Catherine and Heathcliff is rendered 'mythical' as a consequence of its social marginalisation. One of the classic functions of ideology is to provide idealist resolutions to material contradictions, and the logic of Eagleton's argument is that at one level the novel recognises this is precisely what Catherine's 'solution' represents. But there is another sense in which it also colludes with that idealising process, since Brontë's presentation of that love suggests something about it which is '*inherently* convertible to myth', a crucial fact which marks out the 'possible consciousness' of the novel. Here, again, Eagleton is borrowing from Goldmann: 'possible consciousness' refers to a consciousness whose limitations it would require a transformation in social conditions to transcend. What Eagleton means by this is that the novel, for all its grasp of dialectical oppositions, can *only* posit an alternative world of freedom as myth since the social freedom which the novel gestures towards – one which would not require the impossible choice forced on Catherine – has not been historically realised. In other words, the limits of the novel in this respect are not the personal limits of its author's imaginative capacity, but are determined by history. *Wuthering Heights*, then, appears to recognise that the freedom represented by Catherine's and Heathcliff's love is rendered mythical because it is socially unrealisable, but it nonetheless simultaneously participates in the idealisation of that myth.

One of the reasons *Wuthering Heights* has been such a key text for Eagleton is because of its concern with the relationship between nature and culture, and it is to reflections on this relationship that I want to return throughout this book. As we have seen, Heathcliff is associated with nature, in the sense that he is on the 'outside' of society, but the various relations between Heathcliff, nature and society are complex, since nature appears to subsume society: the novel also presents social relations as an extension of natural appetites – in other words, it is invoked ideologically to account for the aggressively acquisitive behaviour promoted by capitalism. Moreover, it is nature that provides the connection between the apparently dissimilar child and adult Heathcliffs, since Heathcliff is transformed from being natural in the sense of being non-social into a figure who is naturally competitive. (But then culture is also similarly contradictory, 'either free-wheeling Romantic fantasy or that well-appointed Linton drawing-room .... Heathcliff's schizophrenia is symptomatic of a world in which there can be no true dialectic between culture and Nature – a world in which culture is merely refuge from or reflex of material conditions, and so either too estranged from or entwined with those conditions to offer a viable alternative' [Eagleton, 1975, 111]. Hence, Eagleton's claim that Heathcliff is 'in one sense an inversion, in another sense an organic outgrowth, of Heathcliff the child' (Eagleton, 1975, 111): that wild freedom – which we saw was also a consequence of neglect – is transformed into the only socially realisable form of freedom available to him once Catherine has abandoned him: he becomes a predatory, capitalist landlord. The hollowness and inauthenticity of this 'freedom', though – a freedom obtained by exploiting others – is figured through the increasingly alienated or mechanical way in which Heathcliff pursues his peculiar form of 'revenge'.

Eagleton's view of Heathcliff as 'contradiction incarnate' (Eagleton, 1975, 112) extends to Heathcliff's relations to both Heights and Grange, since he takes on the cultural characteristics of roughness and even violence intrinsic to the Heights in revenging himself on the Grange, whilst at the same time strategically adopting the capitalist characteristics of the Grange which were historically important in undermining the yeoman world represented by the Heights. Hence, 'His rise to power symbolises at once the triumph of the oppressed over capitalism and the triumph of capitalism over the oppressed' (Eagleton, 1975, 112), representing simultaneously therefore the progressive spirit of capitalism and the archaic world which it has superseded – and, appropriately, Hareton, after first losing the Heights to the appropriative Heathcliff wins it back only for it to be subsumed into the Grange, hence further signifying the demise of that yeoman world from which Hareton comes and which the novel initially values. This incorporation of Hareton into the Grange – symbolising the assimilation of the remaining representative of the yeomanry into the capitalist landowning class – signals for Eagleton the ultimate triumph of the gentry, rather than any compromise, though this is a point to which we shall return. Moreover, Heathcliff's death puts an end to his excessive or parodic version of those capitalist principles which sustain, but which, through its cultured civility, are distanced from, the Grange, allowing the novel to amalgamate Heathcliff's love and his rapacity as components of an outmoded and more brutal existence. Once again, Heathcliff's symbolic qualities are contradictory: his ' "defeat" ... is at once the transcending of such naked power and the collapse of that passionate protest against it which was the inner secret of Heathcliff's outrageous dealings' (Eagleton, 1975, 114).

The adult Heathcliff's conflicts with the Grange, then, represent for Eagleton an imaginative transposition of the historical conflicts between bourgeoisie and landed gentry. Heathcliff, who acquires his fortune outside that close-knit community with which we are presented, ultimately combines cultural elements of the Heights – its violence and lack of civility – with the acquisitive capitalist methods of the Grange, thus placing him in different ways at odds with both: from the perspective of the Grange, he is culturally a malevolent churl, reflecting the cultural affinities between yeomanry and bourgeoisie in opposition to the refined gentry; from the perspective of the Heights he is an overreacher, reflecting the objective alliance between bourgeoisie and landlord which, as we have seen, developed in the period in which the book was written. The project of the novel, then, is to resolve this conflict, though it does so by harnessing, or civilising Heathcliff's crudeness through the cultivation of Hareton by the second Catherine. Hareton, of course, is from the yeomanry whose historical demise is conveyed realistically enough at the end of the novel, but he is also the beneficiary of Heathcliff's methods, so that it is still possible to read Hareton's eventual cultivation as the refinement of the spirit of Heathcliff (after all, Hareton resembles no one else so much as Heathcliff, whether in spite or because of Heathcliff's treatment of him). The further contradiction that Heathcliff represents both capitalist entrepreneur *and* 'metaphysical' protest against the social order which has labelled him outcast is again resolved by Eagleton in terms of the limits of the 'possible consciousness' of the novel: the industrial bourgeoisie, whose spirit Heathcliff embodies, was by Brontë's time no longer a revolutionary class, hence it provided

> no sufficient social correlative for what Heathcliff 'metaphysically' represents. He can thus be presented only as a conflictive unity of spiritual rejection and social integration; and this, indeed, is his personal tragedy.... The novel, then, can dramatise its 'metaphysical' challenge to society only by refracting it through the distorting forms of existing social relations, while simultaneously, at a 'deeper' level, isolating that challenge in a realm eternally divorced from the actual. (Eagleton, 1975, 116–17)

The ending of the novel does present to us some form of rapprochement in the union between Catherine and Hareton, and to this extent bears some comparison with the compromises of Charlotte's work which are symptomatic of her gradualist ideological vision. But whilst this union ends the novel on a note of optimism, it does not entirely dispel what has gone before – after all, the novel is a tragedy despite this, since one thinks of Catherine's and Heathcliff's as *the* love story of the novel – and at the end the spirit of that love, its metaphysical reproach to the social order, lives on, not least in those reported sightings of their ghosts. But it is also the case that whilst symbolically the marriage resolution represents a unity of bourgeois and landed classes, as we have seen, the *fact* of Hareton's yeoman background remains to remind us of the demise of this class which is, after all, preferred in the early part of the novel to the excessively refined yet violently protective Grange. Hence there is an enduring tension between the symbolic and literal significances of the novel's ending.

Eagleton's own introduction to the second edition of *Myths of Power* recognises the limitations of the method he employs in it, but it also grasps these limitations as significantly determined by the historical moment of the book itself: its gender-blindness, for instance, is symptomatic of the relative underdevelopment of feminist criticism in Britain at that time; the uncritical reliance on Romantic terms such as 'the imagination' neglects to interrogate them in the light of psychoanalytic insights. There is also a residual realist aesthetic underpinning Eagleton's value judgements which allows him to pit Emily's unflinching grasp of dialectical oppositions against Charlotte's tendency to assimilate, and therefore falsify, them. It is this latter realist assumption which Eagleton corrects in his next book, *Criticism and Ideology*, in which all texts – including realist ones – are regarded as aesthetic *transformations* of ideology.

There are other questions it is worth considering at this point, and in order to do so I want to examine in rather more detail some of the ideological categories which inform Emily's text, and in particular those which refer to the nature/culture relation, since it seems to me that Eagleton's account neglects these. It is perhaps easiest to begin this reconsideration of the novel by quoting from a contemporary review of it:

> There are scenes of savage wildness in nature which, though they inspire no pleasurable sensation, we are yet well satisfied to have seen. In the rugged rock, the gnarled roots which cling to it, the dark screen of overhanging vegetation, the dank, moist ground and tangled network of weeds and bushes, – even in the harsh cry of solitary birds, the cries of wild animals, and the startling motion of the snake as it springs away scared by the intruder's foot, – there is an image of primeval rudeness which has much to fascinate, though nothing to charm, the mind. The elements of beauty are found in the midst of gloom and danger, and some forms are the more picturesque from their distorted growth amid so many obstacles. A tree clinging to the side of a precipice may more attract the eye than the pride of a plantation.
>
> The principle may, to some extent, be applied to life. The uncultured freedom of native character presents more rugged aspects than we meet with in educated society. Its manners are not only more rough but its passions are more violent. It knows nothing of those breakwaters to the

fury of tempest which civilised training establishes to subdue the harsher workings of the soul. ...

It is humanity in this wild state that the author of *Wuthering Heights* essays to depict. ... [Ellis Bell] displays considerable power in his creations. They have all the angularity of misshapen growth, and form in this respect a striking contrast to those regular forms we are accustomed to meet in English fiction. They exhibit nothing of the composite charac-ter. There is in them no trace of ideal models. They are so new, so wildly grotesque, so entirely without art, that they strike us as proceeding from a mind of limited experience, but of original energy, and of a singular and distinctive cast. (Unsigned review, 1974, 223–4)

There is an assimilation of land and people in this description which is revealing of the relations between politics and aesthetics typical of the period. In all senses, the vicinity of the Heights is considered primitive. That word 'picturesque' is a significant one, relating the novel to debates about landscape which date back to the latter half of the eigh-teenth century, when the vogue for the picturesque became popular. Picturesque landscapes were developed in contrast to what was regarded as the excessive formality and artifice of the landscape gar-dening practised by figures such as 'Capability' Brown and Humphrey Repton, and embodied relatively untamed natural views. But in the politically febrile atmosphere of the 1790s – a decade dominated by consciousness of the political revolution in France – aesthetic debates made explicit political connections. Writing in defence of landscape gardening in 1795, Humphrey Repton wrote:

I cannot help seeing a great affinity betwixt deducing gardening from the painter's study of wild nature, and deducing government from the uncontrouled opinions of man in a savage state. The neatness, simplic-ity, and elegance of English gardening, have acquired the approbation of the present century, as the happy medium betwixt the wildness of nature and the stiffness of art; in the same manner as the English constitution is the happy medium betwixt the liberty of savages, and the restraint of despotic government. (Repton, 1994, 201)

The comparison being made in the first sentence here is between pic-turesque aesthetics and the ideas of Jean-Jacques Rousseau – one of the philosophical influences on the French Revolutionaries – whose defence of the noble savage rejected both Christian and Hobbesian denigrations of the natural condition of humanity as either sinful and depraved or selfish. For Rousseau, humanity in its natural state was possessed of a natural compassion which was the source of all virtue. After 1789, reactionaries in England looking across the Channel saw in the violence and disorder of the French Revolution what they regarded as evidence of the natural sinfulness of humanity unrestrained by either social conventions or State force. This perspective was central to Edmund Burke's crucial response in the early years of the Revolution. The view developed that England, by contrast, had avoided revolution by rejecting the political absolutism characteristic of the French *ancien regime* whilst simultaneously suppressing excessive liberty (hence, in part, that peculiarly English fetishisation of the value of compromise). This is the view expressed by Repton, and the association of the picturesque with primitivism gained ground in the first half of the nineteenth century. It was counterposed with the principle of 'cultivation', a condition which – again by analogy with the state of the land – was both natural, yet entailed development of its best properties. A cultivated person was both learned and, as a consequence, in some sense *more* human, certainly more *humane*. Moreover, this principle of cultivation – the process which generated true 'culture' – contrasted with mere civilisation, which, in the words of the poet Coleridge,

> is itself but a mixed good, if not a far more corrupting influence, the hectic of disease, not the bloom of health, and a nation so distinguished fitly to be called a varnished than a polished people; where this civilisation is not grounded in *cultivation*, in the harmonious development of those qualities and faculties that characterise our *humanity*. (Coleridge, 1976, 42–3)

It seems to me that it is possible to map the three categories I have been discussing fairly neatly onto Emily Brontë's text: primitivism (Heathcliff), civilisation *without* cultivation (the Grange), cultivation (Hareton, under the second Catherine's guidance). This suggests that the ending of the novel is indeed more of an assimilationist blending of qualities than Eagleton's initial reading proposed.

Moreover, the imagery of cultivation – both literal and metaphorical – is crucial to the novel. The ending of the novel famously sees Catherine and Hareton cultivating flowers at the Heights, symbolically replacing the blackberry bushes that had formerly grown there. Nature in its raw and even malign state – think of the thorns – is replaced by something that requires tending and whose value resides in its aesthetic properties rather than its utility. But the language of cultivation is used of characters too. Hareton's potential to transcend the oppositions of the novel is hinted at by Nelly herself (in this respect, at least, a fairly reliable narrator), who at one point discerns in the maturing Hareton

> a well-made, athletic youth, good looking features, and stout and healthy, but attired in garments befitting his daily occupations of working on the farm, and lounging among the moors after rabbits and game. Still, I thought I could detect in his physiognomy a mind owning better qualities than his father ever possessed. Good things were lost amid a wilderness of weeds, to be sure, whose rankness far over-topped their neglected growth; yet, notwithstanding, evidence of a healthy soil that might yield luxuriant crops, under other and more favourable circumstances. (Brontë, 1995, 195–6)

Here the metaphor of cultivation is explicit, but this is complicated by Nelly's ability to read Hareton's capacity for improvement from his physiognomy: his appearance reveals that he is *cultivatable*. Heathcliff's acquired gentility on his return to the Heights, by contrast, is a veneer, something ultimately unassimilable by him, and once again this is betrayed to Nelly by his physiognomy:

> Now fully revealed by the fire and candlelight, I was amazed, more than ever, to behold the transformation of Heathcliff. He had grown a tall, athletic, well-formed man, beside whom my master [Edgar Linton] seemed quite slender and youth-like. His upright carriage suggested the idea of his having been in the army. His countenance was much older in expression and decision of feature than Mr Linton's; it looked intelligent, and retained no marks of former degradation. A half-civilised ferocity lurked in the depressed brows and eyes full of black fire, but it was subdued; and his manner was even dignified, quite divested of roughness though too stern for grace. (Brontë, 1995, 95)

Heathcliff might have acquired cunning, but this will merely be in the service of his malign ends. These references to biology as the determining force of a person's cultivatability ultimately betray the racial consciousness of the novel, its indebtedness to typically Victorian perceptions that certain groups of humanity were inferior to others and that race constituted an obstacle to their 'improvement'. As the reviewer quoted above notes, Emily's novel does not deal with 'those regular forms we are accustomed to meet in English fiction'. Hence, Heathcliff's necessary death in the novel is determined at least as strongly by this ideological trait of his characterisation as by any sense that his love can only be fulfilled in that metaphysical realm to which it has been consigned by the social.

The importance of race is something to which we will return in considering Eagleton's later provocative reading of this novel in which Heathcliff features as an Irish refugee from the potato famine. For the moment, though, we need to consider further the importance of this idea of culture since it is one with which Raymond Williams, a key thinker on the postwar British left, was deeply concerned, and it is in part against Williams's influence that Eagleton was reacting when he wrote *Criticism and Ideology*.

The ideology of 'culture'

Heathcliff's cultivation by Catherine, then, places *Wuthering Heights* in a specifically English idealist tradition, and it is one which I want to examine in more detail. One of the terms which crops up frequently in Eagleton's work is that of 'organicism'. It provides us with a useful starting point from which to consider his Marxist politics specifically in relation to Englishness, since the term is arguably the dominant ideological trope of that culture – indeed, it is constitutive of the very notion of 'culture' – a fact which Eagleton has consistently highlighted. The belief that England and, by extension, Britain has developed historically, as a polity and culture, naturally and in a gradual fashion – both of which are connotations of the term 'organic' – is a consequence of that polity's lack of any experience of a thoroughgoing and sustained revolutionary stage of development. This became crucially important in the period of European revolutions 1789–1848, from which Britain emerged, virtually alone of European nations, reformed but far from revolutionised.[2] The Reform Act of 1832, of course, only extended the franchise to middle-class men, whereas the working-class radicals who subsequently demanded further political change, the Chartists, were actively defeated by the State.[3] In this period, conservative habits of thought emerged which valorised *evolutionary* change over revolution, crediting Britain with that unique brand of freedom which managed to reconcile liberty with duty, resistant alike to ruling-class tyranny and 'mob rule'.

Such conservatism united people who were not always explicitly in agreement on matters political, since the ideal of organicism permits different interpretations of what constitutes gradual change (one of the characteristics of organicist thinking is its rejection of what it labels 'dogma'). Edmund Burke, the father of modern Conservatism, is most often associated with the gradualist position, one which he articulated in his response to a speech given in support of the French Revolution of 1789. Burke sanctioned the social and political order – still at this time dominated by a landed elite – in the following way:

> By a constitutional policy, working after the pattern of nature, we receive, we hold, we transmit our government and our privileges, in the same manner in which we enjoy and transmit our property and our lives. The institutions or policy, the goods of fortune, the gifts of Providence, are handed down, to us and from us, in the same course and order. Our political system is placed in a just correspondence and symmetry with the order of the world, and with the mode of existence decreed to a permanent body composed of transitory parts; wherein, by the disposition of a stupendous wisdom, moulding together the great or young, but in a condition of unchangeable constancy, moves on through the varied tenour of perpetual decay, fall, renovation, and progression. Thus, by preserving the method of nature in the conduct of the state, in what we improve we are never wholly new; in what we retain we are never wholly obsolete. By adhering in this manner and on these principles to our fore-fathers, we are guided not by the superstition of antiquarians, but by the spirit of philosophic analogy. In this choice of inheritance we have given to our frame or polity the image of relation in blood; binding up the constitution of our country with our dearest domestic ties; adopting our fundamental laws into the bosom of our family affections; keeping inseparable, and cherishing with the warmth of all their combined and mutually reflected charities, our states, our hearths, our sepulchres, and our altars. (Burke, 1986, 120)

The development of natural organisms, then, is one which proceeds whilst leaving the form of the whole in tact, and unlike those revolutionary doctrines which aspired to revise social organisation in the light of rational first principles, this analogy insists on the maintenance of a connection between past, present and future, each of which would be co-present at any time in the various generations. Note that this sense of the simultaneity of past, present and future is decisively different from the Marxist, dialectical grasp of history in which these temporal entities are not present as 'generations' but are bound up with conflicting historical forces. Note also that Burke's defence of English political development sets the affections against the intellect by arguing that the basis of the English social order resides in those natural sentiments which bind families, communities and the nation rather than on a constitution constructed afresh on the basis of avowedly rational principles. These affective bonds are necessarily complex and, since they have developed over the centuries, are not amenable or reducible to rationalisation or systematisation. Consequently, for Burke and for the English tradition of organic thought, attempts to change society systemically on the basis of abstract ideas such as liberty and equality are pernicious or even mad (Alderson, 1998, 34–9).

In what sense, then, is 'organicism' ideological? First of all, it is a legitimating perspective. In other words, it renders legitimate a partic-ular historical process and set of values, and it does so, moreover, by naturalising them. Second, the idea of 'organic' change as a descrip-tion of English historical development is both partial and misleading, since it implies a benign, orderly, essentially non-conflictual process in which society develops as a single entity or harmonious totality. This, though, is not how the various defeated radicals of English history experienced things. Those who were transported, imprisoned, spied on, ruined, or killed by the forces of the British State hardly experienced historical change as just as natural, ineluctable and smooth as the passing of the seasons. The description of British historical change as organic, then, is ideological in the sense that it is also a misrepresenta-tion, or at least a partial representation, helping to obscure the reality of what happened in the very process of legitimating it. The term 'ideology', when used in this context, therefore refers to a set of dominant ideas and values which effectively operate in the defence of existing power relations and which misrepresent the nature of that power. As we have already seen, though, ideology is not usually simply a fiction, and organicism in its falsifications of actual historical processes makes a kind of sense because of the lack of a successful and sustained revolution in British history. Finally, note the complexity of this point: the ideology of organicism is determined by actual historical events – and to that extent bears a certain fidelity to them – but the claims that it makes about history are nonetheless false.

The ideological grip of organicism was not confined to Burke's high Tory circles, a fact which serves to illustrate the Marxist under-standing of ideology as not reducible to explicit political affiliation. An organicist perspective, for instance, is integral to the thinking of the eminent nineteenth-century liberal, Matthew Arnold, the major polemicist for the value of 'culture'. Arnold's understanding of culture is avowedly indebted to Burke and other Tories such as Coleridge. In writing his best-known work, *Culture and Anarchy* (1867), Arnold was intensely conscious of the class divisions which characterised nineteenth-century British society. Culture was the cohesive force which would serve to enlighten and humanise a society split between a dissolute aristocracy ('Barbarians') a utilitarian and puritanical middle class ('Philistines') and a potentially unruly and ill-educated working class ('Populace'). In other words, culture would help to secure that harmonious social totality which was necessary for the continued organic development of British society. But Arnold was writing in a different historical context from Burke, since his work was principally an assault on the now dominant middle class. As we have seen in our discussion of Marx, the utilitarian brand of rationalism espoused by this middle class had a demystifying effect on the ideological legitimations of a previous social order, and this created a problem: how might this philosophy, based on self-interest, win the allegiance of society as a whole, including those who palpably did not benefit from it? It was the achievement of a number of figures like Arnold to recognise this problem, though of course they did not couch their arguments in such terms: 'The thrust of Arnold's social criticism is to convert a visionless, sectarian bourgeoisie, pragmatically sunk in its own material interests, into a truly *hegemonic* class – a class with cultural resources adequate to the predominance it has come to hold in history' (Eagleton, 1976, 104).

Arnold's 'culture' is a peculiarly undertheorised phenomenon, since his account of it is heavily dependent on generalisations rather than specifics: 'culture ... is a study of perfection, and of harmonious perfection, general perfection, and perfection which consists in becoming something rather than in having something, in an inward condition of the mind and spirit, not in an outward set of circumstances' (Arnold, 1965, 48). When Arnold does feel the need to be more specific than this, he can only hold up an example of culture for our admiration by counterposing it with an instance of the mechanistic ideas dominant amongst the middle class. Indeed, such a process is an inevitable consequence of Arnold's very grasp of culture, since to define it too rigidly – to theorise it, that is – would be to fall prey to precisely those mechanistic processes against which he is polemicising. Arnold's vagueness is overdetermined, though, since his awareness of the Populace generates different anxieties: 'The Populace are an alien class who must but cannot be incorporated into civilised discourse; accordingly, Arnold must stretch that discourse to the point where it purges itself of all class idiom, but, along with it, of all political substance, or speak a more identifiable class-language which is sharp and substantial only at the price of potentially alienating the Populace' (Eagleton, 1984, 63). The consequence of these contradictions is, as with Burke's writing, a distrust of theorising and an appeal to intuition – one which Burke would unashamedly equate with 'prejudice' – which aids the process of binding the present to the past. Indeed, this tradition of thinking about and valuing 'culture' is constitutive of a deep-seated English suspicion of intellectualism and of 'theory' in general, one which used to be, and in many cases still is, integral to the very discipline of English Literature.

Eagleton's consistent highlighting of organicism as a crucial ideological component of British politics and culture is important in his critique of Raymond Williams, the most important post-Second World War British left intellectual. In *Criticism and Ideology*, Eagleton made a break with Williams's influence – though in more recent years he has tempered his original criticisms – opting for a more rigorous and orthodox brand of Marxism. The principal thrust of his argument is that Williams's career up to the point at which Eagleton wrote *Criticism and Ideology* had demonstrated a naïve and disabling conviction in the 'wholeness' of English culture, inherited from figures such as Burke and Arnold, which Williams simply attempted to wrest from the hands of its elitist proprietors. In this sense, Williams neglected the ideological import of the very term 'culture', even though it was to a study of this phenomenon that he had principally committed himself: 'Alert as he is to its [ie. culture's] political tendentiousness in the hands of a Leavis or Eliot, he would still seem to believe it possible to *redeem* this "neutral" category from the ideological misuses to which it has been put' (Eagleton, 1976, 25). Again we see that the ideological potency of organicism is not limited by political affiliation, and, for Eagleton, Williams's organicist conviction fatally compromises his work right up to the beginnings of his rapprochement with Marxism in his 1973 essay on 'Base and Superstructure in Marxist Cultural Theory' (Williams, 1980). But even this work – which argues that Marxists have erroneously consigned artistic production to the level of superstructures when it should properly be considered as part of the broader *productive* activities of humanity – is marred by its lack of recognition that 'in capitalist formations above all literature belongs *at once* to "base" and "superstructure" – figures at once within material production and ideological formation' (Eagleton, 1976, 41). Indeed, it is worth noting that Eagleton has since elaborated and extended this specific point about literature in order to defend the Marxist base and superstructure model which has more frequently been taken to refer to a rigid separation of spheres:

> 'Superstructure' is a *relational* term. It designates the way in which certain social institutions act as 'supports' of the dominant social relations. ... What is misleading, in my view at least, is to leap from this 'adjectival' sense of the term to a substantive – to a fixed, given 'realm' of institutions which form 'the superstructure'. ... An institution may behave 'superstructurally' at one point in time, but not at another, or in some of its activities but not in others. ... The doctrine [of base and superstructure] ... becomes more plausible when it is viewed less as an ontological carving of the world down the middle than as a question of different perspectives. If it is doubtful whether Marx and Engels themselves would have agreed with this reformulation of their thesis, it is also doubtful in my view whether it matters much. (Eagleton, 1991, 83)

However, this simultaneity of base and superstructure as embodied in certain institutions should not tempt us to abandon the distinction, which remains significant, and is the basis of the extraordinarily complex theory of literary production which Eagleton advances in the rest of *Criticism and Ideology*. Since this remains his most rigorous and complete theoretical statement for reasons to which we shall return, I want to outline its arguments here in some detail.

Theorising literary production

As well as being Eagleton's most sophisticated account of what a Marxist critical practice might entail, *Criticism and Ideology* is also a remarkably dense text, full of necessary elaborations and qualifications. It is also a difficult work, 'certainly nobody's idea of an easy read' (Eagleton, 1990, 79), as Eagleton has himself remarked. Alert to both the material determinants of literary production and the relatively autonomous nature of literary traditions, the book is a scrupulously thought through attempt 'to show the text as it cannot know itself, to manifest those conditions of its making (inscribed in its very letter) about which it is necessarily silent' (Eagleton, 1976, 43).

Eagleton's sense that literary production must be accounted for in terms of both base and superstructure informs his analysis in the two main theoretical chapters, 'Categories for a Marxist Criticism' and 'Towards a Science of the Text'. The first of these provides an account of the various material and ideological pressures on the literary text in the form of ranked but nonetheless complexly related levels of determination, and represents Eagleton's response to Williams's challenge to think about the 'material practices' inscribed in the text. An instance of what Williams means by this phrase can be found in his account of the Romantic artist in his first book, *Culture and Society*, in which he discusses the various related, though uneven, transformations which helped to give rise to this figure in the late eighteenth and early nineteenth centuries. Crucially, he notes the increasing – though not complete – commercialisation of publishing which led to a greater sense, on the one hand, of autonomy on the part of the artist – a freedom, that is, from direct patronage – but a greater sense also of the tyranny of mass taste, which was thereby discountenanced as uncultivated. Increasingly, the Romantic artist was perceived as a figure apart, which in this respect he (mostly) literally was, though this separation encouraged the belief that he had privileged access to a set of insights which were critical of the increasingly utilitarian society which was emerging (Williams, 1958, 48). Such analyses in the earlier, non-Marxist writings of Williams were effectively prototypical of a critical practice which Williams was later to call 'cultural materialism'. Eagleton's chapter on 'Categories' is therefore concerned with material, institutional and ideological contexts in which literary production takes place and which determine aspects of both the form and content of texts. 'Towards a Science of the Text', on the other hand, is effectively an attempt to account for the productive tension the text establishes in relation to ideology, since it would be a drastically reductive form of criticism which simply translated the text into some prior ideological perspective. In this chapter, the principal influence on Eagleton is the work of the French Marxist philosopher Louis Althusser and his follower Pierre Macherey, but Eagleton's arguments are also critical of Athusserian claims and his overall grasp of the process of literary production, its necessary blindnesses and potential insights, is far more subtle than that school of thought would permit. In responding dialectically to the very different influences of both Williams and Althusser, then, we see Eagleton articulating a position which is indebted to but distinct from both.

'Categories for a Marxist Criticism' argues that any literary text is multiply determined – or 'overdetermined' to adopt the Althusserian jargon – by a conjuncture of the following levels of determination: general mode of production (GMP); literary mode of production (LMP), general ideology (GI), authorial ideology (AuI), and aesthetic ideology (AI). The GMP refers to the dominant mode of production – in the classically Marxist sense of the forces and relations of production – at the time when the text was produced. The LMP refers to a specific mode of production *within* the GMP – in other words, the forces and relations of production involved in producing a piece of literature. This would include all those right the way through from the author(s), the mechanical producers (e.g. scribes or capitalist publishers), and distributors, to the processes of exchange and consumption which determine its reception by an audience/readership. Each of these categories – and not just the authorial one, as our post-Romantic assumptions would lead us to believe – is important in determining the form and even, to some degree, content of the literary text. The relations between each stage in the literary productive process would differ according to the mode of production being described. Those I have labelled here the mechanical producers, for instance, transform an authorial manuscript into the final form it will take – a commodity in the shape of a book, for instance – prior to the process of dissemination. (This is not the only possible relation, and in certain, highly specific cases – e.g. oral literature, or William Blake's original literary productions – the author and producer of the finished product might be one and the same person.) Moreover, the kind of literary product which results from this both determines and is overdetermined by the processes of distribution, exchange and consumption, since, for instance, 'The handwritten manuscript can only be distributed and consumed on a hand-to-hand basis within, let us say, a courtly caste; the multiply dictated work (one copied simultaneously by several scribes) is able to achieve wider social consumption; the ballads pedalled by a chapman may be consumed by an even wider audience; the "yellowback" railway novel is available to a mass public' (Eagleton, 1976, 47). Moreover, any given social formation is likely to include a number of different LMPs – our own, for instance, might include private publication, prestige publishing which may be uneconomic (as is the case with some poetry), ordinary commercial publication, and internet publication – though one of these, determined principally by the GMP, will be the dominant one. Each LMP prescribes particular social relations of literary production, and this again will impact on the literature produced. For instance, the position of a successful contemporary novelist is very different in relation to both her publishers and her audience than that of a writer dependent on patronage would have been, and the nature of that audience and of the author's relationship to it will influence the kind of work produced. For all of these reasons, analysis of the LMP is not about considerations 'external' to the text: the LMP will help to determine its 'internal' properties.

GI refers to the dominant set of values, representations and beliefs determined by the GMP which help reproduce the social relations of the GMP (GMP and GI are translatable into base and superstructure). But the determination here is not one way, since GI also has a determining relationship to the LMP: 'All literary production ... belongs to that ideological apparatus which can be provisionally termed the "cultural". What is in question is not simply the process of production and consumption of literary texts, but the function of such production within the cultural ideological apparatus' (Eagleton, 1976, 56). In other words, the institutions which sustain 'culture' – of which those that produce literature and shape its reception are a part – play a role within the GI. Important, in this respect – at least in the developed GMP of capitalist formations – is the role literature is made to play in education. When Eagleton wrote *Criticism and Ideology*, for instance, he saw the role of an education in literature as being, at least in part, the dissemination of liberal humanist values which were considered under threat from a mechanistic society. Its ideological import was therefore in some respects at odds with the capitalist base, though it also, by preserving a privileged space for those liberal humanist values, paradoxically contributed to the reproduction of the dominant GI. Such liberal humanism is not likely to go unchallenged in contemporary English Departments, and to that extent some reassessment of the role of education within the GI is necessary, though it seems to me debatable that this role has changed radically.

AuI refers to the author's particular 'mode of insertion' into the GI, that is those elements of the author's general background – for instance, her class, gender, sexuality, religious affiliation or nationality – which might predispose her to adopt a particular perspective on or relationship to the GI. It is important, though, that we do not conceive of the GI/AuI distinction as the recreation of some public/private split, so that the author's sexuality or religious affiliations are interpreted simply as matters of personal choice or inclination: crucially, Eagleton argues that these two categories *must* be considered together, since 'AuI is always GI as lived, worked and represented from a particular overdetermined standpoint within it' (Eagleton, 1976, 59). Here again, the picture is complex, since in some respects an authorial ideology may differ from the GI, yet in other respects conform. Moreover, the reasons for this difference will vary: an aristocratic writer would clearly have different reasons for being at odds with the GI of a capitalist social order than would a working-class writer.

We might pause for a moment at this point to consider the distinction here between Eagleton's view of the author and that of certain poststructuralist modes of thought for whom the author is simply 'dead' and the text a tissue of textual traces. Neither version regards the author as 'originary' in relation to the text; that is, neither regards her as the point of origin of that particular discourse. But for Eagleton nor is the author merely a kind of cypher, since she is individual in the sense that her perspective is likely not merely to be a distillation or transmutation of already-extant discourses. It makes a difference, for instance, that Jane Austen, was the daughter – and daughter rather than son – of an Anglican clergyman who died relatively young. Austen's financial security and continued status required her to marry well, which she never did, and this resulted in her and her immediate family becoming dependent on the mercy of her wealthier relations in the gentry. Jane Austen's AuI – one ultimately of attachment to a traditional landed elite – is therefore overdetermined by her status as a woman, by her sense of the relations between religious and social – even national – duties, and by her precarious position as a member of the lesser gentry, resentful of the snobbish disdain which was directed towards her, but equally fearful of the collapse of that order on which she was ultimately dependent (on this, see Lovell, 1978, 15–37). Hence, that blend of caustic commentary on the moral foibles of certain members of the gentry, combined with a profound respect for that class's traditional authority.

However, the literary text is not to be read as merely an expression of AuI, since the AuI is only one – though a highly significant one – of the ideological determinations of the text. Another of these is AI, that aesthetic region within the GI which exists in various possible relations to the other elements – religious, political and so on – of the GI, relations which are themselves determined ultimately of course by the GMP. The 'literary' component is only one of the components which make up the AI, and is itself made up of a number of discourses (for instance, critical and creative discourses). Moreover, AI incorporates what Eagleton also calls an 'ideology of the aesthetic' – a formulation which will later receive book-length treatment from him – which relates to the 'function, meaning and value of the aesthetic itself within a particular social formation' (Eagleton, 1976, 60).

As I have already begun to indicate, these different levels are not to be treated discretely, but require consideration in relation to each other, since it is from these various relations that they acquire value and significance. Specifically, we need to think about the various kinds of determination at work between these levels which are not always predictably one way or simple. Indeed, it is a measure of Eagleton's refusal of any vulgar Marxist sense that a text merely 'reflects' or in some way expresses what is happening in the economic base that he wants to stress the highly mediated nature of literary production – that is, its indebtedness to various determining factors which nonetheless always finally relate to the GMP – as well as the internal complexity of the various levels he outlines and the various relations between those levels. Through its general organisation of society – for instance, into scattered rural communities with low levels of literacy and only rudimentary communications between those communities, or into densely populated urban centres with high levels of literacy (at least among certain classes) and frequent traffic between them – the GMP will inevitably affect the LMP. But at the level of *relations* of production – that is, class relations – there may also be points of contradiction between the two which themselves will be ideologically important. For instance:

> The specificity of the articulation between 'general' and literary social relations in capitalist formations is to be found in the fact that although the literary social relations in general reproduce the social relations of the GMP, they do not necessarily reproduce those social relations as they hold between the *particular individual agents of the literary productive process....* The individual functions within the 'general' social relations fulfilled by the LMP agents in capitalism ... are autonomous of the functions they fulfil within the social relations of literary production. An aristocratic novelist may be consumed by proletarian readers, or *vice versa*, but these 'general' social relations of the particular agents are 'cancelled' by the market relations of literary commodity production. (Eagleton, 1976, 53)

This is an interesting point, and we might speculate on its effects on the consumption – and therefore the 'meaning' – of literature. How many readers of Evelyn Waugh, for instance, encounter his work as consumers of a commodity, whilst thereby participating in forms of transaction – mass production and distribution – and being from social classes mostly held in disdain by those novels? This is an extreme example, but the fact is that the self-consciously 'literary' tradition of the twentieth century has been kept alive largely by a leisure class – that is, one indebted, at least initially, to an independent income which provides it with the leisure time necessary for writing – whose values are largely at odds with those determined by the GMP.[4]

There are various other possible relations between the different levels discussed by Eagleton, and again these are not significant simply in terms of the way we consider the literary text, but may be relevant in the development of literary forms. Eagleton cites the instance of the emergence of the novel which was reliant on certain developments in the technology of publishing and the processes of distribution, as well as on broader social relations which created a particular relation between author and readership – all these at the level of LMP – but the form which was enabled by such conditions only came into existence in conjunction with developments in General and Aesthetic Ideological determinants: Ian Watt's classic account of the rise of the novel, for instance, links it to the emergence of an ideology of individualism determined by the rise of capitalism (Watt, 1957, 66–102).

I have done little more here than outline the various categories discussed by Eagleton and give some sense of the ways in which they might account for various aspects of literary production, but it should of course be stressed that the effects of the different determining levels, and their relative importance will vary historically. Nonetheless, this does not exhaust the complexity of the literary productive process, since it neglects to account for that element which is crucial to our perception of the value of literature: that which we label 'creativity'. That said, Eagleton's analysis does not, having provided a rigorously materialist account of the material and ideological determinants of literary production, simply reintroduce Romantic-individualist notions of genius and inspiration to explain the uniqueness of the text, but rather discusses texts in terms of the particular relationships they establish with ideology. It is at this point that the Althusserian context for this work becomes particularly important (though it also influences Eagleton's treatment of the 'levels' of determination in the text's material production). Marxist aesthetics traditionally has struggled with the complex problem about the relationship between literature – not to mention art more generally – and ideology. Two propositions have tended to be forwarded. The first is that literature simply reproduces ideology, whereas the other suggests that literature calls ideology – or, at least, bourgeois utilitarian ideology – into question.

There are more or less sophisticated versions of both arguments, but each tends to take the term 'literature' as a homogeneous category, oddly making little allowance for the clear ideological distinctions between writers – between, say, William Blake and T. S. Eliot – or the historical contexts in which they wrote. But there are other problems with these propositions. The first refuses to engage with the specificity of literature as a mode of discourse – its processes of production, its formal organisation of its material, its particular mode of realising ideology, and even the ideological function it plays in broader society. According to this argument, a literary text might as well be a politician's speech or a political tract. The second does at least recognise some distance between literature and ideology, but its sense of that distance is far too simplistic.

The French Marxist philosopher, Louis Althusser, and his follower, Pierre Macherey – in this brief summary, I will conflate their arguments – attempt to solve this problem by allotting to literature a particular relationship to ideology, one which situates it in some sense *between* ideology and scientific knowledge. In some ways, this represents a kind of back handed compliment: literature is not simply 'illusion' (as Macherey terms ideology at one point), but, then, nor does it reach the status of 'truth' either. Instead, it achieves a distantiation of ideology – that is, it sets itself at a distance from ideology – by giving it a form, and thus rendering ideology all the more visible for us. So, literature is not entirely deluded, but nor does it represent enlightenment. Some have taken Eagleton's text to be straightforwardly derivative of Macherey's,[5] but we have already seen that Eagleton rejects such a crude epistemological division between ideology and knowledge, and rightly so: science, for instance, is far from untainted by ideology (as a great deal of contemporary sociobiology amply demonstrates), whilst other forms of discourse are not necessarily deluded, and ideology itself cannot be described simply in terms of illusion. Religion, for instance, is part of the ideological superstructure of a society, but, whilst it involves the dissemination of rather grandiose fairy stories, it also comprises sacred buildings, potent symbols, and meaningful and affective rites, all of which bear significantly on the way individuals actually live out their lives. It possesses, in this sense, a kind of reality, even whilst it may distort people's knowledge of the true forces of history. Moreover – again, as we have already seen – ideology inheres in some of the very phenomenal forms of capitalist societies, such as the commodity form. (Initially, Eagleton's argument about the reality of ideology is levelled at the Hungarian Marxist, Georg Lukács's under-standing of ideology merely as 'false consciousness', but it is equally relevant to his critique of Althusser.)

So, whilst Eagleton does not accept the division between science and ideology formulated by Althusser, and consequently rejects Macherey's formalism,[6] he does acknowledge the crucial point that the text establishes a *relationship* to ideology without merely reproducing it, and in trying to articulate this relationship, Eagleton begins with a suggestive analogy between the literary text and a dramatic perform-ance. The dramatic performance is a different entity from the text which it takes as its starting point – it is not the realisation of some essence 'there' in the text, nor is it a reflection of the dramatic text: it is rightly termed a 'production' in the most literal sense, since it is the product of a specific labour *on* the text, involving interpretation as well as such things as staging and acting skills. The dramatic performance, whilst retaining some kind of relationship to the text, entails a trans-formation of it into something else quite distinct, and Eagleton argues that we should, therefore, consider the relationship between ideology and literary text in a similar way.

The text, then, is a specific *production* of ideology. Hence, the determining force of the text is, not history directly, but ideology – those 'significations by which the real lives itself' (Eagleton, 1976, 72) – and this is related to the apparent freedom from history demonstrated by the text (after all, one conventional reason given for reading literature is 'escapism'). In its production of a 'pseudo-real' world in which any-thing seems possible, the literary text appears unconstrained by history – unlike historiographical discourse which at least attempts in some way to provide us with an account of what *really* happened – but the literary text's effacement of history is only apparent, since, as a consequence of this freedom from material history, it comes to rely more heavily on the determinations of ideology. The consequence is that in rendering history more 'abstract' it forces ideology to become more 'concrete': 'The text is a tissue of meanings, perceptions and responses which inhere in the first place in that imaginary production of the real which is ideology. The "textual real" is related to the historical real, not as an imaginary transposition of it, but as the product of certain signifying practices whose source and referent is, in the last instance, history itself' (Eagleton, 1976, 75).

This point about the distantiation of history and creation instead of a pseudo-reality is an important element in Eagleton's argument, since it forces us to think, not about the relationship between the text and history – comparing one directly with the other – but about the ways in which the text gives a determinate shape to ideology. So, for instance, realism is not to be treated as giving us a greater access to reality than, say, fantasy, but as a particular production of ideology which is itself ideologically determined. It is this which leads Eagleton to claim that literature's defining characteristic is its fictiveness, though by this he means, not that the text may be in every respect fictional – a text may be autobiographical, for instance, or may refer to particular historical events, just as Dickens's *Barnaby Rudge* is crucially concerned with the anti-Catholic Gordon Riots of 1780. Rather, the text's fictiveness resides in 'a certain dominance (or "excess") of the signifying practice over the signified' (Eagleton, 1976, 78). In other words, even where the literary text makes reference to real historical objects or events, it nonetheless draws our attention to its modes of representing them, and therefore to the text's relations to those broader signifying practices which constitute ideology.

The text, though, is not to be considered merely as a distillation of ideology; rather, it processes ideology in ways 'unpremeditated' by ideology. Here again, Eagleton is careful not to prescribe the ways in which ideology might be produced by a text: it may enter the text in relatively pure forms – as, for instance, with Christian dogma in hymnody, or Stalinism in the case of socialist realism – or it may be manifest in more mediated ways – as transpositions of lived experience, for instance – but in all cases the text through its various aesthetic strategies 'establishes a transformative relation between itself and ideology which allows us to perceive the usually concealed contours of the ideology from which it emerges' (Eagleton, 1976, 82). The task of Marxist criticism is to consider, on the one hand, what kind of ideology informs the text and, on the other, the particular mode(s) by which that text processes its ideological information. This is consistent with Eagleton's refusal of any predetermined understanding of the form and content of ideology, and it allows for the various potential transformations of ideology which might emerge from the process of literary production.

The specific way in which texts transform, or produce, ideology is through their attempts to find solutions to particular problems. Eagleton interprets these terms 'problem' and 'solution' in the broadest possible way to mean that in each text a certain element or group of elements – be it a fictional situation or a poem's metaphorical conceit – is subject to some literary process which changes them. The problems may be philosophical, as in Pope's *Essays on Man*, or narrative, as in a whodunit; alternatively the 'problem' may be something as simple as an image which is elaborated or transformed in the course of a poem. They will be ideological problems cast in aesthetic forms, but those forms will from the outset be cast in ways which are resolvable or '*acceptably* unresolvable' (Eagleton, 1976, 88). In other words, a text is constrained to resolve its problems in certain ways and therefore has a number of options, providing the impression that the text possesses a degree of choice and is therefore 'free' to determine its own development. That freedom, however, is severely circumscribed, since to choose certain options would require a break with the text's ideological determinants.

But things are even more complex than this, since the text, in transforming ideological problems into those aesthetic terms for which it possesses a resolution, may then generate further problems at the aesthetic level which in turn require ideological resolution. Hence Eagleton's comment that the text is 'never at one with itself, for if it were it would have absolutely nothing to say. It is rather a process of *becoming* at one with itself – an attempt to overcome the problem of itself, a problem produced by the fact that the text is the production, rather than reflection of an ideological solution' (Eagleton, 1976, 89), a dialectical formulation, we might note, which is at odds with the allegedly thoroughgoing Althusserianism of this work. What Eagleton means by this is that if texts merely 'reflect' ideological resolutions this would imply that the resolution pre-existed the text, thereby making the text itself redundant. Rather, the text manifests a restless process of solution-seeking generated by its initial aesthetic casting of an ideological problem and the further problems that this form of resolution may precipitate.

All of this requires some illustration, and we can perhaps best do this by turning to the account of George Eliot in the fourth chapter of *Criticism and Ideology*. This reading of Eliot places her work in the context of a society moving away from the class conflicts which characterised roughly the first half of the century towards more corporate forms in the third quarter in which ideas of national or common purpose were increasingly valorised in contrast to the liberal individualist notions which had previously been prevalent in bourgeois ideology. Economically, this later period was one of growth, leading to higher wages and therefore some degree of assimilation of a formerly oppositional working class. It was also a period of various forms of capitalist amalgamation and consolidation and, politically, of State centralisation. Ideologically, this gave rise to a renewed appeal to older organicist ideals of the sort we have seen in Matthew Arnold, but which are to be found too in the writings of Eliot. Hence the pervasive conflict in Eliot's work between individualism (egotism) and duty (often the consequence of acquiring sympathy). (These oppositions often feature in Eliot's fiction in gendered ways: masculine egotism confronts feminine dutifulness.) The novels attempt to find aesthetic resolutions of this ideological conflict, though they do so in various ways. One of the central images of *Middlemarch*, for instance, is that of the web, a metaphor for society itself which provides an aesthetic totalisation of that society at the same time as the novel rejects any theoretical or ideological totalisation. The novel ends up therefore commending to us a liberal reformism grounded in localised activity:

> The web's complex fragility impels a prudent political conservatism: the more delicately interlaced its strands, the more the disruptive consequences of action can multiply, and so the more circumspect one must be in launching ambitiously totalising projects. Yet conversely, if action at any point in the web will vibrate through its filaments to affect the whole formation, a semi-mystical relationship to the totality is nevertheless preserved. ... natural imagery is exploited to signify how a fulfilling relation to the social totality can be achieved, not by ideological abstraction, but by pragmatic, apparently peripheral work. (Eagleton, 1976, 120)

It is in this way, then, that the novel proposes an aesthetic solution to ideological problems (though there is a sense in which the ideological solution has already been so transformed, since the discourse of organicism which ultimately informs the image of the web is already an aesthetic one).

This account also serves to indicate a further distinction between Macherey and Eagleton, since for Macherey, the literary text exposes the contradictions in ideology in the very process of giving form to that ideology. This cannot be the case, since 'there can be no contradiction *within* ideology [whose] function is precisely to eradicate it' (Eagleton, 1976, 95). This seems to me a rather too doctrinaire understanding of ideology, as there is surely no reason in principle why ideology should exclude contradiction. Eagleton's point, though, is that the major contradiction for Marxist theory is between ideology and material history, and that ideology can only become aware of itself through the conflicts that are generated with rival ideological perspectives – that is, between that ideological perspective which has developed on the basis of the dominant forces and relations of production in one society and an alternative which has developed in dialectical opposition to that dominant one. Shakespeare's plays, for instance, evince a clash of ideologies between a conception of the world as ordered and hierarchical and the emergent bourgeois individualism which threatened it with dissolution. A less obvious case, though, would be the one examined in relation to George Eliot which treats those conflicts in search of an aesthetic resolution in her work as determined by changes within a particular capitalist social formation.

In attempting to provide an outline of Eagleton's major arguments here I have omitted his 'suggestive' account of the relation between ideology and the unconscious. This is partly because I find it rather strained and partly because I want to return to the relations between Marxism and psychoanalysis in the next chapter. *Criticism and Ideology*, in my view, represented the high point of Marxism's attempts to think through specifically literary production, but one of its characteristic features – its extraordinarily complex attempt to grasp or at least suggest the various possible relations between ideology and literature – is perhaps a symptom of an assumption in Althusser and Macherey ultimately not fully challenged by Eagleton: 'that there existed a stable entity named "literature" (or "form") to be known, a real object awaiting its adequate concept' (Mulhern, 1998, 59). It is that assumption which Eagleton was later to call into question himself in his interrogation of both the term 'literature' and the institutionalised study of it in the well-known first two chapters of *Literary Theory*. (In part, Eagleton may again have taken his cue from Macherey, whose later work also focused on the institutions which generated 'literature effects' [Balibar and Macherey, 1978]. Literature in this later work was no longer assumed to be an objective category; rather, what counted as literature was seen to be determined by the ideological preoccupations of those who defined it as a discipline).

This was not the only transformation that took place after *Criticism and Ideology*, though. Whereas that work sought to grasp the text in its historical specificity, Eagleton's later work has been characterised by a recognition that no text possesses a stable meaning which can be fixed simply by reference to the historical conditions of its production, since its meaning also depends on its reception: in short, 'there is no reading of a work which is not also a "rewriting"' (Eagleton, 1983, 12).

Acknowledgement of this would seem to introduce a disturbing degree of complexity into the practice of criticism, though it doesn't render meaning wholly indeterminate since readings in all their variety are themselves ideologically determined. What this recognition of greater complexity licences in Eagleton's later work, though, is a different sense of the potential role of Marxist criticism, a revolutionary – rather than 'scientific' – criticism, as the subtitle to his book on the German Jewish Marxist, Walter Benjamin, puts it. To describe that book as being *on* Benjamin is in many ways something of a misrepresentation, since the book presses Benjamin into service both as theoretical resource and exemplum in its eclectic reflections on his preoccupations and those of subsequent literary and cultural theory. After the tenacity of *Criticism and Ideology*, *Walter Benjamin* appears a remarkably, even bewilderingly, diffuse book. Its concerns – the relevance of religious topics to revolutionary politics; subjectivity, the body and the commodity; literary critical practice; the political significance of the relations between comedy and tragedy – bring together old and new preoccupations in Eagleton's work. The diffuseness of the book renders it even more resistant to the kind of summary which the present series aspires to provide, but perhaps its most important shift is in its more fulsome recognition that, just as the meaning of the text cannot be fixed for all time through 'scientific' scrutiny, so the role of the critic and the protocols she observes are historically determined. The shift itself is indicated by the greater attention Eagleton pays to the ideological properties of critical movements themselves, not merely in *Walter Benjamin*, but in other books written at this time, including *The Function of Criticism* and *Literary Theory*. (His own work and that of other Marxists is not exempt from such scrutiny-it too is formulated in, not outside of, historical conditions-as his important introduction to *Against the Grain* (1986) and essays on Macherey and Fredric Jameson in that volume demonstrate.) The revolutionary criticism advocated by *Walter Benjamin* is an engaged criticism which recognises not merely the historical specificity of texts but the uses to which they are put today, including the uses to which they might be put by Marxists. But Eagleton argues that Marxist criticism must aspire to be part of a broader cultural productiveness or *activism*:

> The primary task of the 'Marxist critic' is to actively participate in and help direct the cultural emancipation of the masses. The organising of writers' workshops, artists' studios and popular theatre; the transformation of the cultural and educational apparatuses; the business of public

design and architecture; a concern with the quality of quotidian life all the way from public discourse to domestic 'consumption': in short, all of the projects on which Lenin, Trotsky, Krupskaya, Lunacharsky and others of the Bolsheviks were intensively engaged remain, for all the differences of historical situation, the chief responsibilities of a revolutionary cultural theory that has refused, other than tactically and provisionally, that division of intellectual labour which gives birth to a 'Marxist literary criticism'. (Eagleton, 1981, 97–8)

The creation of a counter-public sphere – to put it in the Habermasian terms of *The Function of Criticism* – is the necessary precondition of a truly Marxist criticism, which, until the point at which this becomes possible, must largely be biding its time. Today, these sound grandly and to some no doubt absurdly ambitious aspirations, but that must surely invite reflection – at least on the part of those who would lay claim to political radicalism – on the extent to which the investment of most of us in academia is more than simply tactical and provisional, as well as on what we envisage the ends of our activities as being. Scepticism towards such aspirations might also be expressed by those who see little evidence of the above activities in Eagleton's own practice, ensconced as he was until recently in the Oxford college system when not delivering bravura performances at academic conferences. This would be to ignore such things as his affiliations with Field Day – a Derry-based theatre company and group of intellectuals which exists precisely to promote cultural and political dialogue in and about Ireland – but, more importantly, such scepticism misses the point that the historical conditions of possibility of the Marxist critic do not currently exist, since they would require both a transformation in social relations and a more coherent and radical working-class political movement. (Indeed, if Eagleton is responding in *Walter Benjamin* to broader theoretical shifts, he is surely also conscious of the influential argument made by Perry Anderson, and first published in the same year as *Criticism and Ideology*, that the general pessimism of Western Marxism, including both the Frankfurt School and Althusser, has been determined by the politically unpropitious circumstances in which it has been produced, and that consequently 'when the masses themselves speak, theoreticians – of the sort the West has produced for fifty years – will necessarily be silent' [Anderson, 1979, 106.])

The above passage – and others like it – raise other issues. They have been read as evidence of the typically directive, even authoritarian voice of Marxism in its claims to speak for 'the masses',[7] whereas in fact

Eagleton's argument points to a different social value for criticism than
that which it currently assumes or has had conferred on it, whilst recognising also that such a critical role can only become possible with a
renewal of socialist politics. Robert J. C. Young, in an essay which unaccountably begins by claiming that the demand for 'theory' to declare its
politics is one which generates a problematic distinction between the
two, states that 'Critics continue to entertain the fantasy that their work
has the power to bring about a major political revolution – as is maintained by books with subtitles such as *Towards a Revolutionary
Criticism.*' This is very nearly the reverse of Eagleton's sense of criticism's potential, since he is acutely conscious of the relative powerless-
ness of the literary critic. Moreover, he has never suggested that 'politics
is already known, that it is self-evident what it involves, that it is positioned outside theory, so that theory can have nothing to say about it –
whereas on the contrary politics can have a lot to say about theory'
(Young, 1996, 84). Indeed, Eagleton starts from the assumption that
'There is…no need to drag politics into literary theory…it has
been there from the beginning' (Eagleton, 1983, 194). The assumption
that there is a distinction is a product of the divisions of labour in our
societies and of the academic institutionalisation of criticism from
whose effects the Marxist cannot claim to be exempt, however conscious of them she may be. In changed historical conditions, the very
theoretical questions we would ask ourselves would be different from
the ones 'theory' – a term whose meaning Young problematically takes
for granted – asks itself now. A similar argument might be made in relation to Geoffrey Bennington's claim that Marxist criticism ascribes a
metaphysical status to 'history' which it situates in some space beyond
either the literary text or theory (Bennington, 1987 and 1999, 105–6).

One of the consequences of Eagleton's revised understanding of the
role of criticism is that his textual engagements have not only acquired
a broader cultural range of reference, but have sought less to situate
texts historically than to read them in relation to subsequent ideological
concerns as these have been mediated by literary and cultural theory.
Hence, in his later writings he is as likely to invoke the terminology of
deconstruction or Lacanian psychoanalysis as that of Marxism, though
his reasons for doing so have less to do with mere eclecticism than a
desire to point up both the positive potential of such thought – the
extent to which it might enrich Marxist analysis – as well as its
limitations and mystifications.

In hindsight, Althusser's significance for literary and cultural debate may not so much have been any direct or even mediated contributions to critical practice, but rather the intellectual climate that he helped to create. Althusser is in many respects a crudely pessimistic thinker, and one can see in his work that tendency – more pronounced in some forms of postmodernism – to see oppositional forces as mere regulators of the system: even Trades Unions were for him Ideological *State* Apparatuses, a status which reflects most, though not all, Unions' accommodation with capital but makes little sense of struggles between them and the State or of the struggles for dominance which take place *within* them. Of greater theoretical significance, though, is his anti-humanist collapsing of subjectivity and ideology – the claim that we become subject to ideology in and through the very process of becoming (individual) subjects. Taking its cue from this argument, literary critical practice either focused on the ways in which the reader was interpellated by the subject position created for her by the literary text (e.g. Belsey, 1980), or led to a scrutiny of the ways in which novelistic characters were themselves interpellated to become subjects. Such an intellectual climate can be seen to have generated favourable conditions for the reception of another French thinker who, though he was Althusser's pupil, was to become a critic of Marxism, Michel Foucault. For Foucault, too, subjectivity was intimately connected with power, though the determining force now was no longer ideology – which in capitalist societies for Althusser ensured the reproduction of a quiescent working class – but 'discourse'. This shift was significant in a number of ways symptomatic of a more general intellectual one, and a brief outline of certain features of Foucault's thought may help us to grasp this.

The principal focus of Foucault's criticism is Enlightenment thought, since according to him it is the Enlightenment which has governed modern forms of subjection. Through medical, psychiatric, penal and sexological discourses, power now became internalised, producing us as particular kinds of subjects governed by 'reason'. Power – a complex term in Foucault's thought – is not primarily therefore negative, in the sense of being a force which 'oppressed' the individual, since it is constitutive of her and even conditions her sense of the possibilities for freedom. In his work on sexuality, for instance, Foucault argues that the sexological discourses which came into being in the late nineteenth century, giving names to the various perverse subjects it claimed to have discovered and encouraging them to confess to their conditions, set the terms for the sexual liberation movements of the twentieth century. Consequently, lesbian and gay movements which emerged in the later twentieth century were, for Foucault, examples of a 'reverse discourse' which remained indebted to the essentialist thought of the sexologists even whilst it rejected that founding discourse's tendency to pathologise them. This scepticism towards the possibility of liberation was another feature of Foucault's rejection of the Enlightenment, since the very concept of liberation suggests a humanistic perspective: the realisation of some human potential unconditioned by discourse. For Foucault, by contrast, there can be no such thing as a false consciousness which might somehow be thrown off (though the conclusion to the first volume of *The History of Sexuality* retains some sense of the possibility of freeing up what Foucault rather vaguely calls 'bodies and pleasures' from the constraints of discourse). Whereas Althusser had declared a rigid and untenable distinction between 'science' – the objective position of Marxism itself – and 'ideology', Foucault rejected any such distinction, seeing truth rather as an *effect* of discourse (see, e.g. Foucault, 1981a, 54–6). Despite its distinctive features, Foucault's work is consistent with certain other postmodern philosophical emphases: a shift, at least in leftist variants, away from 'economistic' thought and its focus on class relations to an attention to discourse and power relations grounded in subjectivity of various kinds; a negative evaluation of the Enlightenment, going much further in its criticisms than the dialectical response of Marxism (in the case of some postmodernist thought, convicting the Enlightenment of all the subsequent horrors committed by the West, from imperialism to the Holocaust); a rejection of teleological thought (the sense – in a strong version of such thought – that history has a predetermined terminus, or – in weaker versions – that it has determinate possibilities); a tendency, at the very least, towards epistemological and moral relativism. Clearly, Marxism was going to be a casualty of any such intellectual trend.

2 Culture and Postmodernism

The most influential claim that we have entered into a postmodern condition has been made by Jean-François Lyotard, who suggests that the 'metanarratives' by which science has claimed legitimacy since the late eighteenth century are no longer credible. The metanarratives he is referring to are philosophical – the Hegelian narrative of the evolution of self-consciousness – and political – that of human emancipation. Marxism, in its indebtedness to Hegel and its emancipatory commitments, is clearly one – possibly the most prominent – school of thought to be subject to such incredulity, and though the term 'postmodernism' seems to be increasingly out of favour these days its intellectual bearings remain largely in place, all the moreso, indeed, for having become almost a sort of common sense. Indeed, the ubiquity of the 'post-' prefix to describe a number of more or less recent intellectual currencies is a testimony to this common sense – poststructuralism, postmarxism, postfordism, postfeminism, postcolonialism (each of which might be taken as symptomatic of or a contributory element to a postmodern consciousness). The ideological bearings of that prefix are worth hesitating over for a moment, implying as it does supersession – historical, intellectual; possibly, though not necessarily, both – and greater sophistication, though such connotations combine frequently with a reluctance to fill the void with (too much) content and a contradictory wariness for the most part about subscribing to a belief in 'progress'. Meanwhile, the constant advocacy in such intellectual movements of the need to think otherwise, differently or in some (pluralistic) way afresh contrasts with, but is rarely related causally to, the observation that 'we' have now reached a 'post-theoretical' condition on this non-progressive journey. 'The engagement with Theory is the experience of an endless promise. Post-Theory promises that "Theory" will only take place when one can "finally see sight" ', write the editors of a collection called *Post-Theory* (McQuillan *et al.*, 1999, xv),

apparently unbothered by any parallels this might generate with mys-
ticism. Equating theory with deconstruction, they nonetheless invoke
a useful Derridean metaphor, demonstrating the kind of philosophical
sophistication claimed by an aggrandised 'Theory' which tends to disdain – though not absolutely, of course – the problems associated with
what we can see.

The issues generated for Marxism by postmodernism are not just
theoretical ones. If it were simply a matter of evaluation, the response –
acceptance or rejection – would be relatively straightforward, but the
term does not simply refer to a set of theoretical claims; it also refers to
an alleged historical transformation, at least in Western societies. It is a
matter of material changes, as well as a change in sensibilities. For
Lyotard, for instance, the change is bound up with the capitalist subordination of knowledge production to a performativity principle in the
language games which provide science with legitimacy: 'in the discourse of today's financial backers of research, the only credible goal is
power. Scientists, technicians, and instruments are purchased not to
find truth, but to augment power' (Lyotard, 1984, 46). Hence the
frequent differentiation between postmodern*ism* (aesthetics or
theoretical pronouncements) and postmodern*ity* (an epochal designation, even if it is one which registers something less than an abrupt
shift from 'modernity') as well as to recognise the interrelatedness of
the two. Amongst Marxists, Fredric Jameson has argued that the disori-
entating features of contemporary life amount to such an epochal shift
(Jameson, 1991), whereas others have been more sceptical, for
instance, arguing – rightly in my view – that Jameson's account is (ironically) an over-totalisation dependent on an extrapolation from a limited number of cultural and architectural phenomena (Callinicos,
1989, 128–32). Nonetheless, the pervasive features of postmodernism –
under which term, for convenience sake, I will subsume theories of
postmodern*ity* – need accounting for in terms other than intellectual
'fashion', which – whilst it may point in the direction of certain material determinations – remains a potentially idealist explanation.

What distinguishes Jameson's account of postmodernism from the
claims of postmodernists is its invocation of a totality, since postmodernism generally is hostile to totalising explanations – that is, to any
grasp of the social as a structured, if complex whole. For Marxism, as we
have seen, the social totality is inevitably contradictory – its contradictions determining its movement forwards – and mediated. Most contemporary Marxists have also been keen to acknowledge the strong
degree of autonomy rightly claimed by social movements not reducible

to class. But postmodernism is suspicious of totalising claims, and its rejection of them may even stand as its definitive feature, stressing, for both epistemological and ethical reasons, the irreducibly plural nature of reality (a term which nonetheless it dislikes because of its association with truth claims) and the tyranny of identitarian thought. Plurality is – effectively, at least – both fact and value. Lyotard's sense that the Enlightenment's legitimating metanarratives have broken down, for instance, leads to a claim that what we now have is an uncontrolled proliferation of micronarratives whose potential in terms of knowledge production is not reducible to the performativity principle:

> Postmodern science – by concerning itself with such things as undecid-ables, the limits of precise control, conflicts characterised by incomplete information, '*fracta*', catastrophes, and pragmatic paradoxes – is theoris-ing its own evolution as discontinuous, catastrophic, nonrectifiable, and paradoxical. It is changing the meaning of the word *knowledge*, while expressing how such a change can take place. It is producing not the known, but the unknown. And it suggests a model of legitimation that has nothing to do with maximised performance, but has as its basis dif-ference understood as paralogy. (Lyotard, 1984, 60)

Resistance can exploit the paralogy generated by such science. At times, Lyotard is prepared to invoke some sense of a totality or 'system' (though in his hands, the term has little more theoretical precision than in most '60s hippy-jargonese). For instance: 'the temporary contract is favoured by the system due to its greater flexibility, lower cost, and the creative turmoil of its accompanying motivations … [but] it is not totally subordinated to the goal of the system' (Lyotard, 1984, 66). However resistance exists at the level of and as a consequence of the micronarratives the system favours. Subversion is therefore dependent on the unintended consequences of the system's productiv-ity, but it is not clear whether the system directly can, or should, ever be the object of revolt. Implicitly it can't because that would require a reversion to the metanarratives of truth and justice, and shouldn't because those metanarratives would subsume the heterogeneity which the system has fortunately generated. Lyotard even suggests that all invocations of a totality in politico-philosophical programmes will, if realised, *necessarily* – not, that is, in concrete historical conditions – produce totalitarianisms. Consequently, he advocates a 'war on totality' (Lyotard, 1984, 82) through the activation of difference and the generation of a sense of the unpresentable (rather than any depiction of the real) as the sublime cause of a postmodern radicalism.

In formulating a Marxist response to postmodernism, it is perhaps first valuable to consider the general sensibility which underpins such thought, since if ideology is not merely a matter of explicit beliefs, but also of such things as mood or predisposition, there are good reasons for beginning by attempting to characterise a specifically postmodern sensibility before attempting to explain it historically. As Lyotard's account of postmodernism progresses, his sense of the negative properties of the system diminishes. As Steven Connor summarises, 'Lyotard [finally] sees the whole realm of the social under postmodernity as intrinsically aesthetic – organised in terms of narrative, linguistic and libidinal structure, rather than in terms of power' (Connor, 1989, 42). To the extent that this is the case, Lyotard's work is rather more optimistic, even utopian, than other forms of postmodern thinking, though it shares certain characteristics with them. It is partly because of this utopian element that Lyotard generally tends to be regarded as a less rigorous thinker than either Foucault or Derrida, whose work is characterised by what Eagleton describes as a kind of 'libertarian pessimism':

> libertarian, because something of the old expression/repression model lingers on in the dream of an entirely free-floating signifier, an infinite textual productivity, an existence blessedly free from the shackles of truth, meaning and sociality. Pessimistic, because whatever blocks such creativity – law, meaning, power, closure – is acknowledged to be built into it, in a sceptical recognition of the imbrication of authority and desire, madness and metaphysics, which springs from a paradigm quite other than the expression/repression model. (Eagleton, 1990, 387)

We have already seen something of this sensibility in Foucault, and will discuss in more detail its manifestations in Derrida; if Lyotard can be said to share in it, he nonetheless tends to forget there might be reasons for pessimism. I want now to attempt a sketch of the ways in which Marxism has accounted for this particular sensibility, as well as the postmodern valorisation of the plural, in materialist terms, and in doing so I want to draw on a more general Marxist discussion to which Eagleton has contributed and on which he has consistently drawn, but which, as Neil Lazarus notes, has tended not to be engaged in turn by postmodern theory (Lazarus, 1999, 11).

Inevitably, Marxism grasps postmodernism as the product of historical change. To take the most recent changes first, the later decades of the twentieth century were ones of capitalist reorganisation and of mixed, but mostly negative, political fortunes for the left. The dismantling of formal apartheid, for instance, was a triumph by any standards, but the hostility towards redistributive justice of the capitalist world order on which South Africa depends for its 'prosperity' has ensured the continuation of economic immiseration for the black majority. And this context – the massive defeat of socialist forces – has been decisive. The economic liberalisation pursued by Reagan and Thatcher from the late 1970s onwards has become the common sense of virtually all nation states – with, in the case of some nominally socialist governments, a few perfunctory genuflections towards the altar of beneficent state intervention – and the collapse from the late 1980s of what was taken to represent the antithesis of capitalism (the neo-Stalinist States of Eastern Europe) helped to clinch the ideological correlation between capitalism and freedom. The fall of the Soviet Union was greeted with triumphalism as the death of socialism, the triumph of capitalism and even – in an ostentatious return to Hegel – the end of history (Fukuyama, 1992). Capitalism and freedom, we are told, was what the people of those States wanted, though since then the purity with which the former has been dispensed has corresponded ill to the majority's experience of the latter. A worker in the heavily polluted Russian mining town of Norilsk, a town absolutely dependent on the company which is poisoning it, declares that 'In Soviet times I felt more freedom. The only aim of our company today is profit. It is the cruellest capitalism' (Walsh, 2003, 4).

It is clear from this global context that an incredulity towards the realisation of socialist possibilities at any rate – even where that incredulity is not explicitly postmodernist – is at least partly governed by both a sense that this would entail a reversal of history, and that capitalism is now so dominant – there are so few chinks in its armour – that it's impossible to know where to begin to defeat it and probably inadvisable to try. If this is an ideological perception, it is not just this, rooted as it is in an awareness of the genuine weakness of organised opposition to capital as a consequence of material changes in capitalist structures and of the determined actions of nation states across the globe in suppressing such opposition through anti-union legislation and other repressive measures, something to which I will return in a moment. The sense of there being 'no alternative' has rarely been so deeply felt as it has over the past decade and more (though, as I write, and over a million people in Britain march against war on Iraq – refusing the claims to legitimacy of the dominant global power and its principal ally, and rejecting the narratives they tell – there are signs that things may be beginning to change). In 'hypothesising' a state of defeat for the left as the basis for the postmodern turn (Eagleton, 1996, 1–19), Eagleton partly has in mind this context, but the cumulative impact of various defeats goes further back than this, as we will see, and must be considered in relation to those changes in capitalism to which I have just alluded.

If the emergence of postmodernism is in part an ideological response to defeat, hence its pessimism, its libertarian dimensions can be related to key features of contemporary capitalism. Something of this is suggested in Eagleton's important essay on 'Capitalism, Modernism and Postmodernism'. As we have seen, Lyotard's potentially critical insight that, as a consequence of the commodification of knowledge, the 'performativity principle' is the dominant feature of contemporary knowledge production leads him not to oppose the order which determines that this is the case, but to offer as a form of resistance 'what amounts in effect to an anarchist version of that very same epistemology, namely the guerilla skirmishes of a "paralogism" which might from time to time induce ruptures, instabilities, paradoxes and micro-catastrophic discontinuities into this terroristic techno-scientific system' (Eagleton, 1986, 134).

This, though, is only one of the ways in which postmodernism is indebted to capitalism. One of the further features of postmodern claims to radicalism lies in its turn to subjectivity, and in particular its theorisation of the subject as dispersed. It is effectively a critique of the 'bourgeois unified subject' – that autonomous, rational figure in possession of himself and his goods we noted in the previous chapter – but for Eagleton, this critique lacks force because it dwells precisely on effects, failing to grasp that that materially constituted subjectivity has been *historically* superseded, and ironically precisely because of the intensification of commodity exchange characteristic of contemporary capitalism:

> The 'unified subject' looms up in this light as more and more of a shibboleth or straw target, a hangover from an older liberal epoch of capitalism, before technology and consumerism scattered our bodies to the winds as so many bits and pieces of reified technique, appetite, mechanical operation or reflex of desire. (Eagleton, 1986, 145)

Whereas Eagleton's arguments tend perhaps to argue on the basis of intuition – a term I don't invoke pejoratively – others have considered the determining role of capitalism in relation to postmodernism more rigorously, and the most important figure to do so is undoubtedly David Harvey. Harvey – though sceptical of any radical break between modernism and postmodernism, and thus of granting postmodernity a properly epochal status – nonetheless sees as crucial in the determination of a postmodern condition and aesthetics the change provoked by the global economic crisis of 1973 onwards which accelerated, if it did not wholly produce, a shift from a Fordist regime of accumulation to one of 'flexible accumulation'. The term 'regime of accumulation' derives from the French regulation school of economists and refers to the complex unity established over a period of time between mode of production, state regulation and patterns of consumption in order at least to attempt to prevent economic crises. I can do scant justice here either to regulation school theory itself or to the profundity of the change described by Harvey, but some account is necessary. Under Fordism, large scale factory production characterised by minute divisions of labour, generated mass produced, standardised commodities directed largely at a market whose fundamental unit was the nuclear family, whilst at a certain stage in the evolution of Fordism, Keynesian state regulation of the economy aspired to full employment and a certain standard of living – ultimately guaranteed by welfare programmes – which ensured a continuing demand for such commodities. Even typical Trade Union activity of this period tended to be bound up with the particular regime of accumulation, for instance by delimiting the tasks for which its members might be responsible. Such constraints on capitalism were tolerable whilst the regime generally held up, but the crisis of 1973 made it imperative that these and other constraints should be broken. The shift to flexible accumulation has brought about diversification rather than specialisation in corporate production, leading to a greater exploitation/creation of niche markets as well as a reduction in turnover time in both production and consumption (hence the astonishing rapidity with which goods become obsolete, are rendered inefficient or simply go out of fashion). Flexible accumulation has been substantially dependent on a remarkable and disorienting expansion of credit, or 'fictitious capital', and has brought about the development of instantaneous modes of communication (as well as an increased commodification of communication itself), a weakening of restrictions on labour 'flexibility' – underwritten by significant levels of unemployment pursued as state policy – in terms of both tasks undertaken and job security, and an increasingly global playing field for capitalism, with businesses able to shift production to parts of the world where labour and other costs are lower. One consequence of this has been an acceleration of 'time–space

compression' – that is, a hastening of our experience of time as a consequence of the rapidity of change and a contraction of our experience of
the world through instantaneous communication and more rapid and
widely available means of transport. At the level of the state, and even of
regional authorities, we have seen a transformation in roles, as each
seeks to guarantee conditions conducive to capital in competition with
other state or regional authorities. Amongst other things, this results in
offering tax breaks and other incentives to business, the endless bid-
ding for and staging of 'events' (hence, in part, an unprecedented
expansion of the values of competition into the sphere of 'culture'), and
the regulation of labour forces.

There are many consequences attendant on the transformation
which Harvey describes, not least amongst them a difficulty in our ability to grasp anything which might be described as a totality (there was
surely something about even the *appearance* of Fordist regimes of
accumulation – the relative homogeneity they produced – which
encouraged such a grasp). Other effects include: greater cultural
eclecticism (across time and space), a greater emphasis on novelty
(rather than standardisation) in the production and consumption of
commodities, and a heightened awareness of cultural capital (if only
through the distinctions between branded goods), all of which
accentuate difference and generate an intensified sense of individuality
based on a multiplication of desires (for commodities) to the point
where it is often difficult for people to make rational decisions about
what they want or even need (the remarkable fetishisation of the
mobile phone is an outstanding example). Harvey's account can be
complemented by Alex Callinicos's suggestion that the appeal of
postmodernism derives from political defeats experienced by the left as
far back as 1968, defeats which led to the disillusionment of many articulate figures caught up in the politics of those years. These figures subsequently joined the ranks of a diverse 'new middle class' which has
grown in size since that time and which mostly benefited from the
redistribution of wealth upwards in the 1980s, thus encouraging an
intensification of commodity fetishism through the phenomenon of
what Mike Davis calls 'overconsumptionism' (Callinicos, 1989, 162–71).
This new middle class in particular, argues Callinicos, constitutes the
collective postmodern subject, the one whom Lyotard seems to have in
mind when he notoriously discusses the eclectic cosmopolitanism of
contemporary existence, thus mistaking a particular class experience
for a universal condition. Importantly – and this must be stressed to

forestall accusations of vulgar Marxism – Callinicos rejects the idea that postmodernism constitutes the unified 'world view' of such a class, which is, after all, itself heterogeneous and includes managers as well as intellectuals; nor does he suggest that postmodern theory is in all cases determined by the conjuncture he describes. He simply claims that the conjuncture he describes accounts for the take up of postmodern ideas; it might even be suggested that it accounts for the *way* in which those ideas have been taken up. In many ways, the best material embodiment of the consciousness Callinicos describes is that of the burgeoning supplements of the Sunday broadsheets in and through which 'lifestyle' has increasingly displaced coverage of politics and 'human affairs'. They both dispense and reflect contemporary taste and assert the class distinctiveness of their readership through the commodities – food, clothing, furniture, travel, films, music and so on – that they promote. They are themselves, then, material embodiments of the dominance of 'culture' in our supposedly postmodern consciousness.

Part of the sophistication embodied in the goods promoted in such newspapers is achieved through the distinctiveness they often claim in relation to the commodities of 'mass culture'. But the pervasive commodification of culture at all levels draws our attention to another feature of twentieth century capitalism which no contemporary Marxism can afford to ignore and which has determined certain aspects of postmodernism: the emergence of a 'culture industry'. The phrase originates in the neo-Marxist analyses of the Frankfurt School, and of Adorno in particular, for whom such an industry extended the principles of instrumental rationality into that sphere which, it was (wrongly) assumed, had resisted it: 'By subordinating in the same way and to the same end all areas of intellectual creation, by occupying men's senses from the time they leave the factory in the evening to the time they clock in again the next morning with matter that bears the impress of the labour process they themselves have to sustain throughout the day, this subsumption mockingly satisfies the concept of a unified culture which the philosophers of personality contrasted with mass culture' (Adorno and Horkheimer, 1976, 131). This kind of perception of the culture industry, though insightful, is one which suffers from a more general problem in Adorno's work. As Eagleton notes, 'Adorno's experience of fascism led him and other members of the Frankfurt school to travesty and misrecognise some of the specific power-structures of liberal capitalism, projecting the minatory shadow of the former sort of regime upon the quite different institutions of the

latter' (Eagleton, 1990, 359). Adorno's sense of the way in which the
culture industry served straightforwardly to undermine critical
consciousness needs to be understood in this context, but the term
itself remains a valuable one for understanding the ways in which
culture itself is now so pervasively subordinated to the demands of
capital, even if the culture industry – as with capitalism more generally –
now recognises the value of differentiation and niche marketing as
supplementary or alternative to mass production. This expansion into
and subordination of culture by and to the productive logic of capitalism has also had the consequence of generating what for some is an
autonomous realm of 'the spectacle': advertising, cinema, news,
virtual reality games, and so on. For Guy Debord, writing in 1967, 'All
that once was directly lived has become mere representation', though
this grasp of the autonomy of the spectacle remains indebted to the
Marxist grasp of commodification: 'The spectacle is not a collection of
images; rather it is a social relationship between people that is
mediated by images' (Debord, 1995, 12). Later, for a postmodernist
such as Baudrillard, on the other hand, the autonomy of the processes
of signification has gone further, leading him to posit the existence of a
'code' severed from any material base, something no longer merely
mediates our sense of the real, but rather constitutes reality for us, in
the process neutralising by pre-assigning a role to any form of political
dissent (see Baudrillard, 1983). Baudrillard endows an almost mystical
quality on this code's omnipresence, and this is probably the clearest
instance of the way in which postmodernism's scepticism about
distinctions between representation and reality serves to reinforce
political quietism by emphasising the complicity between power and
its discontents. For Eagleton, the critic (in his definition of the figure
who participates in the creation of a counter-public sphere) cannot
ignore the dominative nature of the culture industry and the extent to
which it colonises our very subjectivity, but must become involved in
the process of 'reconnecting the symbolic to the political, engaging
through both discourse and practice with the process by which
repressed needs, interests and desires may assume the cultural forms
which could weld them into a collective political force' (Eagleton,
1984, 123). In contrast to Raymond Williams before him, though, this is
not a role which Eagleton has conspicuously taken on for himself and
his cultural criticism has unfortunately shied away from engagement
with the culture industry, continuing instead to privilege literature.
Indeed, one might accuse Eagleton of a certain traditionalism in this
respect: it often appears that, despite his sense that 'literature' is an

ideologically determined object of study and his call for an end to that study, the scope of his radicalism has been constrained by his institutionalisation at Oxford, by its donnish atmosphere and staid curriculum and the particular controversies and battles which have taken place there. Indeed, Eagleton's recently published memoir reveals to us both a strong animus towards Oxbridge traditionalism and a sniffiness about U.S. academia perhaps not entirely unconditioned by the values of those institutions he has mostly inhabited.

One might conclude from this summary that, as far as Marxism is concerned, that is postmodernism done and dusted: whilst there have been qualitative changes in the nature of capitalism, postmodern theory dwells merely on the surface of such changes – indeed, it tends to argue that the distinction between surface and depth is illusory. Certainly, taking issue with postmodernism's reasoning and grasp of the social is one indispensable mode of engagement, but this has not been the only strategy adopted by Eagleton, at least in response to some of the more sophisticated thinkers who have contributed to a postmodern consciousness. Indeed, he has argued against the abruptly dismissive attitude of Marxists such as Perry Anderson. In reviewing Anderson's *In the Tracks of Historical Materialism* – a critique of structuralist and poststructuralist thought – Eagleton notes the *contradictory* character of such thought, which makes possible a dialectical appreciation of it:

> The denunciation of all global theorising as epistemologically indefensible meta-discourse is certainly an assault on Marxism; but it was also a potentially valuable deconstruction of certain 'overtotalising' theories (not least certain versions of Marxism) which did indeed ride roughshod over difference, conflict and specificity. The 'saturnalian subjectivism' Anderson scorns is indeed often enough a politically despairing hedonism, but it has also engaged (in the work of Julia Kristeva) more authentically Bakhtinian themes of the carnival of the oppressed. Foucaultean 'micro-politics' represent at once a politically disastrous dispersal of traditional Marxist forms of political organisation, and a recovery of vital, twilight regions of political work which traditional Marxism has often brutally suppressed. The 'attenuation of truth' is certainly one of the more irresponsible features of post-structuralism; but Anderson writes as though the correspondence theory is quite unproblematic and in good working order, despite the grievous difficulties with which it is beset. (Eagleton, 1986, 94)

There can be no doubting Eagleton's ultimate allegiance to Marxism here, but there is also an appreciation of its vulnerability to certain aspects of postmodern critique. Eagleton's work during the 1980s saw him increasingly ready to appropriate certain postmodern terms and habits of thought to the extent that, to some, he has risked selling out or granting too much legitimacy to intellectual movements irreconcilable with and inimical to Marxism. More than any other Marxist, he has explored the limits of any potential rapprochement between Marxism and certain forms of postmodernism.

Deconstruction

> Terry Eagleton ... I take to be the British Marxist who has most clearly *taken on* deconstruction, in both senses of the expression 'to take on'.
> (Bennington, 1987, 17)

The problem with attempting to grasp the key features of deconstruction is that deconstruction itself disavows any essential qualities, and may better be grasped as a particular way of reading texts which serves to undo those texts' internal systems of logic. Indeed, its advocates doubt whether it can be spoken about as having an existence at all (Wolfreys, 1998, 1–18). In particular, it works to undermine the certainties, or foundations, of the texts on which it goes to work, those things which are required for any systematic thought to be viable. It is not itself a system or set of beliefs, though it does possess consequences for belief, and arguably appeals to, indeed underwrites – despite its avowed distrust of underwriting anything at all – a certain mindset.

To attempt an account of deconstruction, especially in the short space available, is perhaps therefore something of a foolish enterprise, but in order to understand Eagleton's grasp of its ideological features it is necessary to provide some sense of the way it goes about its business and what its operations achieve. It is useful to begin with that principal opposition which underwrites much philosophical discourse and whose absoluteness deconstruction has sought to disrupt: that between presence and absence. The opposition is translatable in various ways as, for example, that between meaning and non-meaning, the essential and the inessential, the necessary and the contingent, inside and outside, voice and writing, life and death – in short, between that which is privileged in a philosophical system as the very ground of that system and that which is secondary, derived, dependent or antithetical. Deconstruction demonstrates that such prioritisations are reversible, though never definitively so. Rather, deconstruction seeks, not in Hegelian fashion to invert an opposition as a stage in the process of reconciliation, but rather to valorise

> certain marks ... that *by analogy* ... I have called undecidables ... which inhabit philosophical opposition, resisting and disorganising it, *without ever* constituting a third term, without ever leaving room for a solution in the form of speculative dialectics.

Derrida provides a list of such 'marks', or terms:

> the *pharmakon* is neither remedy nor poison, neither good nor evil, neither the inside nor the outside, neither speech nor writing; the *supplement* is neither a plus nor a minus, neither an outside nor the complement of an inside, neither accident nor essence, etc.; the *hymen* is neither confusion nor distinction, neither identity nor difference, neither consummation nor virginity, neither the veil nor the unveiling, neither the inside nor the outside, etc. (Derrida, 1981, 43)

This refusal of closure, the insistence on deferral, is crucial to deconstruction. In many ways, Derrida's deployment of the term *differánce* as a means of troubling our conviction that meaning can be straightforwardly present in language is almost paradigmatic of the deconstructive process. Serving in itself to invert the conventional prioritisation of speech over writing, of the apparent immediacy of the speaker in contrast to the distance of the writer, since its specificity can only be marked in written form, *differánce* refers us to the processes by which meaning is produced through a relationality between signifiers usually effaced. Its invocation represents a refusal ever to allow meaning to be present in its purity or identity. This does not mean, however, that we can conclude with Peter Dews that 'the logical consequence of [Derrida's] argument is not the volatilisation of meaning, but its destruction' (Dews, 1987, 30), first because the appeal to this kind of logic is an appeal to that which deconstruction seeks to make problematic, and second since deconstruction is fully aware that the valorisation of 'absolute difference' would represent a lapse back into metaphysics: *differánce* resists any such firm conclusions, and to assert meaninglessness is to establish a certainty of sorts. Meaning, then, cannot be exploded, starting points cannot be dispensed with, and accounts of deconstruction – even of a figure called Jacques Derrida – can be provided (even argued over), though usually only when accompanied by disclaimers of the viability of the project about to be undertaken (see, for instance, Bennington and Derrida, 1993, 1–23).

There is no necessary 'lesson' in deconstruction for literary criticism. To assert such a thing would be to essentialise the phenomenon.

Indeed, there have been a variety of ways in which its lessons have been learnt. In America, the Yale School of criticism has tended to celebrate the literary text's ability to highlight the problems of referentiality. For Paul de Man and others of that School, deconstruction is a way of revitalising the notion of a canon, since the literary is defined by him as precisely that quality of self-knowing undecidability in a text revealed in the 'aporetic' moment in which referentiality is finally frustrated. In de Man's disavowals of any determinate relation between textuality and history, Eagleton discerns a 'silent anti-Marxist polemic running throughout his work' (Eagleton, 1986, 138), and in the privileging of the aporetic moment, Frank Lentricchia perceives 'the formalist's response to a repressed and alienated social existence' (Lentricchia, 1983, 317). Moreover Derek Attridge's claim that Derrida's own understanding of the specifically literary as consisting in those aspects of a text 'which make most demands on us, which are difficult to write about in the conventional discourse of criticism because they shake the foundations of that discourse' (Attridge, 1992, 6) suggests a not entirely different perspective from de Man's, and Derrida's philosophical engagement with literature is the obvious counterpart to his prioritisation of aesthetic questions in philosophical analysis.

Highly self-conscious – since the self is a metaphysical entity – and aware of the ineliminable contradictions which it produces, constitutively resistant to systematisation and even conceptualisation, deconstruction is unsurprisingly a formidable enemy. And, indeed, it is part of Eagleton's achievement to recognise that to declare it an enemy at all is to fall prey to the oppositional thought which it is resourceful enough to be able to undo. Hence such a declaration of opposition would be less problematic for deconstruction to handle than the dialectical evaluation to which Eagleton subjects it. (Possibly this accounts for the failure of many to understand what he is about in his first essay on deconstruction. Antony Easthope's attribution of 'baffled rage' [Easthope, 1988, 174] to it, for instance, is rather more indicative of his own bafflement.) Nonetheless, Eagleton's engagement with deconstruction in *Walter Benjamin* does not let it off the hook: it is indeed one of his finest polemics and conditions his attitude towards deconstruction throughout the rest of his writings. In it, he grasps deconstruction's paradoxes not as the product of philosophical rigour but as determined by ideological impulses.

Of course, polemic is to certain ears inherently, *essentially* vulgar, and in this essay Eagleton deliberately flaunts that vulgarity. Faced with the disavowals of deconstruction – its refusal to be constituted as any kind of entity – he not only affirms but seeks to accentuate its identity by labelling it deconstruction*ism*, something practised by deconstruction*ists*. That identity, though, is discernible less in a set of beliefs – since conviction is not deconstruction's *forte* – than in a familiar temper which betrays its affiliations:

> The modest disownment of theory, method and system; the revulsion from the dominative, totalising and unequivocally denotative; the privileging of plurality and heterogeneity, the recurrent gestures of hesitation and indeterminacy; the devotion to gliding and process, slippage and movement; the distaste for the definitive ... it is doubtless pleasant to find one's spontaneous bourgeois-liberal responses shorn of their embarrassing eclecticism and tricked out as the most explosive stuff around. (Eagleton, 1981, 138)

A few years later, Eagleton was to revisit and somewhat refine this assessment:

> deconstruction is ... a liberalism without a subject, and as such, among other things, an appropriate ideological form for late capitalist society. Classical liberalism was always wracked by a conflict between the autonomy of the self and its plurality, seeking to fold back the latter within the regulative unity of the former; deconstruction takes up this contradiction, in a later stage of bourgeois society where the humanist doctrine of autonomy is increasingly implausible and discredited, and boldly sacrifices that traditional liberal shibboleth to the cause of a plurality which might just give ideology the slip. (Eagleton, 1984, 99–8)

It should be noted here that in both these quotations he is dealing principally with the Anglophone assimilation of deconstruction – though the ideological features of that assimilation cannot be entirely divorced from deconstruction's philosophical origins – in which the term 'difference' has acquired an almost unquestionable *value*.

The specific ideological character of deconstruction is determined for Eagleton by its particular way – there are different possibilities – of dealing with the 'metaphysical' opposition between inside and outside, initially by going to work laboriously on the texts it seeks to deconstruct only to gesture towards the collapse of the very structures by which we make sense of things. It is an ideology, Eagleton suggests, characteristic of times of working-class defeat or of classes who perhaps never had much faith in socialist politics (it would appear Eagleton has both of these in mind at different times in the essay). The particular way of dealing with the inside/outside problematic just outlined is distinctive to deconstruction, but the problematic is not itself unique and represents a displacement onto the terrain of philosophy of the political opposition between social reformism and ultra-leftism. The first of these is too wedded to the system as it exists and is sceptical of the possibility of revolutionary transformation whilst the second can only conceive of change as something utterly incommensurable with the present (deconstruction combines 'Minute tenacity with mad "transcendance" ' [Eagleton, 1981, 134]). For Marxism, however, the transition to an outside is achievable by a collective agent present within that system – indeed, one whose existence is structurally necessary to that system and whose agency is determined by it: 'What deconstructs the "inside/outside" antithesis for Marxism is not the Parisian left intelligentsia but the revolutionary working class' (Eagleton, 1981, 133).

Eagleton has consistently argued for the ultimately social reformist nature of deconstruction as a consequence of its refusal to think in terms of a totality and therefore to conceive of the forces necessary for the transformation of that totality. In various meetings between deconstruction and Marxism, that signal failure has been evident. Thus Eagleton writes of Michael Ryan's attempt at a rapprochement in *Marxism and Deconstruction*: 'if the liaison between Marxism and deconstruction is to be more than any idly theoreticist affair, it would seem necessary for it to make some difference to political practice; yet whenever Ryan sketches out a possible "deconstructive politics" it seems instantly assimilable to the well-meaning, flexible, participatory if somewhat theoretically diffuse political programmes of the traditional New Left' (Eagleton, 1986, 86–7). More recently, he notes of Derrida's engagement with Marxism in *Spectres of Marx* – which, as its title indicates, involves a deconstruction of the opposition between materialism and idealism – that whilst it indicts liberal-capitalism, it nonetheless proposes in response merely 'the ultimate post-structuralist fantasy: an opposition without anything as distastefully systemic or drably "orthodox" as an opposition, a dissent beyond all formulable discourse, a promise which would betray itself in the act of fulfilment, a perpetual openness to the Messiah who had better not let us down by doing anything as determinate as coming' (Eagleton, 1998, 264).

Poststructuralism and politics

We still need to consider, though, that other sense of 'taking on' noted by Bennington, and – despite its general hostility – there is some evidence of this aspect of Eagleton's response in the *Walter Benjamin* essay. Eagleton comments, for instance, on the potential value of deconstruction's attentions to and valorisations of those forces which have been rendered 'marginal': 'one only has to think of the productive ways in which, in the hands of feminism, they can be used to deconstruct a paranoid, patriarchal Marxism that reaches for its totality when it hears the word "residue" ' (Eagleton, 1981, 138). This brings us to one of the familiar criticisms of Marxism alleged by postmodernism: that it has traditionally disregarded, merely co-opted, assimilated or in some other way dissipated the radicalism of other social movements as a consequence of its prioritisation of anti-capitalist class politics – in other words, that it has sought to tame the 'differences' those movements make since, if it took them seriously, they would so multiply the aims of Marxism (or any other political project) as to make it incoherent as a singular force. In fact, the argument that Marxism has traditionally not taken other political struggles seriously is not so much an allegation as a truism, though its truth has been impressed on the left over the years more by those movements themselves than by deconstruction. Nonetheless, the language of deconstruction has since been adopted by academics associated with such movements and has proved congenial to the expression of a detotalising left politics which has become known as 'post-Marxism', a term which suggests continuity as well as supersession and one to which we might therefore expect Eagleton to be sympathetic. In fact, though, post-Marxism – at least in the version which originated that term – has been more appropriately described as a fairly straightforward kind of ex-Marxism which relies on travestied versions of that which it claims to have superseded (Geras, 1987, 40–82).

Ernesto Laclau and Chantal Mouffe's *Hegemony and Socialist Strategy* was the first text to declare itself post-Marxist, and since then Laclau and Mouffe have become editors of a series of books, *Phronesis*, which seeks to explore the relations between poststructuralism and Marxism in the belief 'that an anti-essentialist theoretical stand is the sine qua non of a new vision for the left conceived in terms of a radical and plural democracy'. So far, though, there are few signs of post-Marxism advancing beyond theoreticism, and indeed their own work bears the marks of such an orientation: it suffers from the elevation of discourse to the status of 'new "transcandental" hero' in which it appears as 'prior to everything else' (Eagleton, 1991, 219). It also relies on a particular way of grasping the complexity of social formations.

Laclau and Mouffe at one point sum up their rejection of Marxism and embrace of 'radical democracy' in the following terms:

> The rejection of privileged points of rupture and the confluence of struggles into a unified political space, and the acceptance, on the contrary, of the plurality and indeterminacy of the social, seem to us the two fundamental bases from which a new political imaginary can be constructed, radically libertarian and infinitely more ambitious in its objectives than that of the classic left. (Laclau and Mouffe, 1985, 152)

The term 'political imaginary' refers to the process of identification by which, for instance, Marxism sees itself in relation to eighteenth-century jacobinism as culminating in a single moment of transformation (revolution), and 'radical democracy', by contrast, sees itself as open to a plurality of causes thrown up by the 'indeterminacy of the social' which therefore cannot be reconciled in a single moment. Even from this brief summary, we can begin to formulate questions which highlight the difficulty of reconciling postmodern thought with left politics. For instance, if 'the social' is *constitutively* indeterminate and plural – a claim about its *reality* rather than any discursively constructed grasp of it – in what meaningful sense can it be said to exist at all? (Famously, for Margaret Thatcher there was no such thing as society.) Meaningful discussion of the social entails a recognition that there are certain necessities which require us to come together in the first place and certain forces and structures in place which organise the production of our needs – for instance, capitalism or patriarchy – providing some degree of coherence which can then become the focus of political struggle. Not that 'coherence' should be taken to imply a lack of complexity or contradiction. David Harvey comments of money, for instance, that it 'forms the basis for a wide-ranging individual liberty, a liberty that can be deployed to develop ourselves as free-thinking individuals without reference to others. Money unifies precisely *through* its capacity to accommodate individualism, otherness, and extraordinary social fragmentation' (Harvey, 1990, 103). It is determinate complexities such as these – not an abstract, presumed and therefore idealist *in*determinacy – that make politics difficult, including the attempt to construct hegemony. The assumption, on the other hand, that a proper grasp of complexity *necessarily* implies a refusal of determinacy might be said to be definitive of postmodern thought.

Such arguments go to the heart of any attempt to reconcile deconstruction and other forms of poststructuralism with left politics.

Indeed, if Laclau and Mouffe are true to their word, there can be no way of determining which social movements we might regard as detotalising *in a good way*. After all, 'the social' throws up all sorts of movements, and the status of those who comprise such movements as 'subordinate' or even 'oppressed' is no necessary guarantee of their progressive characteristics. It is not finally clear, then, that the radical democracy advocated by Laclau and Mouffe necessarily underwrites a specifically left wing politics.

Moreover, the invocation of plurality as a value in itself generates its own problems for the kinds of 'new social movements' valorised by Laclau and Mouffe, since, if those social movements have played a significant part in detotalising Marxism, they cannot themselves resist the force of a deconstructive politics: they too have traditionally organised around collectivities which require some kind of identity, as many of the more rigorous poststructuralist versions of political theory have recognised. We can, then, discern contradictory forces at work in recent cultural and political debates. On the one hand, there is the legacy of identity politics which, through the appropriation of the language of poststructuralism, have sought to undermine totalising projects with the assertion of particular (collective) identities – a process which ultimately Eagleton, following Raymond Williams, regards as 'militant particularism' – and on the other there is that poststructuralist logic which seeks to undermine even those identities through the assertion of even more specific particularities or differences. Certain kinds of feminism, for instance, consider the universalising term 'woman' contemptuous of cultural differences, arguing especially that it has served to privilege Western women's concerns (Butler, 1990, 1–6). How new such arguments are, though, is another question. The demand 'But what about *us/me?*' is surely a familiar one in political debates; it is just that poststructuralism has provided a newly legitimised vocabulary for such appeals. Which is not to say that the validity or otherwise of the appeal can be decided in advance: there will inevitably be merits and demerits in every case, priorities which need to be asserted if a political programme is to be effective, and rights and sensitivities which need to be upheld and respected in the assertion of those priorities. All political movements have experience of this process of negotiation; some handle it more or less effectively, others fall apart.

In this context we need to consider Eagleton's own reassertion of dialectical thought, one which acknowledges that identities are necessary insofar as they contribute to a transformative process – that they may be the agents of change – but also potentially limiting and disabling; that they should neither be deconstructed prematurely – before the political task in hand has been accomplished – nor be clung to as if their value was absolute or transhistorical. At the same time, Eagleton refuses to accept that the philosophical category of 'the universal' is the enemy of such forms of self-realisation:

> What is it to 'be' a woman, a homosexual, a native of Ireland? It is true, and important, that such excluded groups will already have developed certain styles, values, life-experiences which can be appealed to now as a form of political critique, and which urgently demand free expression; but the more fundamental political question is that of demanding an equal right with others to discover what one might become, not of assuming some already fully-fashioned identity which is merely repressed. All 'oppositional' identities are in part the function of oppression, as well as of resistance to that oppression; and in this sense what one might become cannot be simply read off from what one is now. The privilege of the oppressor is his privilege to decide what he shall be; it is this right which the oppressed must demand too, which must be universalised. The universal, then, is not some realm of abstract duty set sternly against the particular; it is just every individual's equal right to have his or her difference respected, and to participate in the common process whereby that can be achieved. Identity is to this extent in the service of non-identity; but without such identity, no real non-identity can be attained. To acknowledge someone as a subject is at once to grant them the same status as oneself, and to recognise their otherness and autonomy. (Eagleton, 1990, 414–15)

There are problems with this formulation, some more difficult than others to resolve. Not every difference, for instance, is one which demands respect. This is why liberal theory has always added the proviso that one's freedom shouldn't impinge on the freedom of others (a formulation which, incidentally, has more profound implications than liberals would want to acknowledge, since the freedoms of capitalists impose considerable burdens on others). But then Eagleton has argued elsewhere frequently enough that it is absurd to ascribe an unquestionable value to the term 'difference'. Some might want to point out that there is also a conflation of collective – 'oppositional' – identities with individual ones which arguably serves to raise further questions about the relations between them. For instance: can a collective identity be oppressive? The implicit answer to this – already hinted at above – is yes, insofar as it has outlived its oppositional value, though the precise point at which this might be said to have happened may also present problems. (Some, for instance, argue that the term 'gay' has outlived its usefulness; others – possibly because differently positioned – vehemently disagree.) The point is made by Eagleton in a slightly different formulation elsewhere:

> This is the kernel of truth of bourgeois Enlightenment: the abstract right of all to be free, the shared essence or identity of all human subjects to be autonomous. In a further dialectical twist, however, this truth itself must be left behind as soon as seized; for the only point of enjoying such universal abstract equality is to discover and live one's own particular difference. The *telos* of the entire process is not, as the Enlightenment believed, universal truth, right and identity, but concrete particularity. It is just that such particularity has to pass through that abstract equality and come out somewhere on the other side, somewhere quite different from where it happens to be standing now. (Eagleton, 1988, 11)

This seems a more satisfactory account, but there remain points which require clarification. There is, for instance, the question with which Eagleton opens the first of these quotations: what does it mean to 'be' any of these things? Not everyone would accept that the categories cited are merely 'oppositional' or – as the passage suggests – cultural. If we disregard crude racial theories, being Irish is clearly contingent on the way the world is carved up and thus might conceivably be rendered anachronistic in some post-national future, but can the same be said for being a woman? As Eagleton himself has acknowledged, feminism doesn't seek to abolish women just as anti-racist politics don't seek to abolish non-whites, and both are therefore constitutively different from Marxism which *does* seek to bring an end to the existence of an exploited working class (Eagleton, 1998, 288–90). But there are nonetheless some analogies between that which Marxism seeks for the working class – an end to its very existence through the demise of that social order which renders that existence necessary – and that which feminism and anti-racism seek cognitively for women, black people and others – an end to pejorative or otherwise demeaning perceptions of them. There may, then, be a sense in which the terms 'women' and 'black people' might cease to be *significant,* or at least cease to possess the significance they currently possess. The consequence in the case of both class and other politically significant groups would be the liberation of those differences undetermined by power from the constraining grip of social or ideological determinations. We will see in the discussion of *The Merchant of Venice* below the ways in which Eagleton's privileging of social and political identities and their relationship to universal principles informs an apparently deconstructive literary criticism.

All of these issues I raise in response to Eagleton's argument are ones which might be raised by postmodernism, though in a different language – of difference, essentialism, teleology, for instance – which carries with it a set of values which inevitably impact on the possible conclusions one might reach. It is frequently not the case, then, that much political postmodernism is asking new questions – though it may be asking old questions with a greater sense of urgency – just that its way of formulating them is distinctive and, with its fetishisation of certain terms, often unhelpful. It may be that it is becoming possible to move beyond any requirement to speak in those terms in order to engage in political dialogue.

The material body

Marxism has not generally proved particularly receptive to psycho-analysis; or, where it has, the results have mostly been unsatisfactory. Eagleton, though, has been rather more enthusiastic about the pot-ential of psychoanalysis. The problem for Marxism is that it appears to confirm the private nature of subjectivity, the individual's separation from the social. Moreover, it does so – through its narrative of the threat, separation and identification experienced by the infant in rela-tion to the mother and father – in the context of bourgeois familial relations which are historically and culturally specific, despite the pre-tensions of psychoanalysis to transhistorical and transcultural expla-nation. Once again, Eagleton's response has been dialectical, and his later work in particular demonstrates an increasing readiness to deploy a Lacanian rhetoric in contexts which might well have outraged Lacan himself. In Eagleton's hands, psychoanalysis becomes a resource for thinking through the relations between subjective and objective dimensions of social being, as well as the mediation of them by the ideological. In the process, he demonstrates an alertness to the complexity of these relations, as well as an awareness of the necessity of maintaining the distinctions between the various terms, and, in this respect, his brand of Lacanian Marxism – if that is an acceptable designation – is very different from the reductivism of Althusser, though unlike Althusser, Eagleton's sense of the value of psychoanalysis is suggestive and provisional rather than fully theorised.

But if psychoanalysis offers the prospect of remedying a lack in Marxism – its inability to theorise subjectivity – it also functions in Eagleton's handling of it to highlight once again the undialectical nature of other recent theoretical discourse. Eagleton's objection to contemporary theorisations of the body is to their 'culturalism', their focus on the body's 'constructedness', its discursive representation, its plasticity and capacity for dissident signification. By contrast, rather than emphasise the body's apparent capacity for self-invention, Eagleton, prefers to stress the body's limits and frailties, the very things which make us *weak*. Surprising perhaps, this, given certain perceived associations between Marxism and the heroic, its celebration of progress and potentiality, and the representations of the indomitable, optimistic, muscular figure of the worker in Stalinist propaganda. But Stalinism was no respecter of bodies, and the dialectical aspect of Marxism proper also stresses the broken figure, the negative underpinning of progress in oppression. The bleak conditions which gave rise to Frankfurt School theorising, for instance, determined a tragic sense of history such as that evident in Walter Benjamin: 'Whoever has emerged victorious participates to this day in the triumphal procession in which the present rulers step over those who are lying prostrate. According to traditional practice, the spoils are carried along in the procession. ... there is no document of civilisation that is not at the same time a document of barbarism' (Benjamin, 1973, 248). Moreover, it is through a sense of the body's claims that Eagleton seeks to assert an ethics of Marxism, since limits and potentialities exist in a dialectical relation, both at the individual and collective levels (if we take drugs we get wrecked; what our bodies put on in Manchester is paid for physically by workers in Bangladesh), but this is something which the one-sided optimism of the intellect discernible in much contemporary cultural theory neglects to recognise. Eagleton's writings on the body, then, draw on traditions within Marxism which have been marginalised. In particular, he focuses on Marx's sense of our 'species being' which informs Sebastiano Timpanaro's discussion of our materiality (Timpanaro, 1975, 29–54), claiming that it is in our material being that we can assert certain universals which genuinely do transcend cultural and historical differences in practices and representations. As Eagleton sardonically puts it, 'Perhaps the dead are not really dead, just differently capacitated. But we die anyway' (Eagleton, 2003a, xiii).

In this respect, one of the values of psychoanalysis, asserts Eagleton against its Marxist critics, is that it represents a materialist theory of subjectivity rooted in the relationality of the body of the infant to itself as well as to its mother and father, though he also notes that the specific roles taken up by the bodies in this arrangement are culturally determined (Eagleton, 1983, 163). I do not have the space here to rehearse the familiar Freudian narratives, but it is worth noting that in his own account of those narratives Eagleton begins with that feature of psychoanalysis which possesses the potential to complement Marxism: the point that civilisation entails repression (significantly, perhaps, he prefers to stress this rather than the more healthy term 'sublimation'). Our social assimilation – and, in particular, the labour which civilisation demands – requires our self-denial, since the 'reality principle' is at odds with the 'pleasure principle'. It is this which, through the Oedipal process, produces the unconscious and therefore the division which is constitutive of our subjectivity, and from which there is no escape back into wholeness, even though this is what we are doomed to desire. It is in Lacan's reworkings of Freud that Eagleton finds the most valuable theoretical resource, representing as it does an awareness that the body is not merely a possession of the mind and that the self is not reducible to its physical being: 'It is not true that I have a body, and not quite true that I am one either. This deadlock runs all the way through psychoanalysis, which acknowledges that the body is constructed in language, but which knows too that it will never be entirely at home there' (Eagleton, 1996, 75). In this respect, then, psychoanalysis avoids the reductivist errors of Cartesian dualism and postmodern antihumanism, but it also provides a language for thinking about the relationship between nature and culture, need and desire, since for Lacan it is the accession to the symbolic order – the world of signs – that establishes the division in the subject which is constitutive of desire. The Real in Lacan – not to be confused with either reality or Freud's reality principle – is that force which recalcitrantly resists symbolisation, the consequence, nonetheless, of our entry into the symbolic order. It is an ever-present impossibility; also known as 'the Thing', Lacan describes it as 'the beyond-of-the-signified' (Lacan, 1992, 54), that towards which we are oriented in our relation to the signified and yet which we cannot reach (since what that we could possibly know could be *beyond* the signified, the supposed destination of all our signifiers?). In Eagleton's rather than Lacan's words – since they reveal something of the significance the term possesses for Eagleton – the Real is 'the primordial wound we incurred by our fall from the pre-Oedipal Eden, the gash in our being where we were torn loose from Nature, and from which desire flows unstaunchably' (Eagleton, 2003, 197). In discussing the Real in this way, Eagleton establishes a connection between individual human life and the life of the species, at least as that collective life is explained in what for most of us is myth. Eagleton is perhaps too ready here to assimilate the pre-Oedipal infant to the natural, since that plenitude which Lacan discerns in the period before the accession to the symbolic order is a strictly *imaginary* one, though this may partly explain Eagleton's recourse to myth.[1]

The reference to Eden, though, is also indicative of Eagleton's theological preoccupations and his attempt to reconcile these with Marxism. It is in an early text, *The Body as Language*, that he first formulates the argument that our linguistic capacity which constitutes our propensity for practical thought is definitive of our species being, and at the same time establishes 'man's estrangement – from others, the products of his world, the constraints of his own sensuous being. To enter into significant relation with another person demands as its pre-condition the possibility of objectifying him as "other": only in this case can we speak of *relationship*' (Eagleton, 1970, 23). There is in this – and certainly in Eagleton's later restatement of this case – an echo of the Adornian argument that in separating itself from nature – nature in general as well as its own nature – humanity has necessarily alienated itself from that nature. For Adorno, this separation is a consequence of that desire to dominate nature which culminates in and is intensified by Enlightenment thought. For Eagleton, focused more on *human* relations, the possibilities generated by this separation are more open, since they establish the possibility of exploitation, or sin, as well as creative fulfilment both on the part of the individual and in human history. If there is a tension here between the Christian understanding of sin as an individual act and the Marxist understanding of exploitation as socially determined rather than personally malicious, it is one which invites a rethinking of Christian traditions as much as, and possibly more than, Marxism. Eagleton retains this sense of the tragic duality inherent in our linguistic ability throughout his work, and it has recently become the focus of one of his most important texts, one which in many ways recapitulates and brings up to date his concern with both the body and tragedy, *Sweet Violence*. In the final chapter of that book, Eagleton develops further an argument again first to be found in *The Body as Language*, treating the figure of the scapegoat, or *pharmakos* – that ancient figure made to bear all the ills of society before being outcast, the prototype indeed of Christ – as an allegory for dialectical change. That figure – a kind of moral purgative onto which the social order projects its own deficiencies before expelling or sacrificing it – might be a figure of social stabilisation if it remains merely reviled, or alternatively, if identified with – *pitied* – a force for transformation, the figure whose very abject condition demands change because it represents the failure of that social order. Despite their usual social status and because of their very abjection, Eagleton finds in the tragic heroes who are made such scapegoats the potential to

> inaugurate a revolutionary ethics by their death-dealing, heroically tenacious commitment to another order of truth altogether, a truth which discloses the negativity of the subject rather than legitimating a positive regime, and which figures for Jacques Lacan as the terrifying abyss of the Thing or the Real. Such figures represent a truth which the system must suppress in order to function; yet since they therefore have the least investment in it of any social group, they also have the strange, hallowed power to transform it. They incarnate the contradictions of the social order, and so symbolise its failure in their own. (Eagleton, 2003a, 280)

The tragic hero read in this way becomes a type of that dialectical movement known dialectically as the negation of the negation, and if the significance of that hero's destitution can be universalised, her status can be made to parallel Marx's collective subject, the working class, which precisely by being rendered nothing carries the potential to bring an end to class society. That invocation of Lacan again connects the subjective with the social, since the symbolic order is of course a social phenomenon, that through which we articulate determinate relations with others, whereas the Thing is that force which generates desire but which cannot be accommodated by any particular configuration of the symbolic. There remains nonetheless a problem in such a short-circuiting of the relations between the subjective and the social, since Eagleton's sense of social negation is one which implies a remedy, whereas Lacan, as Malcolm Bowie points out, 'expects the permutations of his triad [the Symbolic, Imaginary and Real] to be enlightening across the entire range of human classes, societies and cultures' (Bowie, 1991, 91), and for Lacan communist society is one which continues to demand a sublimation of the desire on which he urges us not to give up (Lacan, 1992, 318). One alternative account of the relation between the subjective and the social which may stand up to scrutiny is that the reaffirmation of a new social order following any reconstitution of society is bound to generate new exclusion(s) and therefore a new dialectic. This is how Eagleton envisages things in *The Body as Language*, at any rate: here, the 'dialectical process of death and rebirth, of revolution and consolidation, of the sacrality of the negative power of the oppressed and the sacrality of positive restructuring, is the very form of salvation history, and open only to eschatological resolution; it is only in the kingdom of heaven that this creative dialectic within the inner life of the sacred will reach its synthesis, and a structure be created which will not disclose its own deficiencies in the act of being realised' (Eagleton, 1970, 69). If this remains the (unstated) perspective of *Sweet Violence*, it may begin to resolve some of Eagleton's problems, but its sense that humanity can only ever reconstitute society on the basis of new forms of exclusion, that it is irredeemably fallen – however fortunate that fall may be – owes more to Christian dogmatism than to Marxist dialectics.

If the possibility of some rapprochement between psychoanalysis and Marxism breaks down in such an attempt to map subjective onto historical development, it remains possible nonetheless that psychoanalysis may be of use in thinking through the problematic relations between subjectivity, ideology and authority. Once again, the tragic hero is of value to us, reminding us in her abjection of our bodiliness, though not in some immediate sense, as if we could step outside our cultural condition and somehow know again what it is to be 'natural'. Eagleton's Marxism is not of the naïve and implicitly puritannical sort which would simply dismiss the claims of desire in a reassertion of the primacy of need, and indeed he performs a deconstruction of the two in his recognition that 'The supplement of culture is no mere superaddition to human nature, but is needed to fill a structural lack at its core' (Eagleton, 2003a, 286). On the other hand, if we can never simply know what it is to be natural, we can only harm ourselves by forgetting our corporeality and falling for the undialectical alternative to such naturalism: the culturalist, postmodern myth that we are entirely 'constructed' beings. Indeed, the reassertion of the body's primacy is the necessary, indispensable basis of ethical and political solidarity, of the connection between self and other which carries with it the potential to provide the basis for a just social order: 'Human dependency is prior to freedom, and must provide the ground of it' (Eagleton, 2003a, 286). There are echoes here and elsewhere of Merleau-Ponty, an influential figure in Eagleton's thinking about the body: 'Once the other is posited, once the other's gaze fixed upon me has, by inserting me into his field, stripped me of part of my being, it will readily be understood that I can recover it only by establishing relations with him, by bringing about his clear recognition of me, and that my freedom requires the same freedom for others' (Merleau-Ponty, 1962, 357). That reference to a state of dependency is also, though, one which unites political and psychoanalytical concerns, since dependency is our earliest and uniquely protracted human condition, one which not only involves provision for need, but, through the relations through which those needs are met, conditions our subjective development, including our very sense of the other (Eagleton, 1990, 285).

Eagleton's latest reflections, then, reaffirm the materiality of the body, but they also represent a continuation of similar speculations in *The Ideology of the Aesthetic* and elsewhere which highlight the extent to which the body's materiality and its lived experience in culture are bound up with class and other political conflicts. The philosophical category of the aesthetic is, indeed, one which relates precisely to the body, to its senses and the relations between these and rationality. The philosophical discourse of the Enlightenment is produced by and necessarily caught up in the political conflicts of its time. The aesthetic is that category which, on the one hand, might be deployed conserva-tively to emphasise that political power is inscribed in our subjectivity, and on the other, to highlight the autonomy of the subject which might be the basis of resistance to authority:

> If the given social order defends itself in Burkeian fashion through 'culture' – through a plea for the values and affections richly implicit in national tradition – it will tend to provoke an abrasive rationalism from the political left. The left will round scathingly on the 'aesthetic' as the very locus of mystification and irrational prejudice; it will denounce the insidiously naturalising power which Burke has in mind when he com-ments that customs operate better than laws, 'because they become a sort of Nature both to the governors and the governed'. If, however, the existing order ratifies itself by an appeal to absolute law, then the 'subjec-tive' instincts and passions which such law seems unable to encompass can become the basis of a radical critique. (Eagleton, 1990, 26)

Moreover, the 'ambivalence' at the heart of aesthetic discourse lies in the fact that it can never protect itself absolutely against the pos-sibility that the feelings and impulses it is vindicating are 'authentic' rather than socially determined, a valorisation of the individual rather than of established relations. After all, even the emergent bourgeois society of this period required order, and a philosophical advocate of bourgeois freedom such as Hegel locates in the aesthetic – in an appeal to communal ties – the means of defence against the 'bad particular-ism' of bourgeois selfishness and greed. But if Eagleton's sense of aesthetic discourse as riven undecidably from its inception by these two impulses, the source of that contradiction is not located internally, within philosophical texts, as it might be for deconstruction; rather, it is bound up with historical conflicts and imperatives which might only be resolved historically (hence the persistence of this contradiction down to the present). Moreover, that very contradictoriness, grasped dialectically, makes possible something other than the monistic Foucaultian view of Enlightenment discourse as constituting the subject to the roots of her being, as bringing the body under the sway of reason. Rather, the potential liberated in aesthetic discourse is 'dangerous' because 'there is something in the body which can revolt against the power which inscribes it; and that impulse could only be eradicated by extirpating along with it the capacity to authenticate power itself' (Eagleton, 1990, 28). Hence, Eagleton's account of the aesthetic can never be anything other than profoundly ambivalent, neither valorisation nor dismissal, despite Isobel Armstrong's claim that the category of the aesthetic is simply 'repugnant' to him (Armstrong, 2000, 29). In his consideration of each of the thinkers covered in this text, Eagleton considers the permutations of this contradiction at the heart of aesthetic thought.

This duality at the level of the subject might be expressed differently in terms of desire – the desire on the one hand for fulfilment and, on the other, to be obedient. That obedience might yield its satisfactions is not an idea congenial to the Marxist tradition which has tended to regard repression as a force set over and against the individual, one which only various forms of mystification could prevent her from perceiving clearly. Yet one of the enduring problems considered by Western Marxism has been why exploitative capitalist societies have proved so durable. The Italian Marxist Antonio Gramsci influentially makes an important distinction between those regimes which hegemonise their rule – that is, govern largely by winning the consent of their people – and those which are merely repressive. But even such a formulation fails to address obedience as bound up with desire, and this, for Eagleton, is one of the values of the psychoanalytical category of the superego, that social conscience set *internally* against the ego which is the locus of both idealism and self-denial. It is not good enough in constructionist fashion merely to talk of the internalisation of the law: for psychoanalysis, that internalisation is prepared for in the psychic life in a highly complex way which involves identification and the conversion of repressed (pleasurable) instinctual energies as well as inherently masochistic ones. One of the aims of psychoanalytic therapy, indeed, is to attempt to subdue the hostility of the superego towards the ego. At the level of the subject, though, the superego deconstructs the opposition between coercion and hegemony, being, on the one hand, an imperious ruler which feels no need to rationalise its demands and, on the other, that very internal principle of obedience through which the law achieves hegemony.

This imbrication of law and desire, challenging older repressive models, has been influential, but Eagleton characteristically refuses merely to submit to its negative political implications, stressing not merely the grounding of law in the constitution of the subject, but also that we should not take the demands of the law at face value:

> If the law really were transcendentally disinterested, then the political left would most certainly be in trouble. That the law is not, ideologically speaking, how it would like to present itself is at once political obstacle and opportunity. If its grounding in desire is what deepens its virulence, it is also what renders it precarious and problematic, as a genuinely transcendental authority would not be. Marked by the sign of castration, concealing its lack beneath its logocentrism, the law has something of the instability of the unconscious as well as of its drivenness. The very excess of its zeal is the chink in its armour – not only because it involves the law in a ceaseless self-undoing, arousing the yearnings it interdicts, spreading havoc in the name of creating order. The law is out of hand, and if its decrees become insupportable then it leaves its victims with no choice but to fall ill of neurosis or rebel. Both courses of action have their ambiguous pains and pleasures. (Eagleton, 1990, 174)

Hence, there are also (narcissistic) pleasures to be derived from dissent, iconoclasm and revolution which exceed any rational satisfaction to be derived from challenging one's enemies (though Eagleton neglects the point that such feelings too should be regarded ambivalently by the left, since their particular form of excess carries the potential for mere revenge – a point the left perhaps still has sufficiently to learn from Burke). Moreover, there is in Freud a recognition that the healthy process of sublimation is only possible for a minority in most civilisations and that for many the unsatisfactory, because unstable, process of repression embodied in work is the necessary condition for the majority (Eagleton, 1990, 277), a situation which renders those civilisations inherently unstable.

Eagleton's invocation of Freud, then, is necessarily critical, alert to the limitations of a theoretical paradigm which for all its insights is also steeped in bourgeois assumptions. Amongst these – and Eagleton's awareness of this is again determined forcefully by his specifically *Christian* Marxism – is Freud's excessive focus on *erotic* love rather than one which may be said to be impersonal and therefore more obviously social, one grounded in the recognition of our mutual dependency. Nonetheless, if we are tempted to see in Eagleton's critical appropriations of psychoanalysis a conflict between his Christian instincts and the Jewish founder of psychoanalysis, there is no question of Eagleton's awareness that a specifically Christian appeal to love rather than the law can itself be profoundly ideological. By way of a conclusion to this chapter, I want to turn to another of Eagleton's literary readings which brings together his critical interest in deconstruction and his concern with the body, culture and ethics.

Deconstruction and criticism

The possibilities for articulating a Marxist critical practice informed by deconstruction would seem unpromising, but it was to this end that Eagleton devoted himself in the 1980s. Eagleton's most extended literary analysis to be so informed – as well as by psychoanalysis and feminism – is *The Rape of Clarissa*, a complex work which, in an account of the material and ideological conditions of the production of that novel, discusses the ways in which ideologies of class and gender combine in the anti-aristocratic ethos of the book, whilst nonetheless recognising – and even locating in the text – a sense of the limitations of a specifically bourgeois feminism. Such a historically alert sense of the novel's contradictions, and of what it might be *persuaded* to say in a politicised reading, contrasts with an interpretation he attacks at one point as an instance of 'the truly reactionary nature of much deconstructionist "radicalism", once divorced from the social and political contexts it so characteristically finds hard to handle' (Eagleton, 1982, 67–8) for its unequivocal allegiances to the rapist, Lovelace. Later, the series 'Rereading Literature', edited by Eagleton, produced a number of often influential texts on individual authors, and if that series is open to the criticism that it operated to reconfirm the canon, it nonetheless provided resourceful critical accounts of figures still dominant in university syllabi. The strategic aim seems to have been to demonstrate the flexibility of a Marxist critical practice to students who were increasingly schooled in (then) recent theoretical trends and thereby to demonstrate to them that Marxism was not simply last year's fashion.

Eagleton's discussion of Shakespeare in this series is one which elicits from the plays' various forms of instability and undecidability revelations of hollowness (of identity, authority, meaning) where there should be repletion. Indeed the plays are often rendered non-identical with themselves, as when we are informed that 'Meek women, military carnage and aristocratic titles are supposed by the play to be natural; witches and regicide are not. Yet this opposition will not hold even within *Macbeth's* own terms, since the "unnatural" – Macbeth's lust for power – is disclosed by the witches as already lurking within the "natural" – the routine state of cut-throat rivalry between noblemen' (Eagleton, 1986a, 6). As this passage indicates, such forms of non-identity are less the product of some arbitrariness on the part of language, or of some asocial conceptualisation of desire, than of a historical non-identity, of a period in which the static, hierarchical values of feudalism are being increasingly dislocated by those of bourgeois individualism. Hence, the apparent anachronisms of the plays as Eagleton reads them: Lady Macbeth is a ' "bourgeois" feminist' (Eagleton, 1986a, 6), Coriolanus is 'a bourgeois prototype rather than Roman patrician', and the hollowness of the character Hamlet appears to us so modern because he is a character 'strung out' between two social orders, at the beginning of a historical epoch which, in certain respects, our own times seem to be superseding (Eagleton, 1986a, 74–5). However, this latter way of making Shakespeare our contemporary – ironically by placing him historically – brings me to another distinction which I want to make briefly before considering in detail one of Eagleton's readings. If the approach in this book is historicist – 'an exercise in political semiotics, which tries to locate the relevant history in the very letter of the text' (Eagleton, 1986a, ix) – it is far from being a New Historicist one. Whereas New Historicism – highly indebted to Foucault – is concerned to lay bare the alterity generated by historical distance, at least partly in order to challenge humanist assumptions, a very different understanding of history comes through in Eagleton's writing, in which history appears as *longue durée*, as constituted by epochs which establish connections between past and present despite what are by no means insignificant changes (on this, see Eagleton, 1986a, 49–52). If there is a describable entity called capitalism, if we can trace its emergence at least as far back as the sixteenth century, and if it still exists – even in some necessarily transformed manifestation – there must be some common features between then and now.

The unifying theme which underpins the various reflections on Shakespeare's plays is the tension between exactitude and excess which in language is manifest, on the one hand, in the desire for a stable relation between signifier and signified and, on the other, in the realisation that no straightforward correspondence between the two can be predicated. That tension can be signalled in other ways too, not least in the relation between body and history. In Shakespeare, the body is often made to stand figuratively for a social order which is bound by ties of kinship and by economic production which is less abstract – more a matter of use than exchange value – than under capitalism, and one which is also hierarchical. This is in conflict with the transformative, 'progressive' – and thus properly *historical* – features of the emergent bourgeoisie, who effectively call into question the order of self-identity and stability by inaugurating one of economic abstractions through commodity production and constant change. In a move characteristic of Eagleton's later criticism informed by deconstruction, though, the terms are characteristically reversible too, since the bourgeois order's conception of the body is crudely biological, valorising a figure which pursues its selfish interests, one which is thus too absolutely self-identical. For a Shakespeare who is revealed in his plays to be disturbed by these new commercial values, the body possesses a different significance from this, then, one which, though ultimately conservative, nonetheless possesses a dialectical value, since it is

> an inseparable unity of fact and value: to be a human body, biologically speaking, is also to be constrained to behave in certain culturally and ethically sanctioned ways, to feel one's flesh and blood inscribed by a set of discursive norms. Bourgeois naturalism or materialism ruthlessly reduces this complex unity, dividing off facts into dead matter and values into hollow pieties to be pragmatically exploited. (Eagleton, 1986a, 100)

Moreover, exactitude – knowing the price of everything – is also a feature of commodity exchange, whereas the excesses of feudalism are naturalised as 'the kind of largesse or superabundance of Nature which Shakespeare depicts in his last work' (Eagleton, 1986, 100). These complex, reversible and ultimately undecidable contradictions between exactitude and excess are manifest different forms in the various themes Eagleton traces in the plays: 'the respective claims of justice and mercy, inherent and conferred value, law and humanity, art and Nature, or ... the semiotic riddle of an ideal language, at once metaphorically transformative and sensuously precise' (Eagleton, 1986a, 102). The undecidable relations between these two terms to be found in Shakespeare's plays are therefore ones which refer us back to history – as well as forwards to the possibility of a historical transformation of the relations between them – rather than ones which insulate or 'liberate' us from history, as they might have done for the Yale School.

The principal theme of *The Merchant of Venice*, is, of course, justice. But the question it raises is: in what does justice consist? In the rigid application of the law, or in a willingness to make exceptions? If in the latter, then it carries the potential to undermine the general applicability of the law which at least claims to be the means of delivering universal justice (if all cases are merely 'individual', generalisations cannot be made). All legal cases seek a balance between these two elements, but that balance is always going to be a precarious one. (The comparison Eagleton makes is with the deconstructable relationship between *langue* and *parole*: if *parole* – an individual utterance – depends on some prior linguistic system, *langue*, it also exceeds that system in its particularity in a way which frustrates any sense of the determining relations between them.) In the play it is in fact Portia who threatens to undermine the law which Shylock upholds, since it is Portia who insists on the most literal interpretation of the bond made between Antonio and Shylock in an attempt to get Antonio off the hook. In doing so, she goes against the 'spirit' of the law, that which exceeds the letter of the bargain but which is nonetheless essential to its meaning – since the shedding of blood is implicit in that bargain – and thereby threatens to undermine law. Shylock, indeed, understands this – 'If you deny me, fie upon your law!/ There is no force in the decrees of Venice' (IV: i, 101–2) – but, as Shylock also appears to appreciate, that law is far from genuinely universal: it is the law of the Venetian ruling class – in large part capitalist and exclusively Christian – made by and for them. Its pretended universality therefore masks its interestedness – something which complicates any purely formalist deconstruction of system and event, law and individual case. (As the disguised Portia comments in *rejecting* Antonio's offer of payment, 'My mind was never yet more mercenary' [IV: i, 414]). The significance of the interestedness of the law – in terms of both framing and execution – is itself complex: Eagleton speculates that Shylock surely 'knows' that the ruling class will not allow a Jew to get the better of it (we will come back to this point), but, at the same time, Antonio points out that the law must be seen to be upheld to ensure that international capital retains its confidence in the State's legal system (III: iii, 26–31).

The conventional interpretation of Shylock is that he is inhuman in his inflexible exaction of the penalty forfeited by Antonio, constitutively incapable as he seems to be of showing mercy. This – in the cultural history of anti-semitism to which this play has contributed and which forms one of the contexts for Eagleton's reading – is simply to say that he is a Jew, since – at least from the Christian perspective – it is God's punitive legalism which characterises him in the Old Testament, whilst in the New his gracious mercy is both redemptive and gratuitous – 'gratuitous' because it is unmerited by humanity. Portia, indeed, gives Shylock the opportunity to redeem himself:

> The quality of mercy is not strain'd,
> It droppeth as the gentle rain from heaven
> Upon the place beneath, it is twice blest,
> It blesseth him that gives, and him that takes,
> 'Tis mightiest in the mightiest, it becomes
> The throned monarch better than his crown.
> His sceptre shows the force of temporal power,
> The attribute to awe and majesty,
> Wherein doth sit the dread and fear of kings:
> But mercy is above this sceptred sway,
> It is enthroned in the heart of kings,
> It is an attribute to God himself;
> And earthly power doth then show likest God's
> When mercy seasons justice: therefore Jew,
> Though justice be thy plea, consider this,
> That in the course of justice, none of us
> Should see salvation: we do pray for mercy,
> And that same prayer, doth teach us all to render
> The deeds of mercy. (IV: i, 180–98)

Here, mercy is a 'higher' principle than fear-inducing government, and the language is replete with Christian values. In the spirit of Eagleton's reading which reveals an interested law and a knowing Shylock, we might speculate that the plea being made here is actually no plea at all – Portia, of course, knows she still holds her trump card when her entreaty will fail – but a tendentious speech about the superior virtues of Christianity which consequently, and predictably, falls not so much on deaf as defiant ears. In such an interpretation, the word 'Jew' would carry the full weight of a condescension consistent with the 'mercy' finally shown to Shylock by the court which requires his forced conversion under penalty of death. But Eagleton's strategy goes further, rejecting Portia's initial claim that mercy's sway is, or should be, unlimited, bound up with creation itself (another of God's gratuitously benevolent gestures, of course). If this is the case, what happens to justice? The point is made with reference to a telling modern instance: 'Would it have been admirably merciful, or an obscene insult to the dead, to have allowed a later anti-semite [than Antonio], Adolf Eichmann, to go free?' (Eagleton, 1986a, 47). And it is in this respect that Eagleton points to the value of Shylock's apparently vengeful insistence on his bargain: law is the basis of justice and of rights, and therefore sacrosanct to a socially despised figure such as Shylock, whereas the mercy demanded by Venice's Christian rulers is less a gen- uine principle than that which they can afford to dispense given their privileges: gratuity doesn't cost them.

But Shylock also commits an act of gratuity in making his bargain in the first place, a generous one in the eyes of Shylock *and* Antonio (though not Bassanio), since no one expects that Antonio's ships will apparently not come in. His demand for a pound of flesh is one which, in a sense, recognises that the body is 'invaluable' – that is, falls outside the logic of exchange value – and is both all and nothing: all, in that it represents a human life, and nothing in that it is worthless to Shylock in monetary terms. Moreover, as we have seen, the body is that which unites us as that which we all have in common, *demanding* recogni- tion of our commonality, spontaneously uniting fact and value. This is the import of Shylock's famous speech drawing attention to his own emotional and corporeal humanity, a humanity which has been violated in his treatment at the hands of Antonio in particular and Christian society in general. Hence, the 'bond' he makes with Antonio is a 'dark, bitter inversion of the true comradeship Shylock desires' (Eagleton, 1986a, 43), of the objective claims of our physical condition (though I find Eagleton's depiction of Shylock's intended exactions as 'a kind of black mass or grotesque parody of eucharistic fellowship' insufficiently cautious, however licensed by the text, given the history to which his reading alludes). In this respect too the terms of the play can be reversed: Portia and the others see Shylock as inhuman because unmerciful, whereas his demand all along – perverted through ill treat- ment into vengeance though it is – is that his humanity be recognised, a demand consistent with Shylock's faith. Moreover, 'for [Shylock], love is not the subjectivist whims of Eros' – as it is for the various bourgeois romantic lovers of the play, for whom love is, in idealist fashion, neces- sarily placed beyond the (capitalist) terms of social valuation – 'but the ruthless impersonal requirements of *agape* (charity), which demands precise services, obligations and recognitions' (Eagleton, 1986a, 46–7).

The relationship between humanity and writing is one of the crucial themes of this reading of the play. For the Christians, humanity resides precisely in the mercy which Shylock would deny in his insistence on his *written* bargain, but the irony of such an appeal is that, if the human is that which is somehow above, beyond or in excess of the written, Venetian society is itself constituted by legal and contractual relations. Hence, 'The human is not that which goes beyond writing, but the way in which writing goes beyond itself ... One of the problems the play faces ... is how to distinguish this positive mutual involvement of language and the body from that tyranny of the letter which destroys the body's substance' (Eagleton, 1986a, 39), how therefore to disentangle properly universal claims from those which oppressively deny (bodily) particularity. If Eagleton is – on the whole, though not wholly – on the side of a Shylock a who represents the universalism of the law and the body, it is as a means of correcting the particularistic logic of Venice's rulers, a particularism which masks their interestedness. The reading carries necessary lessons for deconstruction and postmodernism, since, whilst it refuses any *definitive* privileging of these terms, it nonetheless seeks to alert us to the necessity of speaking up for Shylock in the context of the historical power relations which are written into the text, rather than by merely emphasising his difference.

Finally, there are two related points I want to make about this reading, both of which relate to critical practice and to the philosophical relations between language, or culture, and the body. First of all, there is the licence taken by this reading. Of course, it is a 'partial' one against which many objections could be raised. There is, for instance, a sense in which Antonio's flesh *does* possess monetary value to Shylock, since one of Shylock's reasons for hating Antonio is that his gratuitous – that is, non-profitable – loans threaten the 'rate of usance' in Venice (I: iii, 40). Elsewhere, though, Shylock declares that a pound of human flesh 'Is not so estimable, profitable neither/ As flesh of mutton, beefs [sic], or goats' (I: iii, 162–3). Here, by contrast, Antonio's body is worthless to him, negatively incommensurable in value with commodities in flesh. Indeed, the motivations of Shakespeare's villains are notoriously overdetermined, so much so that it is difficult to pinpoint the finally determining factor in their malice. Which is another way of saying that all interpretations are, and must be, creative, just as all performances are (and the knowingness attributed to Shylock in Eagleton's interpretation suggests one possible way of dramatising his character on stage). It is also to say that there is no 'essential' meaning to be discovered in the text (though this is *not* to say that there are no limits to what the text might mean). And here we might observe an instructive contrast between the critical practice commended to us in *Criticism and Ideology* and that which Eagleton has developed since 'taking on' deconstruction. Whereas that earlier text drew parallels between history and dramatic text, and ideology and performance – the latter in each case 'creatively' responding to the determinations of the former – his more recent, more philosophical criticism rejects much of the scientism of that earlier approach, the purpose of which was to lay bare some essence of the text and which consequently failed to historicise the act of interpretation. In this account of *The Merchant*, Eagleton's reading not only situates the text in a particular historical moment but recognises its own situatedness and presses the play's meanings into service in relation not merely to twentieth-century anti-semitism, but also contemporary politico-philosophical debates. The reference to Eichmann's trial in this account of *The Merchant* is, on the one hand – from a certain kind of historicising vantagepoint – unwarranted in its ahistoricism (how could Shakespeare or his audience have access to a knowledge of the future?) and, on the other, both ethically necessary and hermeneutically unavoidable (how is it possible *not* to view the play through a post-Holocaust optic?). The gesture, then, is both gratuitous and necessary – it is a necessary gratuity – akin therefore to that which Eagleton is unafraid to call human nature, a fact which brings me to my second point.

The body, Eagleton claims, provides a necessary ground for our ethics and politics. But one of the features of human nature – indeed *the* distinctive feature of *human* nature, our *species* being – is that we out-strip any sense of nature as a fixed propensity (necessity), go beyond it in the creation of history and, through that, generate culture in its broadest sense (culture which is thus gratuitous, and, from a Christian perspective, a gracious dispensation). So, there is no discourse of nature which is not also and inevitably cultural, but then culture is what comes naturally to us. If this is the case, though, it is of the utmost importance that this deconstructive insight should not lead us to dissolve either term into the other, either by 'naturalising' culture (a gesture which has always been supremely ideological) or, in the name of anti-essentialism, dispensing with any talk of 'nature' at all. Rather, the imperative must be to be true to our nature by continuing to create history in ways which make that history fully respectful of our bodies, honouring their needs and making possible the full creative potential of all. Eagleton's literary critical practice is less concerned now merely to reveal the text's produc-tion of ideology than to render its meanings accountable to that project.

3 Marxism, Culture and Irish Studies

If Eagleton's career has been beset by controversies, these have largely been the fairly predictable consequence of a Marxist's interventions in academic debates dominated by liberal assumptions, even if dressed up in contemporary theoretical language. His recent work in Irish Studies, though, has generated a range of controversies whose complexities are not easily reducible to left-liberal antagonisms. At the same time, his contributions to this field have been more consistently travestied than elsewhere as various hostile commentators have attempted to fix his image as the stereotypical 'plastic Paddy' or offspring of a sentimental and excessively romantic Irish émigré culture. There is something of this in Edna Longley's reference to 'Thomas Kilroy's *Double Cross*, largely a play about residual inferiority complexes. (Though Kilroy's scenario, in which Brendan Bracken and William Joyce strive to become "English", might be complemented by another drama in which figures such as Micheal MacLiammoir or Terry Eagleton would reinvent themselves as "Irish")' (Longley, 1994, 223). Alternatively, his political affiliations with Irish nationalism have been represented as compensation for the decline of Marxism as a political and intellectual force. Thus R. F. Foster comments, not so obliquely, that 'The old form of the [nationalist] narrative continued to exert a compelling attraction for lost souls from the larger island, beached by receding tides of intellectual fashion (structuralist as well as Marxist)' (Foster, 2001, 20). A similar point is made in spruced up theoretical language by Martin McQuillan:

> Given that history has been so undialectical as to produce Tony Blair and New Labour, Eagleton's search for the New Jerusalem has taken him to the satanic mills of Irish history. It is easier to tell the goodies from the baddies in a postcolonial struggle, and the binary of coloniser and colonised bears a reassuring similarity to Hegel's master/slave dialectic. In such a scenario the colonised Irish (Eagleton has never equivocated

about whose 'side' he is on) become a substitute for the lost working class dispersed by the neo-liberalism of Mrs Thatcher. (McQuillan, 2002, 34)

Here the claims are more detailed and more clearly symptomatic of a particular ideological perspective than in Foster. For a start, to represent New Labour's emergence as undialectical is – apparently at any rate – to take the discourse of the Third Way at its own word rather than see it for what it is: one instance amongst many of the global reassertion of the bad side of history's dialectic. The failure to recognise this is consistent with the ambiguous assertion that Thatcher 'dispersed' the working class. The ambiguity is itself significant. Insofar as Thatcher assisted the decimation of traditional industries and forms of organised labour, enabling the growth in non-traditional employment in which labour organisation has been weakened, this might be said to be true; insofar as it implies some form of dissolution or 'disappearance' of a structurally determined agent called the working class it is false (from the perspective of capital, call-centre workers are little different from machine operators). Second, it's not clear what a postcolonial – as opposed to anti-colonial – struggle might be, but the slippage between these terms is indicative of the extent to which postcolonialism appropriates its supposed radicalism from anti-colonial movements without subscribing to the very dialectical logic by which those movements have brought about their ends. (McQuillan's use of inverted commas in relation to the word 'side' is indicative of this.) As Eagleton has noted – drawing on the work of Aijaz Ahmad – 'postcolonialism gets off the ground [as an academic theoretical movement] in the wake of the crushing or exhaustion of the various revolutionary nationalisms which dealt world imperialism such a staggering series of rebuffs some twenty years ago' (Eagleton, 1998a, 125). Nor is it clear (to me at least) that in the (northern) Irish conflict sides are easier to tell apart and more readily evaluated than in anti-capitalist struggles: that perception is also surely historically determined. Finally, Eagleton has not been quite so unequivocal about nationalism as his parodists make out (the militaristic language which McQuillan consistently projects onto Eagleton in his article suggests his acceptance of such parodies). Anti-colonial struggle is not, for Eagleton, a substitute for working-class struggle, but rather a precondition for the effective emergence of socialist politics. These are all matters to which I want to return.

I would not be the first, then, to remark on the extent to which such comments say at least as much about their various authors as they do about Eagleton himself, representing as they do pejuration, misrepresentation or confusion rather than genuine intellectual engagement. Eagleton's particular relationhip to Irishness is not a consequence of 'reinvention', but of having been born into an immigrant Catholic Irish family in Salford at a time when anti-Irish racism helped structure relations between such families and the society into which they emigrated. He is not unaware of that émigré culture's propensity for sentimentality and false consciousness. Writing of his father in his memoir, he comments that 'He could be dewy-eyed about Ireland, and once described it to me with caught breath as "sacred soil"; yet his memories of the place seemed blurred and probably for the most part thoroughly unpleasant, and he had not the slightest intention of ever returning' (Eagleton, 2001, 120). Of his grandmother, he notes that 'She appeared to be the archetypal, long-suffering, don't-mind-me-I'll-make-do-with-a-scrap-of-badger-droppings Irish mother, though this concealed a self-centredness which would have put Caligula to shame' (Eagleton, 2001, 117). That said, he recognises a certain Benjaminian critical value to sentimentality in relation to modernity. Writing of Roy Foster's *The Irish Story*, he points out that one of 'Foster's briskly modernising myths ... is that nostalgia for the past is always morbid, and this in an age of Chris Evans, nuclear missiles and the IMF' (Eagleton, 2003, 232). Moreover, Eagleton's concern with Irish culture cannot be dismissed as a recent one. Indeed, it predates the emergence of Irish Studies as an identifiable or institutionalised academic field. Anyone who cares to reread *Criticism and Ideology*, for instance, will discover a substantial treatment of the cultural production of the *filí*, the specifically literary figures amongst early Irish tribal bards, and of the effects on literary production of the seventeenth-century colonial subjugation of Ireland – inclusions which must have bemused and possibly even astonished early readers of the book by demonstrating an apparent obsession with 'marginal' matters. His only novel, *Saints and Scholars*, is set in Ireland and stages a debate between the Irish Republican Marxist James Connolly, Wittgenstein, Leopold Bloom and Nikolai Bakhtin, and Irish issues dominate his recently collected plays. Nor is it fair to accuse Eagleton of trotting out nationalist platitudes, since his sympathetic, yet critical, attitude to Irish nationalism is conditioned by a continuing primary political commitment to Marxism whose political goals are internationalist. His writings do not merely disparage the work of 'revisionist' historians such as Foster, though they certainly aim to demonstrate those historians' ideological limitations, and his reflections on the relations between historical events and the narrative fashioning of those events, as well as on the complexity of the relations between England, or Britain, and Ireland are substantially more sophisticated than Foster's slight allows, as we will see in considering his reflections on Emily Brontë's novel. On the other hand, he has fallen foul of others who might have been expected to demonstrate some sympathy with him on political grounds, but whose theoretical absorption in postcolonialism has led to attacks on his attempts to integrate an understanding of Ireland into a Marxist grasp of historical processes. I am thinking here in particular of David Lloyd's critique of Eagleton's first collection of essays on Irish culture which I consider below in a fairly sustained comparison of the two writers' work.

Most of the debates central to Irish Studies are historical in one sense or another. Indeed, Irish literary and cultural criticism is less likely to find controversial the proposition that cultural production is determined in some sense by history than its British counterpart at one time was. Rather more controversial, however, are the questions of precisely how the relationship between culture and history should be handled and, more fundamentally, how one interprets history. Hence, any attempt to outline salient features of Irish history for the student or general reader new to such debates is likely to fall prey to accusations of partiality, selectivity, terminological anachronism and teleological thinking, amongst others (I also return to these questions below). Nonetheless, some preliminary account of that history appears to me necessary before going on to consider what is at stake in the debates generated by it.

The orthodox nationalist history of Ireland asserts that the country was England's first colony, the initial period of colonisation dating from the twelfth century, even though Henry II's decision to bring Ireland under the sway of the English crown was a complex one prompted by internal Irish divisions as well as Norman expansionism. The resulting governance of Ireland, was characterised not merely by domination, though, since these colonising rulers, who later came to be known as the 'Old English', were to some extent assimilated to Irish ways. Catholic and gaelicised, they were not wholly culturally distinct from those they ruled. That distinction between rulers and ruled was established later during the recolonisation of Ireland, a process determined by the need of the Tudor state to consolidate its authority when, after the Reformation, Protestantism became increasingly associated with loyalty and Catholicism with disloyalty. Ireland's recalcitrant Catholicism – on the part of Old English settlers as well as native Irish – required the establishment of a ruling class whose religious affiliations were indicative of their allegiance to the English crown. It was effectively under Elizabeth I that the brutal process of expropriating the land of Catholics and replacing them with Protestant (Anglican or Presbyterian) English and Scottish 'planters' was initiated, though it was under Cromwell that the policy was most brutally prosecuted. This strategy of plantation was particularly successful in Ulster, generating that distinctiveness from much of the rest of Ireland which would persist down the centuries. What also distinguished this process of recolonisation was a desire to replace formerly feudal relations between landlord and tenant with the kind of capitalist agriculture which had already been pioneered in England: a capitalism which sought increased productivity through 'improvement' of the land and which established the relationship between landlord, tenant and labourer on a purely economic, rather than customary, basis (Wood, 2003, 73–88). The achievement, however, lagged far behind, less because certain exceptional customs – particularly in Ulster – persisted, but because over time landlords in Ireland displayed significantly less interest in improvement than their English counterparts. The relatively poor, backward state of much Irish agriculture remained a theme of visitors to Ireland throughout the nineteenth century and the blame for it was consistently levelled at neglectful or absentee landlords where it was not considered a consequence of the innate slothfulness of the Irish race.

Thus colonisation in Ireland was bound up with the religious conflicts of Britain, and the religious inflection of Irish anti-colonial movements and political nationalism would continue to be determined significantly by the sectarian nature of class and colonial rule in that island, not least through the various anti-Catholic Penal Laws passed from 1695 on as part of the settlement of those religio-political conflicts (however rigorously enforced these might have been). This Catholic inflection to Irish nationalism has continued in spite of progressive attempts from the later eighteenth century on of the Republican tradition in particular to achieve a secular nationalism. Religion, then, has played a significant part in determining the cultural differences which have also structured Anglo-Irish relations. The native Irish and Old English were perceived as the colonists' others, effectively as barbarians, and this perception of Irish inferiority – that is, in historical terms, of their 'backwardness' – has persisted, though the terms for describing that inferiority were to change, consolidated as they were in the nineteenth century by the 'scientific' racism which defined an emotional and often abject Celticism antithetically in relation to the rational and freedom-loving Saxons. In this process, religion came to be regarded as symptomatic of fundamental racial distinctions.[1]

For most of the eighteenth century, Ireland possessed a parliament subordinate ultimately to Westminster, but during the nineteenth century and up to the establishment of the Free State in 1922, Ireland was incorporated into the Union, sending MPs to and being governed from London. The Union was effected in response to the Republican Uprising of 1798 – by far the most radical 'internal' threat to British authority in these years of more general European revolution, during which Britain emerged as the leading counter-revolutionary force – and the legacy of that uprising was visible to many English visitors who noted the disfigurement of Ireland's picturesque landscape by the military barracks which were erected throughout the country. The various forms of proto-nationalism and nationalism which characterised Irish life throughout the century secured various reforms designed to bring about its assimilation: the idea of converting Irish Catholics to Protestantism was all but abandoned in favour of the erosion of institutionalised Protestant privilege – though it should be noted that even liberals such as Matthew Arnold argued that the creation of a more secular and rational culture in Ireland through non-denominational State-sponsored educational institutions would be conducive to the spread of the Protestant faith by liberating Catholics from their superstitions – and land reforms enacted by Parliament in the later nineteenth century eventually undermined the landlords' economic and political domination by the effective redistribution of their property, thus enabling the emergence of a largely Catholic and nationalist middle class. Such attempts at reform and pacification – including the promise of Home Rule prior to the First World War – were ultimately unsuccessful as the initially unpopular military Easter Rising of 1916 was transformed into a successful awakening of Irish nationalist consciousness in response to the State executions of its leaders. The Irish Republican Army (IRA) led the military campaign to achieve Irish independence, though the final settlement with Britain also resulted in the creation of the Northern Irish State whose unprecedented borders were determined purely by the need to secure a

Protestant majority. This was in response to persistent Protestant Unionist opposition to greater independence for Ireland throughout the later nineteenth and early twentieth centuries (though Unionist fears of being incorporated into an autonomous Ireland were certainly both stoked and exploited by forces at Westminster, and members of the Conservative and Unionist Party supported the principle of armed resistance to legislative Home Rule).

The terms of the 1922 settlement ensured the carnival of reaction on both sides of the border predicted by the Irish Marxist, James Connolly, as social divisions were effectively given State sanction: in the Free State an illiberal Catholicism dominated, whilst the majority in Northern Ireland ensured that it became, in the notorious words of its first Prime Minister James Craig, 'a Protestant State for a Protestant people'. Catholics were severely discriminated against socially and politically, giving rise finally – in conditions globally conducive to such movements – to the emergence of a Civil Rights Association in the late 1960s. That movement was short-lived, as loyalist mobs and the State's own security forces brutally suppressed it, and the chaos which ensued led to the introduction of British troops into the province. That the role of those troops was less to 'protect Catholics' – the conventional account – than to restore order was confirmed as the original troublemakers were targeted and State violence was increasingly turned on the largely nationalist radicals. In this process, Bloody Sunday – the killing of fourteen Irish men by British paratroopers – in 1972 was a watershed, convincing many Catholics that the Northern Irish State was unreformable and that an armed struggle was necessary in order to bring an end to its existence. The rest, until relatively recently, was not so much history as bloody stalemate in a struggle between Republicans, Loyalists and State forces. The terms of the conflict, whose persistence has generated the ideological tensions and certainly the febrile atmosphere so characteristic of Irish Studies, require some interrogation.

British State policy in the north of Ireland has been fatally riven by its contradictoriness, pursuing simultaneously policies of reform of the illiberal, thoroughly sectarian institutions and civil society of Northern Ireland in an attempt to assimilate Irish nationalists, and repression, principally of that same Irish nationalist community, in its attempts to suppress Irish Republicanism. The latter has been the overriding imperative and has led the British State in various ways to placate, bow down to and even collude with its most avowedly 'loyal' subjects in a variety of ways, including – as the peace process is increasingly bearing witness – the most murderous. The extent and the nature of collusion between the security forces and loyalist paramilitaries may never be fully known, but there is sufficient evidence to suggest that it was far from casual; certainly it was motivated by strategies other and even less defensible than simple intelligence gathering on Loyalism (the usual justification). The contradictions into which the British State has been driven – or, at least, the symptoms of these contradictions – has often enough been blamed in racist fashion on the intractability of the Irish themselves, or, in a liberal displacement of this case, on the 'impossibility' of the 'Irish situation', but it is in fact the product of a history largely determined by British policy. The response of revisionist historians to such a claim might predictably be that this itself displaces blame from internal Irish forces onto a conveniently 'other' British State, but it is rather merely to acknowledge that the role of the British State has been to underwrite – albeit reluctantly, contradictorily, even at times naively – one brand of sectarianism and thereby to forestall the possibility of any genuine reconciliation between those very internal forces.

Focus on events in the north has, however, tended to distract the British left from changes in the Irish Republic which are also significant in determining the ideological features of current debates. Crucially, from 1959 onwards, the Irish Republic actively and successfully courted foreign capital investment, encouraging urbanisation and undermining the economic primacy of rural society which had been ideologically symbolic of a specifically Irish way of life. With urbanisation has come greater social liberalism and a consequent relaxation of the grip of the Catholic Church, which saw its privileged status in the Republic's constitution formally brought to an end in 1972. (This is not to say, of course, that the Church does not still exert considerable influence in moral debates such as those over abortion.) Enthusiastic membership of the European Community, at least on the part of governments, has enhanced the Irish Republic's performance, helping to transform it into the kind of 'thriving modern economy' which inevitably brings with it intensified disputes between labour and capital – even if official Irish politics are still dominated by the two parties which emerged from the Civil War, Fianna Fáil and Fine Gael, rather than by class-based parties. At the same time, Northern Ireland's conflict has brought about economic disinvestment and has necessitated a huge annual subvention by the British government in order to keep the State going (just about). All of which rendered Irish governments' attachment to their 'fourth field' largely rhetorical, so that the recent repeal of constitutional claims to sovereignty of the north was largely a formality.

The function of this brief, manifestly inadequate and some will say partisan account of crucial features of Irish history is not simply to serve as an introduction for those largely ignorant of it; it is also to highlight the ways in which Irish history appears to challenge certain fundamental convictions about historical processes. Modern Irish historiography has provoked considerable debate, and not merely in academic circles, about both the accuracy of a formerly orthodox or traditionalist – which is to say, nationalist – Irish history and the contemporary purposes which such history serves. In this context, revisionist historians have presented themselves as the progressive demystifiers of a narrative whose sacredness precluded self-criticism. But Irish history also forces us to interrogate the ways in which temporal processes are conceived, not least because of its relations with and proximity to a former imperial power whose own temporal imaginary was determined crucially by its post-Reformation Protestant identity, its contributions to Enlightenment rationalism, and its economic precocity amongst European nations. All of these determined England's, if not always Britain's, confident sense of its inevitable, yet gradual progress (and the declining influence of all of which more latterly precipitated a peculiarly English melancholia from which it is only beginning to recover). The majority in Ireland however have remained steadfastly Catholic, despite attempts throughout their history to Protestantise them, whilst Irish society was socially characterised until the late nineteenth century by an absent middle class and developed a Gaelic nationalist ideology often consciously at odds with bourgeois values. In all of these ways, it has appeared premodern, as has the endemic 'atavistic' violence which remained a pervasive feature of Irish society throughout the nineteenth century but which has apparently still been with us until recently in the north-east of Ireland. Even here there are complications, since the best elements of Republican tradition lay claim to a tradition – one of secularism in politics and of democracy and human rights – which is definitively modern, whilst the discourse of Unionism/Loyalism, where it is on its best behaviour, is often indebted to a specifically British Protestant notion of civil liberties (though it has to be said that that tradition has always had problems with a Catholicism it deems irredeemably illiberal). In the context of this present juncture, academic attempts to modernise nationalist politics by integrating them into current cultural theoretical concerns have produced what some consider strange alliances. In a relentlessly hostile account of Irish nationalism, which I cite here without approving it, Stephen Howe remarks:

> The premodern [ie. Republican violence] and the postmodern form uneasy solidarities against the claims of modernity, setting themselves against not only prospects of European or wider transnationality but also against universalist conceptions of democracy, citizenship, human rights and equality. Ironically, much that defines 'republicanism' in its usual international meanings is repudiated by such currents of Irish Republicanism and its friends.[2] (Howe, 2000, 234–5)

Moreover, to the extent that a modernised Irish Republic still dwells on its history of colonisation and trauma, it is regarded by many as living in the past. R. F. Foster's scathing account of Ireland's 150th anniversary memorialisation of the Famine (Foster, 2001, 29–32) and Francis Mulhern's critique of contemporary cultural nationalism as 'postcolonial melancholy' (Mulhern, 1998, 161) are two instances of this conviction, related in their insistence on the contemporaneity of Ireland, though very different in ideological complexion. The list of ambiguities, contrasts and paradoxes could be extended, but at the heart of them remains Ireland's peculiarly warped – a term I don't intend pejoratively – relations to history as most of us have been persuaded to understand it.

History, narrative and famine in Ireland

The Irish potato famine of the mid-nineteenth century focuses many of these issues about history, and – conveniently enough for my purposes – Eagleton returns to consider *Wuthering Heights* in the first chapter of *Heathcliff and the Great Hunger* in a way which partly revises his earlier reading of this text, but which also enables him to move freely and with an extravagant licence (which outraged certain critics of the book) among various themes which are at the heart of his engagement with Irish Studies. Still central to his analysis is an understanding of the relationship between nature and culture, since the latter is the product of a surplus generated from the former but which in socially unequal conditions is a more conspicuous feature of the lives of those such as the Lintons than those who lead the rather more hand-to-mouth existence of the Earnshaws. This, though, enables Eagleton to reflect on the very different relations between nature and culture in Britain and Ireland, relations which were pointed up most dramatically and catastrophically by the Irish Potato Famine of 1845–48 which claimed around a million lives – it is difficult to arrive at a precise number – through starvation and diseases caused by malnourishment, whilst more than a million emigrated as a response to the Famine and its aftermath. More specifically, Eagleton is concerned with the ways in which the Famine can be grasped as an historical event, influencing not only the subsequent material basis of Irish society but also our sense of its relations to previous and subsequent events, since it was, writes Eagleton, 'the greatest social disaster of nineteenth-century Europe – an event with something of the characteristics of a low-level nuclear attack' (Eagleton, 1995, 23). The interweaving themes of this essay, then, concern the various relations between nature, social structure, culture and history.

Eagleton's gambit is that Heathcliff can be interpreted as a refugee from the Famine, since he is brought home from Liverpool – the main port for Irish immigrants fleeing the Famine – and is said by Nelly Dean to have spoken a species of 'gibberish' on his first arrival at the Heights. He is also, as we have already noted, racialised as other, someone whose later cultural accomplishments are merely a veneer for an obdurately vicious character signified by his physiognomy. (It has been less commonly noted, however, that Eagleton speculates that Heathcliff may have acquired some of his Byronic features from the fact that Emily's information about Liverpool is likely to have been mediated by her rakish brother, Branwell, who led a 'flamboyant stage-Irish existence' [Eagleton, 1995, 1].) But the point is less that Eagleton wants to assert that Heathcliff *is* Irish – he explicitly mentions a number of problems with this interpretation – than that his characterisation reveals something of the role that Ireland and the Irish played symbolically in relation to English sensibilities. Hence Eagleton's recourse to the language of psychoanalysis in describing Ireland as Britain's 'unconscious', that which is repressed in the civilised discourse of British life. Crucially, nature in the Irish context is resistant to that characteristic aesthetic ideology, organicism, which compares the natural world with the gradual, evolutionary trajectory of British history. In Ireland the interaction with nature in the nineteenth century was for most more conspicuously about scraping together a living than gaining pleasure from a certain perspective on it, and consequently Ireland confronts Britain's organicist sensibility with that other characteristically British materialist discourse on nature 'which speaks of men and women as labouring instruments and fertilising mechanisms' (Eagleton, 1995, 8), and with which organicism is at odds: political economy. As we have already seen, though capitalism has been the source of Britain's wealth, the principles of political economy were hardly calculated to produce social cohesion, hence the recovery of organicism by a tradition of influential nineteenth-century thinkers. This repression of the facts of labour which culture and the organicist perspective necessarily require, is symbolised for Eagleton in the novel by the Lintons' expulsion of Heathcliff:

> Ireland is the biological time-bomb which can be heard ticking softly away beneath the civilised superstructures of the Pall Mall clubs; and its history offers to lay bare the murky material roots of that civility as pitilessly as does Heathcliff. When the child Heathcliff trespasses on the Grange, the neurasthenically cultivated Lintons set the dogs on him, forced for a moment to expose the veiled violence which helps prop them up. (Eagleton, 1995, 9)

Characteristically, though, Eagleton notes various permutations and inversions of the different relations between nature and culture in and between British and Irish societies. In another tradition, for instance, Ireland is regarded as culturally resistant to the discourse of British political economy. But the repression of Irish realities is the one which is most insistently pursued in this essay, and, indeed, this repression can be discerned in the trajectory of Patrick Brontë himself, a figure whose remarkable career saw him rise from lowly status in Ireland to Tory Anglican vicar of Haworth. (The Brontës themselves rarely make explicit reference to Ireland in their work, except in negative ways.)

What further distinguishes this essay and yet makes it in many respects typical of Eagleton's contribution to Irish Studies is its treatment of the Famine itself. Eagleton dwells in particular on the unrepresentability of the Famine, noting that until relatively recently the Famine has been occluded in various sorts of discourse, not least literary and historiographical, in Ireland itself. Hence, Eagleton's own essay is one of a number of more recent accounts which recognise the centrality of the Famine in Irish history. That unrepresentability is a product of various factors – of the shame which Irish people felt in relation to the Famine, of the inherent problems it poses to representation (how does one adequately convey such an enormity?) – but amongst these, one of the most significant is that the Famine defies representation in and through the various narrative modes through which we make sense of events, since it was caused not by some tragic villain, but by an agent, nature, which, if it can be personified at all, can only be so as blankly indifferent and unmotivated. Moreover, if the Famine is considered as the culmination of a particular 'stage' of Irish history, then both the necessity driving events and the end to which those events led bear no relation to anything conceivable within the British organicist conception of history: 'Irish history would appear to have all the necessity of that teleological drive, but to absolutely no beneficent end. A necessity, in short, without a telos, implacable but distinctly unprovidential' (Eagleton, 1995, 14). (This, however, is not to say that there weren't many in England who regarded the Famine precisely as a providential, salutary and necessary corrective to human social mismanagement not to be ameliorated by governmental interference [see e.g. Hilton, 1988, 108–14].) Moreover, this catastrophe is both end and origin, since it also marks the beginning of Ireland's emergence into modernity, not least through its effects in clearing the land of 'excess' numbers of peasants and enabling the development of a middle class whose presence English commentators had always considered essential to the reform of Irish social structures, and this rural middle class would ultimately constitute the political force for the construction of the Irish Free State. Again, in comparing this moment in Irish history to Brontë's novel, the analogy is with psychoanalysis:

> Because of the Famine, Irish society undergoes a surreal speed-up of its entry upon modernity; but what spurs that process on is, contradictorily, a thoroughly traditional calamity. ... This deathly origin then shatters space as well as time, unmaking the nation and scattering Irish history across the globe [through emigration]. That history will of course continue; but as in Emily Brontë's novel there is something recalcitrant at its core which defeats articulation, some 'real' which stubbornly refuses to be symbolised. In both cases, this 'real' is a voracious desire which was beaten back and defeated, which could find no place in the symbolic order of social time and was expunged from it. ... Some primordial trauma has taken place which fixates your development at one level even as you continue to unfold at another, so that time in Irish history and *Wuthering Heights* would seem to move backwards and forwards simultaneously. Something, anyway, for good or ill, has been irrevocably lost; and in both Ireland and the novel it takes up its home on the alternative terrain of myth. (Eagleton, 1995, 14–15)

The Famine achieved what the political economists of the time wanted: the conditions of possibility for modern agriculture in Ireland – that improvement of the land which had been desired by England/ Britain since the recolonisation – through the eradication of barely subsistence farming, and yet the moment of the Famine continues to haunt Irish progress just as Catherine and Heathcliff's maturity is conditioned by traumatic loss. What is not clear, though, is what exactly Eagleton intends by invoking the Lacanian category of the real, other than as a synonym for the unrepresentable. If we understand what is meant by 'a voracious desire which was beaten back and defeated' in relation to *Wuthering Heights*, it is less clear what this means in relation to the Famine, even if the claim that this moment of 'origin' became seriously mythologised, makes sense. This invocation of a psychoanalytic category again risks mystifying actual historical events by suggesting a singular or collective agency at work in Irish history.

This allegorical reading of *Wuthering Heights* goes on to flaunt its own outrageousness by taking Heathcliff as the embodiment of the fate of Irish agriculture itself, moving from dispossessed soul to rural labourer, exploitative tenant farmer to expropriator of the gentry (the Linton's) themselves. In a comparable way, Irish farmers effec-tively expropriated the land of the Irish gentry, except in their case the expropriating was done for them by the British State, thus bringing about the downfall of the Irish ruling class formerly installed and sustained by that same State in its previous incarnations. It is an irony to which Eagleton repeatedly returns in his various essays, not least in the magnificent chapter 'Ascendancy and Hegemony'. Here he explores in more detail the contrasts between Britain and Ireland, elaborating on the argument that the failure of the Irish Ascendancy class was to hegemonise its rule; that is, to establish consent for that rule in the hearts and minds of those over whom it ruled, not least since 'Their power was too visibly traditionalist to present itself as mere *rentier* wealth, but too nakedly profit-oriented to permit them to pose as the traditional guardians of the poor' (Eagleton, 1995, 59). Consequently, it failed to achieve the characteristically ideological move of naturalising its social superiority. There were factors other than directly economic ones which determined this failure – their social position resulted from an historic expropriation of land, their religious contempt for Catholicism often compounded their disdain for their tenants, and their lack of attachment to Ireland itself was often enough demonstrated by their physical absence from the country – and, crucially too, over the course of the nineteenth century they increasingly became a neo-feudal anachronism for the modernising British State itself.

Once again, Burke figures prominently in this discussion, since he recognised the necessity of binding a social order through sentiment, the law being an inadequate means of doing so, a last resort to be invoked once a more instinctive obedience on the part of the State's subjects has broken down. Such reflections lead Eagleton once again into a consideration of the relations between subjectivity and ideology which combines an assessment of the role and situation of the Ascendancy class with more theoretical reflections on the relationship between power and consent, and moves freely between accounts of the eighteenth-century discourse of sentiment – an abiding theme in his work on Irish writing which will find its impressive culmination in the later essay, 'The Good-Natured Gael' (Eagleton, 1998b, 68–139) – and its relationship with aesthetics and post-Freudian psychoanalysis in a way which again connects his work in Irish Studies with broader concerns already discussed.

But throughout the 'Heathcliff' essay there is an engagement with another kind of discourse, one which, if it has not exactly attempted to exculpate the Ascendancy from blame for their treatment of the Irish tenantry – even, ultimately, for the Famine itself – has nonetheless been instrumental in reviving that class's reputation in the face of nationalist accounts of it as unremittingly callous and exploitative. This is the discourse of Irish historiographical revisionism, a phenomenon about which Eagleton has been particularly polemical in recent years, though that polemicism is far from being as straightforward as some have assumed. It is to this I now want to turn. Such a topic may not seem directly relevant to the study of literature, but Eagleton's engagement with it relates not merely to his disagreements with certain historians, but to his perception of the ideological constitution of a larger body of work within Irish Studies, including cultural and literary studies.

Revisionism and its discontents

One of the problems with discussing revisionism is that of adequately establishing the common features of a diverse phenomenon, since its very existence and intentions are in dispute: for some, insofar as the term is used to describe a determined agenda, it is something of a chimera; for others, it is merely another name for a more rigorous application to historical investigation, a process which has had unappealing consequences for those wedded to nationalist myth; more recently, it is said to be passé, its supersession marked by the emergence of – wait for it – post-revisionism, a phenomenon which itself cannot be said to be unified. Moreover, the revisionism that is said to exist, or to have existed, is characterised by internal differentiation: it may, for instance, be Marxist, liberal or Unionist (and this last category may, but does not necessarily, imply an incompatibility with the previous two categories). Its provenance, though, lies in the professionalisation of the discipline of Irish historiography initiated in the 1930s by the historians Theodore William Moody and Robert Dudley Edwards, though the debate prompted by revisionism is a more recent one and owes something to a scepticism which has emerged in recent decades towards 'traditional' nationalist historiography, and which has arguably been determined by both the economic modernisation and liberalisation of the Irish Republic and the re-emergence of armed conflict in the north. In one sense, then, revisionism in Irish historiography is a mark of Irish nationalism's partial obsolescence. As Ireland has modernised – that is, as it has been integrated into a European capitalism destructive of local economic autonomy – the grip of a largely insular and repressive national culture in the Irish Republic has loosened. Certainly in cosmopolitan Dublin, there is a scepticism about nationalist perceptions of the Irish past, even an iconoclastic sensibility towards that past and its major figures, which is far from confined to historians. But the particular ideological characteristics of revisionist history and cultural criticism are also determined by the fact that Irish nationalism is not as obsolete as many would like it to be, revitalised as it was in response to the brutal suppression of legitimate demands for political and social equality for Catholics in the north.[3]

On the face of it, the characteristics of revisionism have little to do with this relatively recent history. Revisionist historiography is probably more likely to take as its subject matter the eighteenth-century Penal Laws against Catholics or fluctuations in farm rents in the nineteenth century. Moreover, revisionists have frequently enough disavowed the term attributed to them, no doubt in part at least out of a distaste for labels which perhaps suggest to them a factionalism or partisanship at odds with their sense of their own objectivity. R. F. Foster writes of the 'historiographical revolution['s] ... deliberately even-handed determination to give all sides their due' (Foster, 1993, 33), though, in its context, this comment is not entirely uncritical of that historiography. Truth, it seems, should be disinterested, able to deal judiciously with different points of view and thereby raise itself above them. But this in itself is ideologically revealing, since for the left truth is likely to be partisan, bound up inevitably with ascertaining how and why certain groups are or have been oppressed. This, however, is not to say that the revisionists' claims to impartiality should be taken at face value: it is not that their pronouncements are somehow *too* even-handed. Rather, their claims to have revised previous, nationalist forms of historiography evince motivations which are not reducible to a desire merely to correct the record through a more scrupulous detailing of the facts.

The allegation of revisionists is that the kind of nationalist historiography which was effectively institutionalised after the establishment of the Free State told a story which underwrote the legitimacy of the Free State itself, one in which the Irish fought for centuries against and finally emancipated themselves from the colonial grip of the English/British. It is a teleological history which therefore stresses continuity. R. F. Foster notes that the Department of Education after 1922 issued instructions that, in Irish schools

> 'the continuity of the separatist idea from Tone to Pearse should be stressed'; pupils should be 'imbued with the ideals and the aspirations of such men as Thomas Davis and Patrick Pearse'. Thus history was debased into a two-dimensional, linear development, and the function of its teaching interpreted as 'undoing the conquest'. (Foster, 1993, 15)

In part at least Foster's scepticism towards such a narrative proceeds not merely from a sense of the reductivism of that version of history, but from his critical, liberal stance towards the State as it was founded. This highlights a problem for those radicals such as Eagleton who would wish to retain some sense of the value of Ireland's history of anti-colonialism, since that history appears ultimately to have served reactionary ends. Arguably more serious, though, is the sense to which we will return that the falsifications of nationalist history have legitimated claims on the part of armed Republicanism in the north to be the latest agents in this incomplete project of liberation.

The scepticism of revisionist historiography towards the nationalist narrative manifests itself in a variety of ways, three of which are particularly important for my purposes. First, there is a tendency to examine critically the supposed continuities and totalisations of Irish nationalist history, to insist on historical differences which disrupt our ability to grasp history as an unfolding narrative and to emphasise local phenomena which problematise the very notion of a more or less homogeneous nation. Second, there is a greater emphasis placed on relativism, a suggestion that we cannot appreciate the historical specificity of given periods if we insist on imposing our own terms and values on them. Third, there is an interrogation of prior claims about the enormity of the sufferings of Irish people frequently amounting to a scepticism towards those claims, one which arguably mimics the attitudes towards Irish complaints of many English commentators throughout history. In some cases, claims Brendan Bradshaw, this has amounted to a wilful ignorance of the violence that has been visited on Ireland throughout its colonial history as well as a sanitising distortion of that history which does not take into account its 'catastrophic' dimension (Bradshaw, 1994, 199–205). For Eagleton, moreover, objectivity is not achieved through the kind of avowedly neutral obser-vation which eschews moral reflection, since the kinds of catastrophic events noted by Bradshaw possess inherent moral significance: 'If one does not see this, then one does not see what actually took place' (Eagleton, 1998, 323).

It is clear that each of these features of revisionism is consistent with an attempt to produce a more objective view of history, and indeed – as Eagleton for one has noted – such work has challenged the complacencies, distortions and insularity – narcissism, even – of aspects of nationalist historiography. Reading essays in *Heathcliff* such as 'Ascendancy and Hegemony' or, even moreso, 'Changing the Question' – a dissection of the paradoxical status of Ireland as both colony and member of the Union which challenges familiar claims that Ireland's integration into the Union is incompatible with any claims about its colonised status – one is struck by his willingness to accept, yet reinflect revisionist claims (though, of course, not being a historian he is not best positioned to assess them). But ultimately, the 'factual' corrections of revisionism – to what extent, for instance, landlords were absentees or callous – are beside the point: 'What such controversies typically repress is the whole structure of social relations as such, displacing such embarrassingly global issues with moralistic gesture or econometric myopia' (Eagleton, 1995, 64). Some grasp of social relations as a totality might lead, not to an apprehension of individuals' moral or economic 'performance' but to a critical grasp of the social structures which set limits to agency, benevolent or malevolent, and a consequent belief that it was these which required transformation.

If, as revisionists have claimed, certain features of nationalist historiography have legitimated northern antagonisms, it is possible to perceive in the very features of revisionism outlined above an ideological perspective determined by a simultaneous detachment from and embarrassment about the conflict in the north, as well as a consequent disdain for Republicanism in particular. The nationalist narrative of history has not only served to underwrite an illiberal State, much revisionist history claims, but its 'myths' provide ideological sustenance to the IRA which, if it is not seen implicitly as the *cause* of the conflict, is at least held primarily responsible for the violence. The conflict itself is often enough reductively regarded as merely sectarian, and the British State's claims to being a neutral peacekeeper have gone largely unquestioned, even if there has been acknowledgement that Britain has resorted to 'excessive' force on occasions. Seamus Deane notes in relation to Roy Foster's comments in his book *Modern Ireland* about atrocities committed by British forces in Ireland that 'it seems that actions can be tailor-made to suit a pre-existent language, as when the British foolishly commit atrocities and thereby make a "propaganda gift" to the IRA. ... It is not killing people that turns the populace against the Black and Tans; it is IRA propaganda' (Deane, 1994, 244). Such rhetorical slips are profoundly revealing. Regarded in this light, the desire for objectivity manifest in the revisionism of the last thirty years in particular may rather be seen in part as a projection of present concerns onto the past. Even those continuities which revisionism does stress in Irish history – replacing those which were characteristic of nationalist historiography – are consistent with such contemporary anxieties. Hence the tendency to dwell on the persistence and pervasiveness of sectarianism, thereby shifting the focus from colonial context to 'internal' divisions. Such an emphasis carries with it its own implicit teleology.

Eagleton's critique of revisionism, though, goes beyond this, finding in its principal characteristics certain affinities with a discourse with which it apparently has little in common. Revisionism on the whole rejects theoreticism, seeing this as more typical of a certain kind of nationalist discourse which employs an unwieldy and abstract vocabulary disdainful of empirical data. But we have already met with a theoretical discourse which rejects totalising claims, which insists on micro- rather than grand narratives, and which celebrates difference and plurality as a means of undermining the constraining force of identity. In these respects – and in spite of the manifest differences which characterise its various works – Eagleton argues that revisionism is ideologically compatible with postmodernism, and indeed that the conflict between nationalism and revisionism is a conflict between ideological assumptions which underpin modern and postmodern perspectives, however counterintuitive this may appear. Ideology, as we have seen in other contexts, runs far deeper than 'theory' as such: it unites figures who speak different languages and, in some instances, don't necessarily understand one another. Eagleton outlines the basis for this improbable unity:

> The political discourse of modernity is one of rights, justice, oppression, solidarity, universality, exploitation, emancipation. Nationalism, along with liberalism and socialism, belongs to this world-view. The political language of postmodernity is one of identity, marginality, locality, difference, otherness, diversity, desire. With some important qualifications, revisionism is part of this milieu. There are those for whom the former language is now effectively bankrupt, and there are those for whom the second way of speaking is no more than a disastrous displacement of the first, one consequent on the failure of that discourse to realise itself politically in our time. (Eagleton, 1998, 326; see also Eagleton, 1997)

This is a significantly more sophisticated contextualisation of revisionism than has been proposed by others, since it relates revisionism to postmodernism's ultimate compatibility with contemporary capitalism. The perspective of revisionists is at one with such a worldview, and the resolution of the tension outlined by Eagleton between different political discourses is one which will continue in the absence of some historical resolution (and not merely in the north of Ireland, though such a resolution may set precedents for other sets of competing claims). But Eagleton goes on to speculate that global history might itself have some ironies in store for Irish history as he suggests that the future will see an increasing conflict between postcolonial nations of the south and the advanced political economies of the northern hemisphere which exploit them (granting, for the moment, that not all southern nations are impoverished). In such a struggle – in which capitalism will no longer be able to represent itself in quite such a triumphalist way as it has at least since the collapse of 'communism', but will come to seem distinctly *un*progressive in its oppressiveness – it is likely that those who emphasise Ireland's colonial past will be regarded as most forward-looking and those liberals whose embarrassment about Ireland's northern 'atavisms' has been determined by their enthusiasm for the Republic's economic and political liberalisation will come to seem reactionary.

Ireland, nationalism and postcolonialism

Eagleton is only one of many who have criticised the ideological tendencies of revisionist historiography. One frequently heard retort to such critiques is that they have generally come from cultural theorists rather than historians. The claim is not entirely true, but nor is it entirely without validity. Historians frequently regard this as a self-evident vindication of the revisionist position, though in fact their unwillingness to dwell on the philosophical underpinnings of their discipline often makes them easy prey for those on the look out for inconsistencies. Take, for instance, Stephen Howe's comment that the ideas of Walter Benjamin 'have recently gained a somewhat modish popularity among those who want excuses for not taking history seriously' (Howe, 2000, 94). Howe has at least taken the trouble to acquaint himself with cultural and postcolonial theory, but this kind of comment is virtually meaningless, since Benjamin's writings invite us to reconceptualise history and consequently to take history very seriously indeed (I leave aside at this point the *value* of Benjamin's reflections). Howe's grasp of what constitutes 'history' is therefore a complacent one and, in a sense, it is Howe who doesn't take his discipline seriously. His brief summary and critique of the main features of colonial discourse theory (Howe, 2000, 107–10) hits certain targets but is mostly parody and one imagines him flicking impatiently, even imperiously, through his material pausing only to tut loudly.

Eagleton's critique of revisionism is clearly informed by his views on Irish nationalism, though since these have been consistently travestied – despite what seem to me entirely lucid reflections on the subject – I want to take some time to differentiate his position in this regard from that of others. Ultimately, Eagleton's views are not easily reconciled with the postcolonial theory which has inflected many attempts to reconceptualise the nationalist tradition.

As with most words prefixed in such a way, the 'post' in 'postcolonial' denotes intellectual affinities as much as it does historical actualities as Neil Lazarus indicates in his claim that 'access to the field [of colonial/postcolonial studies] and – even more – visibility within it, has tended to be contingent on the presentation and display of the appropriate "post"-theoretical credentials' (Lazarus, 1999, 9). Postcolonialism's affinities with postmodernism centre on the question of history and the rejection of 'metanarratives' of progress which, it is claimed, consign non-Western societies and cultures to a non-historical premodernity, a condition of stasis out of which it is implicitly desirable they be dragged – forcibly if necessary. Hence, Enlightenment thought is said to be at best complicit with and at worst as having determined both a Western disdain for the East and the 'improving' ideology of colonialism. Marxism's Enlightenment credentials therefore make it similarly complicit with colonialism, and Marx's brief comments on the Asiatic mode of production are said to be symptomatic of this:

> Indian society has no history at all, at least no known history. What we call its history is but the history of its successive intruders who founded their empires on the passive basis of that unresisting and unchanging society ... England has to fulfil a double mission in India: one destructive, the other regenerating – the annihilation of old Asiatic society, and the laying of the material foundations of Western society in Asia. (Marx, 1973, 320)

It was Edward Said who first highlighted Marx's comments as instances of the way in which Orientalist orthodoxies overtook any more genuine engagement with actualities and even precluded sympathy with the inhabitants of the East on his part. Marx's comments have since become virtually ubiquitous citations in postcolonialism's condemnation of Marxist thought, and Eagleton has therefore been criticised for adhering to a Marxist, rather than postcolonial, framework in his accounts of Irish culture. Martin McQuillan notes that Eagleton, through his dramatic spokesperson, James Connolly, in the play *The White, The Gold and the Gangrene* 'seeks to bring Ireland into the dialectical narrative of class struggle in the way that Marx reads Indian colonisation' (McQuillan, 2002, 31). This kind of claim short-circuits any serious evaluation of Marxism, since it is not Eagleton, Connolly or even Marxism which brings Ireland into the dialectical 'narrative' – if we must use that quasi-pejorative term – of class struggle, but the capitalism which Marxism claims to describe: it is the adequacy of this claim which requires assessment.

The governing assumptions of postcolonialism have been contested from the outset, however, by Marxist critics such as Benita Parry, and, more recently, Aijaz Ahmad, Timothy Brennan and Neil Lazarus.[4] Indeed, as Ahmad notes, there is a certain irony about academicist anti-Marxist postcolonialism, since

> The Marxist tradition had been notably anti-imperialist; the Nietzschean tradition [including post-structuralism] had had no such credentials. Now it transpires that that is precisely what had been wrong – not with Nietzschean intellectuals but with anti-imperialism itself. It *should* have been Nietzschean and now needed to do some theoretical growing up. (Ahmad, 1992, 222)

Ahmad, moreover, returns to Marx's writings on India and, without exonerating them of European ignorance or positivism – and, indeed, ultimately castigating them for their insufficiently materialist methodology – provides a more complex context for them. For Marx, colonialism in India was an extension of capitalism's potential to transform the globe in ways which were destructive of previous orders, with both positive and negative consequences. Capitalism was and is destructive, brutally so, but this was true for Marx in colonising as well as colonised nations. Moreover, since the social structures which Marx believed would be destroyed in India included the caste system, claims about the progressiveness of capitalism should not be taken lightly (though, in fact, Marx considerably overestimated the destructive capacity of capitalist colonialism in this and other respects). To claim, then, that Marx supported colonialism is rather like saying he supported capitalism. Moreover, Marx consistently argued that, in order to enjoy the progress which capitalism had visited on colonised nations, those nations would rightfully need to assert their independence. Postcolonial critics rarely cite other parts of Marx's letters on the Asiatic mode of production and British rule in India:

> All the English bourgeoisie may be forced to do [in India] will neither emancipate nor materially mend the social condition of the mass of the people, depending not only on the development of the productive powers, but on their appropriation by the people. But what they will not fail to do is to lay down the material premises for both. Has the bourgeoisie ever done more? Has it ever effected a progress without dragging individuals and peoples through blood and dirt, through misery and degradation?
>
> The Indians will not reap the fruits of the new elements of society scattered among them by the British bourgeoisie till in Great Britain itself the now ruling classes shall have been supplanted by the industrial

proletariat, or till the Hindus [Marx's generic term for Indians] themselves shall have grown strong enough to throw off the English yoke altogether. (Marx, 1973, 323)

Marx in other words was unreservedly pro-nationalist, whereas the thrust of Said's and others' arguments about Orientalism as a discourse is that it functioned to help disable demands for auto-nomous government (Ahmad, 1992, 221–42). Ahmad, moreover, points out that just about all strands of Indian nationalism accept Marx's judgement 'that colonial capitalism *did* contribute "new ele-ments of society" in India, some of which have a very great need to be preserved' (Ahmad, 1992, 236). In fact, a more dialectical impulse may be discernible in Said's more recent argument that we need to think of relations between nations, cultures and histories 'contrapuntally', whilst rejecting the power relations which assume the dominance of any single nation, culture or history (Said, 1993, 341–408). (It is also important to note that Ahmad's discussion of Said elsewhere in *In Theory* both seriously misrepresents Said's career and writings and fails to note that – unlike many subsequent academics working in post-colonial studies – he has 'repeatedly praised the Marxist intellectual legacy in print' [Brennan, 1994, 233].)

Amongst those who have tried to locate Ireland in a postcolonial framework, one of the most sophisticated has been David Lloyd. Though a great deal of work in Irish Studies has been influenced by postcolonialism, some of which is at odds with Lloyd's, I turn to his work in particular in order to foreground the ways in which Eagleton's arguments are at variance with certain postcolonialist emphases. Lloyd's theoretical quarrels with Eagleton were foregrounded by Lloyd himself in a review of *Heathcliff and the Great Hunger* and return us to debates about the progressive nature of capitalism and the coercive features of modernity in relation to local cultures. On first reading, Lloyd's review appears unfathomably hostile, but after consideration of his later work in particular, the reasons for its animosity become clearer. Effectively, Lloyd accuses Eagleton of his own kind of colonisation by comparing him unfavourably with 'many [other] "non-Irish" scholars who have sought to learn from current work in Ireland [but] who have conse-quently produced work that genuinely dialogues with it rather than seeking to master it' (Lloyd, 1997, 89). This is, in one respect, a familiar criticism of Eagleton – that he does not sufficiently acknowledge others' work in the field with which he is engaged[5] – but this attempt to 'master' others' work is, for Lloyd, bound up with another feature of Eagleton's writing: 'an insistent recurrence of the dichotomy "modern" / "premodern" and ... the assumption that Ireland's cultural forms carry forward the force of the "archaic" '. Hence, Eagleton's perspective remains the familiar one of a British leftism all too beholden to metropolitan liberalism for its critical rhetoric, and 'It is as if Eagleton can't quite help regarding the Irish as a "bizarre" or "alien" people' (Lloyd, 1997, 90). Moreover, Eagleton's inattention to critiques of modernisation paradigms of development and of nationalism allegedly leaves him 'finally dependent on the very revisionist history he disdains' (Lloyd, 1997, 91). But it is not true that Eagleton is merely disdainful of revisionist work, and this has a bearing on the argument about the modern/premodern dichotomy which requires lengthier consideration.

Lloyd's most recent work evinces something of the depth of his disagreements with Eagleton, and indeed Lloyd's review of *Heathcliff* ends by prefiguring a future for Irish Studies which just happens to coincide with his own project. In the essays collected in the recent book *Ireland After History* he develops a theorisation and political valorisation of those cultures which he claims to be 'non-modern'. By this he means not the traditional or the antiquated – terms which can only be understood in relation to a modernity which Lloyd appears to denounce wholesale – but those cultures or aspects of a culture which are contemporary with, in some sense responsive to, rather than outside or beyond, yet not assimilable by modernity. By modernity he means bourgeois civilisation in its totality – capitalism, instrumental reason, bourgeois democracy, and, crucially, that form of nationalism which looks to and has its end in the establishment of the very nation-state whose function is to integrate its citizens into the capitalist world order (the universal): 'the desire of nationalism for the state is congruent, for all the particularism of national identification, with the universalism of which, indeed, the nation-state is the local representative' (Lloyd, 1999, 27). The rationality of the state must achieve this by a kind of violence, by demonising as irrational, nonsensical or atavistic those aspects of the cultures of its people which, through their particularity, resist assimilation or incorporation into the universal. Lloyd takes Walter Benjamin's argument that 'progress' may be resisted by the recovery of that which has been repressed by a unilinear historical consciousness as support for his own. Further, he argues that nationalism comes into being alongside and intersects with other emancipatory movements – he instances feminism and socialism in relation to the 1916 Easter Rising in Ireland – and that 'Moving at different paces, these movements attend to a time determined not by a single end but by their distinct ends' (Lloyd, 1999, 28). Lloyd is therefore directly addressing the claim – often disingenuously forwarded in the Irish context – that nationalism is hostile to pluralism (for which, frequently enough, read 'Unionism') by recognising that radical movements are rarely reducible to one cause and combine multiple impulses. Moreover, many of the forces mobilised by nationalism, insofar as they are hostile to the bourgeois project of nation-state building, are therefore resistant to the homogenising force of the universal (capitalist modernity). Lloyd's position here is specifically distinguished, not only from bourgeois theory, but also from Marxism, since – at least as they are presented here – there is barely any difference between them: 'With differing degrees of self-reflection, historians narrate history as the history of its own end, in the reconciliation and resolution of contradiction, finding closure predominantly in an orderly civil society and reformed state or occasionally in post-revolutionary socialism' (Lloyd, 1999, 17); or again, 'Nationalism is ... a vehicle or detour on the way to the cosmopolitanism or socialism that are the proper end of history, for liberal and left thinkers respectively' (Lloyd, 1999, 21). At the very least this gives the impression that for Lloyd the Marxist project of achieving international socialism is more or less comparable with the homogenising impulses of bourgeois political thought. For Marxists, that assertion of equivalence is an astonishing, outrageous move, since the universalism to which socialism aspires is the general condition of genuine, rather than merely abstract, equality and may be regarded as the precondition of establishing differences – individual, social or cultural – undetermined by power. Here, then, we need to note the idealist abstraction of Lloyd's thinking, since it often appears that it is a presumed 'homogeneity', whether in the service of capitalism or anti-capitalism, which for him demands resistance.

It should be acknowledged that there are aspects of Lloyd's thought which distinguish him from 'post-' theory. First, he has argued consistently and with admirable conviction for solidarity between left wing intellectual work and political activity in relation to Ireland and that undertaken in relation to other postcolonial nations. Second, he is willing to acknowledge a totality called 'capitalist modernity' which it is the purpose of the left to resist, though, as we have seen, Lloyd envisages a plurality of resistances predicated on their particular cultural incompatibilities with modernity and has also argued that the differential, because uneven, nature of capitalist expansion necessitates specific forms of resistance (Lloyd and Lowe, 1997, 1). That said, the general thrust of his work is sceptical of Enlightenment's 'metanarratives' of reason, progress and universality precisely because he is enamoured of such marginal forms of resistance.

If we have learned anything from 'post-' theory, though, it is that an attentiveness to language, and especially to figuration is important. In respect of the effectiveness of the resistance Lloyd envisages, his terminology is significant, since, rather than a language of overcoming or revolution, he adopts a quasi-Yeatsian metaphor of disturbance, declaring that he is devoting himself to a recovery of the 'debris [and] remnants' of official history which 'on occasion ... may trouble history's stream with interference, eddies and counterflows' (Lloyd, 1999, 1). This, I think, is genuinely symptomatic of what at some level Lloyd himself realises: that, despite the upbeat tone of this book's conclusion, the forms of resistance he valorises – or, at least, those forms of resistance *as theorised by him* – are unequal to any task of *transformation* (and it is not finally clear from his work what kind of transformation is desired: in an earlier piece, Lloyd argues that the recovery of 'subterranean and marginalised practices' is integral to 'an expansion of the field of possibilities for radical democracy [without which] the critique of representative national democracy and the state formation remains more or less formalist' [Lloyd, 1993]). Indeed, in discussing Lloyd's work, Colin Graham has alerted us to its tendency to idealise subalternity, to celebrate it 'only when it is unsuccessful' (Graham, 2001, 110). The realisation on Lloyd's part that the agenda he argues for may ultimately be ineffective – though how we might assess its effectiveness remains unclear to me – manifests itself at various points in his book in the form of an acknowledgement of the ultimately *overpowering* stream of history. He writes for instance that 'both the terms "postcolonial" and "subaltern" designate in different but related ways the desire to elaborate social spaces which are recalcitrant to any straightforward absorption – ever more inevitable though this often seems – of Ireland into European modernity' (Lloyd, 1999, 77). Contrast this with Eagleton's dialectical grasp of this same situation:

> Modernity in Ireland means among other things divorce, abortion, women's rights, a secular polity, civic and rational notions of citizenship to replace all that tribal *Gemeinschaft*; it also means shutting up about the Famine so as not to annoy the Brits (not even the dead, Walter

Benjamin warned, will be safe from the enemy if he is victorious), revising Irish history in order to sanitise colonialism and slander republicanism, canonising the urban businessman while castigating the countryside, and abandoning small farmers and the working class to the mercies of a brutally neo-liberal Europe. (Eagleton, 1998a, 132)

Some of the claims made here are rather too casually invoked: disavowing responsibility for the Famine, for instance, is not so important to the Brits any more and apologies for British culpability in that event are more easily granted in the name of reconciliation than admissions of responsibility for more recent brutalities. Nonetheless, this dialectical grasp of the underside of modernity's genuinely positive developments is intended to highlight the way in which the Enlightenment promise of freedom might be deployed to push beyond the limits established by capitalist modernity, and this is surely a more hopeful – if neither sanguine nor naïve – political project than the celebration of recalcitrance. In this respect, many of those movements invoked by Lloyd – socialism, certain kinds of feminism – are specifically modern because of their antagonism to capitalism. But then there is a vagueness about Lloyd's sense of the relation of 'non-modern' movements to modernity: they are described at one point as existing in a 'dynamic' relation to modernity (Lloyd, 1999, 2), but a great deal depends on the specificities of those dynamics, a point I want to develop.

In fact, not all the forms of resistance Lloyd invokes as examples of non-modernity can be adequately depicted as 'recalcitrant', but it is far from clear that these forms of resistance conceive, or conceived, of themselves in terms compatible with his theorisation of them. This, of course, raises questions about the extent to which his work is faithful to the impulses of those with whom it claims some sympathy, even where those forces are manifestly oppositional. The case of contemporary Irish Republicanism, whose stated political aspirations – admittedly honoured more often in the breach – include the creation of a socialist republic, is an obvious one. To what extent does his desire to think Ireland in a postcolonial frame and yet maintain solidarity with that movement entail a misrepresentation of it? Invoking Bernadette Devlin McAliskey's criticisms of Republican involvement in the peace process for its betrayal of popular democratic forces is one thing (Lloyd, 1999, 107), but assimilating this to a project of 'non-modern' resistance on the grounds of its valorisation of plurality and opposition to aspects of what constitutes modernity under capitalist conditions is quite another. Or is it that Lloyd imagines his arguments are likely to have some impact on Republicanism's theoretical grasp of itself? The latter question is surely sufficiently rhetorical to highlight a problem which seems to me symptomatic of the separation of theory and practice attendant on the division of labour in modern societies: a constitutive tension in much recent 'political' academic work between its analytical properties and its prescriptive dimensions which has the effect of undermining the validity of both. If Eagleton's work in Irish Studies has been less innovative than Lloyd's, certainly at the theoretical level, it is nonetheless not so deluded about its likely purchase on political movements, and these qualities are related.

Neil Lazarus has argued that 'the West' is a fetishised term in postcolonial theory. Whilst it draws our attention to the Eurocentrism which was ideologically integral to colonialism, and which remains important in global terms, its frequent invocation to describe a geographically coherent civilisational entity responsible for judging 'the East' and attempting to impose on it an alien, homogeneous and largely *cultural* modernity is, first of all, complicit with the Orientalist discourses which consolidated and continue to sustain such an opposition in the first place and, consequently, blinds us to the *material* forces at work in determining colonialism and modern day imperialism whilst also demonising as 'Western' even those forms of reason which might contribute to our effective resistance to capitalist modernity (Lazarus, 2002, 43–64). Since Ireland is precisely that apparently oxymoronic entity, a postcolonial *Western* nation, Lloyd is to some extent conscious of this fetishisation, but he none the less continues to subscribe to its undialectical grasp of modernity. Hence, whereas Lloyd finds in all forms of state-directed nationalisms a mere accommodation with capitalist modernity, Benita Parry, for instance – writing with the particular example of sub-Saharan African Marxist nationalist movements in mind – acknowledges a more complex view of the relationship to modernity of such movements:

> If colonialism was the messenger of modernity's transformative capacities and emancipatory potential in colonial spaces, its message installing exploitation, inequalities, and injustice was refused. These disjunctions suggest a particular sensibility to modernity on colonial terrains, its intellectual and imaginative horizons extending from indigenous cultural and cognitive forms, to premonitions, not blueprints, of the *post-capitalist.* (Parry, 2002, 147)

The relationship to modernity outlined here evinces an engagement with it partly on its own terms and partly on 'indigenous' terms.

Consequently, such movements resist cultural homogeneity even though they are state-oriented, and are not adequately theorisable as 'non-modern' since they are indeed products of modernity. Moreover, the engagement of such movements with capitalist modernity on terms partly indebted to that modernity becomes the basis of a potential – indeed, has informed an actual – supranational political solidarity and grasp of the universal which surely must be the basis of forms of resistance adequate in terms of mass involvement, geographical scope and theoretical coherence to the transformation of that common modernity. The continuing value of nationalism in such contexts can be demonstrated in the situation in Iraq as it unfolds at the time of writing. It is likely that effective non-Ba'athist – and hopefully secular or at least non-sectarian – resistance to US and British occupation and the wholesale privatisation of Iraq's nationalised industries will still draw on the nation's anti-colonial tradition.

Finally, it is worth dwelling further on this fetishisation of the West in postcolonial theory, since it begs other questions of both the theory in general and Lloyd in particular. There are other particularistic national cultures beyond Ireland, but within Europe, which are, or at least proclaim themselves, resistant to 'modernity', and still other determinedly universalising cultural and political movements external to and hostile to 'the West'. How progressive they are is an entirely different question, but the test of progressiveness is one which Lloyd cannot logically extend to them, since progress – at least for the left – entails some sense of the supersession of the present on the basis of that present's inability to live up to its own potential. Once again, Neil Lazarus has put the case well. He reminds us of Adorno's sense that modernity has itself paradoxically become a tradition – that is, that its modes of thought have become intuitive, habitual, unexamined – and that we must learn to hate it properly: 'To hate tradition properly is ... to mobilise its own protocols, procedures, and interior logic against it – to demonstrate that it is only on the basis of a project that exceeds its own horizons or self-consciousness that tradition can possibly be imagined redeeming its own pledges' (Lazarus, 1999, 7). Indeed, Lloyd is crucially silent on the issues of how we might – or even whether we should (would this be an imperialist, because 'Western' gesture?) – *evaluate* non-modern forms of resistance and the ends they serve. He is also silent on what postcolonialism has to offer those who are oppressed within capitalist modernity but can hardly be said to possess any 'non-modern' cultural resources with which to resist it. Presumably we are not to discount such people as mere 'Westerners' – though their occlusion from the perspective of so much contemporary cultural theory is surely symptomatic of some form of disdain – but is it really impossible to grasp, indeed *theorise*, some common purpose between such people's struggles against capitalist modernity and those of the peoples of the postcolonial world? Are their experiences so truly incommensurable? Lloyd does not say they are, but it is one implication of his argument.

Eagleton's critical affiliations with nationalism, then, are determined by a specifically Marxist tradition which postcolonial theory has disdained with results that would have been disastrous if they had not been largely confined to academic circles. But that very tradition also determines a specific form of ambivalence towards both the nation-state and nationalism:

> Nationalism is a child of the Enlightenment, one application among several of the principle that human beings should be as far as possible self-determining. Since this applies to collectivities as well as to individuals, and since in the modern world those collectivities have taken the primary form of the nation state, nationalism is simply the logical offshoot of the democratic principle of self-determination in this particular region. The principle itself, however, is far wider than the nation-state itself, an historically transient affair which has so far meant little but trouble, and which it would be good to see the back of. Nationalism, which is an equally ephemeral current of thought, can either be a constructive step towards this wider self-determination, as socialists have traditionally affirmed of most anti-colonial movements, or it can be a form of festering narcissism which thwarts its attainment. (Eagleton, 1998, 316)

Despite appearances, this is not an attempt to steer some middle path between two positions, to maintain some fidelity to the cause whilst nonetheless attempting to appease nationalism's critics, a kind of having-it-both-ways all too common in Irish Studies. Rather it is a properly dialectical account and therefore sincere in both its advocacy of nationalism and its recognition of the limitations of nationalism's potential for liberation. In its assertions of independence, nationalism is necessary, desirable and progressive, yet potentially insular and an obstacle to human freedom. In a sense, its most desirable characteristic is its future obsolescence, that moment at which its work has been done and people can move on. Hence, Eagleton commends an ironic advocacy of it in a pamphlet which has been consistently, and possibly wilfully, misread by revisionist critics (Eagleton, 1988).

The inability of Ireland to 'move on' from the national question – as much on the part of those who revile as those who revere nationalism – is, according to Eagleton, the consequence of an incomplete project, one thwarted by partition. Edna Longley's response to Eagleton's pamphlet is to question who the Irish people are in whose name the continuing nationalist project is being undertaken (implicitly, they are not the majority within the partitioned north who do not identify with Irish nationalism, ironically or otherwise), and, indeed, Eagleton's pamphlet is vulnerable to the accusation that it deals in sophisticated yet ultimately abstract, insufficiently materialist terms with the dialectics of liberation, since it does not engage with the realities of the north where national aspirations are divided. Moreover, it is not merely revisionists such as Longley who are keen to point this out, since Marxism's dialectical assessment of nationalism's liberatory potential licences a quite different interpretation of the Irish national question, one articulated recently by Francis Mulhern. If nationalism's value lies specifically in its rejection of colonial domination – thereafter inhibiting socialist internationalism – it is possible to argue that Irish nationalism has long since outlived its historic value. Mulhern, from a Catholic background in Enniskillen, remembers the momentary promise of the progressive, genuinely leftist Civil Rights Association and the way in which, for him, it degenerated into nationalist claims which were reactionary:

> One night late in 1968 I stood in the crowd below the campanile. Civil rights organisers spoke, then the student leftists from the university, and finally, the local Nationalist MP. At a loss, I suppose, to match the language of the platform – fascists came from Catholic Italy, didn't they, and what in God's name was a Green Tory? – he made no effort at a speech, but just gave us one of the old songs.
>
> That was it. They were finished, all of them, now. (Mulhern, 1998, 12)

The shifting tenses in the final part of this passage are clearly intended to alert us to the allegorical significance of this scene, and indeed one consequence of the resurgence of Republican struggle following the defeat of the Civil Rights Association was to licence new brands of romantic nationalism. But I use the word 'defeat' here deliberately, since the movement's failure was not principally the result of internal weaknesses – even if some have argued that the movement did not do enough to reach out to disaffected Protestants – but of the strength of the Northern Irish State's own police forces, the loyalist mobs (with whom they collaborated) and ultimately the British army in violently suppressing it. That many drew from this the conclusion that the Northern Irish State was unreformable and that the necessary political struggle was a national one against the political power which – however 'reluctantly' and with whatever reservations – underwrote that State seems to me not to have been an entirely mistaken one. Moreover, it is also the case that the best elements within the Republican tradition were shaped by the experience of the Civil Rights Association, and in the arid political terrain of the north of Ireland it is that tradition which has continued to offer most promise. David Lloyd is surely correct in his assessment that in the past thirty years republicanism 'more fully than at any previous moment ... has affirmed its links with other insurgencies globally' (Lloyd, 1999, 106), though some of those insurgencies – the Basque struggle in certain of its manifestations, for instance – are not necessarily ones with which many socialists would feel comfortable.

In later writings, and no doubt prompted by the attacks of revisionist critics, Eagleton has recognised the greater complexity of the situation in the north, and has also been strongly critical of the sectarianism of Republican militarism. In these writings there is still a scepticism towards the cultural 'pluralism' which obscures the question of political power – 'To view the conflict in the North as primarily one between alternative "cultural traditions" fits well with postmodern culturalism in general, and so sounds reasonably persuasive; it is just that it also happens to be false' (Eagleton, 1998, 326) – and there is also a rejection of the Unionist veto on political change in the north, as when, in reviewing a recent account of Northern Irish politics by two constitutional nationalists, he argues that 'in appearing to pitch everything upon what the Unionists of Northern Ireland will currently countenance, McGarry and O'Leary are in dire danger of transgressing their own proper insistence that the rights to self-determination of the nationalist minority in the North must be accommodated too' (Eagleton, 1995b, 136). Still, there is also a recognition that the political potential of the peace process is to develop new relations between the local and the universal, the national and the global, in ways which are as yet unrealised; indeed, which can only be realised historically rather than in the realms of theory (Eagleton, 1998a, 134).

Poetry and nationality in Yeats

All of this once again appears to take us a long way from literature, but in concluding with Eagleton's discussion of Yeats, I hope to reconnect some of these general historical and theoretical issues with textual specificities. Yeats's social, political and cultural affiliations make him a complex figure, and therefore appropriable for various purposes. Edward Said reads his early work as a poetry of decolonisation in which Yeats 'joins his people to its history, the more imperatively in that as father, or as "sixty-year-old smiling public man", or as son and husband, the poet assumes that the narrative and the density of personal experience are equivalent to the experience of his people' (Said, 1993, 286). Others, though, have argued that this overestimates the seriousness of Yeats's political rather than cultural nationalism (Regan, 1995, 66–84). Moreover, Yeats's lifetime saw the emergence of an increasingly prosperous Catholic middle class, the demise of the Ascendancy, partition and independence. His work might be said either to express the marginalised status of Protestants in the Free State or a protracted melancholic lament for Protestant domination (or both).

In his essay 'Yeats and Poetic Form' Eagleton eschews both biography and any detailed discussion of these complexities, though knowledge of them is implicit in his argument. Hence, it is necessary to provide some outline of these. Yeats's problematic and contradictory relations with his nation became more pronounced over time in response to historical developments to which he contributed (at least ideologically) but which finally left him disillusioned and isolated. He was a Protestant nationalist who, partly in consequence of his love for the figure of Maude Gonne, became associated with Irish Republicanism, especially in the 1890s, but who in subsequent years reacted against that Republicanism, claiming that it gave licence to uncontrolled feelings of hatred. This perception of nationalism became indissociably linked with the figure of Maude Gonne (and, indeed, other female Republicans) as is evident in his reflection that 'Nationalist abstractions were like the fixed ideas of some hysterical woman, a part of the mind turned into stone, the rest a-seething and burning' (Yeats, 1995, 234). This provides an important gloss for Yeats's most famous poem, 'Easter 1916', and in it femininity is characterised by two opposing traits: the cold, rigid, death-like form of the stone and the uncontrolled, animated passion which he found vulgar and intimidating. The attempt at some successful reconciliation of such traits is crucial to his work and is played out in the dialectic between form and content on which Eagleton focuses in his discussion.

In his later years Yeats increasingly expressed neo-feudal, sectarian views which lamented the fall from dominance of the Ascendancy and what he perceived as the attendant cultural impoverishment of Ireland. Though not strictly speaking a member of this class – he was of merely petty bourgeois provenance – Yeats certainly idealised it, and its 'big houses' – those eighteenth-century centrepieces of the landown-ers' estates – became for him a melancholy symbol of what was the Ascendancy's former glory. Insofar as Yeats retained a fidelity to Irish nationalism, the tradition he celebrated, and of which he saw himself a representative, was an emphatically Protestant, if heterogeneous, one: Swift, Berkeley, Burke, Tone, Emmett, Parnell. His increasing alienation from Irish Republicanism was in large part a consequence of its domination by Catholics who constituted the largest portion of the Irish middle class. These people he regarded as philistine, commercially minded and puritanical, an attitude most notoriously expressed in 'September 1913', which was prompted by the refusal of the Dublin Corporation to provide the money to house a collection of pictures offered as a donation to them by Sir Hugh Lane. The opening condenses many of Yeats's attitudes:

> What need you, being come to sense,
> But fumble in a greasy till
> And add the halfpence to the pence
> And prayer to shivering prayer, until
> You have dried the marrow from the bone?
> For men were born to pray and save:
> Romantic Ireland's dead and gone,
> It's with O'Leary in the grave. (ll. 1–8)

The contrast, of course, is between a present which lacks vitality because of its combination of commerce and religion – 'men were born to pray and save' being Yeats's derisive parody of middle class sentiments – and an inspired and heroic Romantic past characterised by what the poem later refers to as 'that delirium of the brave' (l. 22). That reference to the middle class 'being come to sense' suggests not only that they have acquired self-consciousness but also that that con-sciousness is limited by the five senses and does not embrace imagina-tion. (There is too, perhaps, in this respect a hint of sexual disgust for this class – one to be found elsewhere in the poems – in Yeats's reference to '*greasy* till'.) To pre-empt Eagleton's discussion of these matters, the historical moment which is the subject of this poem represents a kind of death-in-life, one which has 'dried the marrow from the bone', though this contrasts negatively with images of the interpenetration of life and death which occur in Yeats's other poems – 'Byzantium', for instance – where the emphasis is on the imaginative contact between corporeal and non-corporeal existence rather than the soullessness of existence.

A combination of Romantic nationalism and anti-democratic elitism was a potent force for evil in the first half of the twentieth century, and indeed Yeats was briefly drawn to a specifically Irish version of fascism in 1933 in the form of Eoin O'Duffy's Blueshirts. But, at least after his six-year stint as a Senator of the Upper House of the Free State Parliament, his involvement in public politics in his later years was exceptional, and they were characterised by greater isolation, his main concern being the elaboration of an esoteric system for understanding history and personal development whose absurdity disfigures much of the later poetry (and an understanding of which, contrary to the assertions of many literary critics for whom systems and theories per se are anathema, *is* important to that poetry). The symbols which he adopts in his later work were, he believed, communicated to him from a spiritual storehouse of such images, the *Anima Mundi*, one in principle open to all but in practice limited to those whose imaginations were most developed. One of these symbols in the later work is the tower – Yeats himself had bought one of the medieval towers of Ireland, Thoor Ballylee, in 1917 – representing for him his sense of spiritual connection with his Protestant forebears as well as his (consequent?) isolation from contemporary Ireland. In a comment intended to point up the marginalisation of Protestants in the Catholic Free State, Edna Longley may be right to claim that 'Yeats did not set out to be solitary' (Longley, 1994, 46), but the terms he set for his own reconciliation with Irish society were both politically undesirable and historically unrealisable.

As early as 1909, one of Yeats's diary entries records his belief that 'To oppose the new ill-breeding of Ireland, which may in a few years destroy all that has given Ireland a distinguished name in the world … I can only set up a secondary or interior personality created out of the tradition of myself, and this personality (alas, only possible to me in my writings) must be always gracious and simple' (Yeats, 1995, 463). Once again, this concern with the elaboration of a poetic persona in response to the vulgarity of the present will be a feature of Eagleton's discussion.

Yeats's relations with his contemporary poets are complex. Influenced stylistically in his later poetry by the sparer style and more concrete imagery of Ezra Pound, he nonetheless retained many of the Romantic impulses which dominate his earlier work, and Eagleton presents him in comparison with Eliot as less typically modernist. If Eliot's cultivation of impersonality in his poetry resulted from a 'classicist' dislike of Romantic individualism and emotionalism which was itself consciously reactionary – Eliot saw himself as part of a broader European movement, embodied in the figure of French proto-fascist Charles Maurras, which emphasised form and authority over expression and individuality in culture, religion and politics – Yeats's cultivation of masks, or personae, in his work was indicative of an aristocratic love of self-fashioning. (There were, then, ideological distinctions between the two which did not preclude a significant degree of convergence: Eliot's admiration for order can be traced to his American Puritan roots, even though it resulted in Anglo-Catholic convictions.) In their use of language, Eliot foregrounds ambiguity, whereas Yeats, on the occasions he does present a complex perspective rather than a lordly conviction that things are or should be so, is more likely to express himself through an ambivalence which is revealing of his dislocation from the trajectory of Irish politics or the realities of the nation's social order.

Eagleton's account of Yeats is complex because of his desire to do justice to his subject matter, to make the paradoxes and contradictions in Yeats's poetry yield a determinate ideological vision. His focus is on the various tensions between form and content, in which form acts not merely to shape content, but often in a way deceptively to tame it. The result is that an often potentially disruptive content – evincing doubt, uncertainty, ambivalence, or demonstrating bizarre or obnoxious perspectives – is contained by the specific use of diction or by formal devices such as regularity of metre, the deployment of rhetorical questions or even the consoling, memorialising listing of names to give the impression of control. This focus on form in part accounts for the relationship between universal and particular in Yeats's verse, since his descriptions of things mostly lack the degree of concretion which is characteristic of a highly prized tradition in English verse and which, along with his Romanticism, distinguish him from the symbolist influences on modernism, the influence of Pound notwithstanding. In

Yeats, the symbolic, or emblematic properties of a thing tend not to be revealed by a more detailed presentation of their features (as in, say, Hopkins's 'The Windhover') but in their apparently effortless revelation of some more universal significance. There is, indeed, a quality to this lack of focus on the particular in Yeats which is indicative of his affiliations with the Ascendancy, since

> he scorns a mimetic art, as slavishly dependent on reality as the clerk on his employer. Yeats finds such naturalism English and low-bred, terms which might well be synonymous in his book, and wants a poetry which like the aristocrat lives only from its own self-delighting resources . ... The task of poetry is not to express the world, or even directly to express the self – the theory of the mask provides an alternative to that – but to take up a stance towards the world, a stance which will fashion a particular self as well as a particular reality. (Eagleton, 1998, 28)

The typically performative utterance of Yeats – a legislating of things into being on the authority of the imagination – is a further instance of this. This idealism at its most extreme results in the conviction that the world is the creation of the mind, though that mystical source of Yeats's symbols, the *Anima Mundi*, rather than the imagination itself is at other times the grounding for Yeats's symbols.

There is to be found in Yeats, though, an epistemology partially at variance with this idealism, as he often attempts to reassure himself that there is a correspondence between mind and world, symbol and thing, 'And these conflicting epistemologies, in which a mind-created universe seeks to compensate for one all too solidly given, are reflected in the vicissitudes of the word "dream" in Yeats, which is used in his poetry almost as many times to mean dangerous illusion as it is to signify creative imaginings' (Eagleton, 1998, 287). Eagleton doesn't spell it out fully, but this discrepancy may well have something to do with divisions precipitated in him by his ambivalence towards the romanticism of the Irish revolutionaries, who in one sense in 'Easter 1916' he imagines as having been brought into being through art, and yet in another represent a degenerate version of that art. A masculine transcendence at variance with bourgeois reality – 'That delirium of the brave' – attributed to Protestant revolutionaries in 'September 1913', is transformed into a feminine hysteria, embodied in the now 'shrill' Contance Markievicz, which refuses both the 'grey' reality of the (formerly resplendent) 'Eighteenth-century houses' as well as the offer of a Home Rule deferred until after the War. The lines 'We know their dream; enough/ To know they dreamed and are dead' which evince a characteristic ambivalence – suggesting identification yet witholding praise ('enough') – clinches the point here. Rather than dwell on this, though, Eagleton is more concerned with the social roots of Yeats's apparent philosophical convictions, suggesting that the Romantic transcendence of Yeats is 'a consoling epistemology for Anglo-Irish gentlemen whose mundane selves seem less and less essential' (Eagleton, 1998, 185).

There is, though, another revealing tension in Yeats, which is partly evident in a further tension between form and content and which Eagleton compares with the Freudian conflict between Eros and Thanatos. Since Eagleton is making a comparison between Freud and Yeats which doesn't depend on any claim that Yeats had actually read Freud, it presumably matters little that *Civilisation and Its Discontents* was published in 1930 and not 1920, as Eagleton mistakenly claims. In this text, Freud argues that Eros – that instinct towards love which is the basis of social relations – is in conflict with our destructive instincts (Thanatos). Since society requires that these destructive urges be checked, we turn these in on ourselves through the workings of the superego, itself formed out of a redirection towards the ego of the aggression felt by the male infant towards the father, the rival with whom he comes to identify. 'Since civilisation obeys an internal erotic impulsion which causes human beings to unite in a closely-knit group, it can only achieve this aim through an ever-increasing reinforcement of the sense of guilt' (Freud, 1991, 326). Hence the requirement that we sublimate our destructive impulses paradoxically results in a self-destructive turning inwards of those forces. Yeats's poetry at different times manifests alternately the civilising impulse of love and other, more anti-social impulses, but Eagleton is keen to demonstrate the social bearings in Yeats's work of these two abstract principles, relating these once again to his aristocratic pretensions:

> Because he is essentially above the law, the nobleman resembles no one quite so much as those who fall outside it, the swarm of beggars, rogues, lustful geriatrics, and amiable idiots who troop their way through Yeats's stanzas. These are acceptable figures to him because like the gentleman they are radical individualists, and so a very different proposition from the anarchy of the mob. ... For Yeats as for Nietzsche, unbending or disman-tling the self is just another instance of its lordly power, and so ultimately strengthens rather than weakens it. The middle classes, by contrast, give themselves away ultimately out of timidity. (Eagleton, 1998, 290)

But the opposition between life and death in Yeats is ultimately more radical than this would suggest and manifests itself in his attitudes to woman who 'in a familiar paradox, is both the bearer of civility and its anarchic destroyer'. Here, of course, we are dealing not so much with Yeats's own masks as with his perception of these principles as they are directed *towards* him. As object of his desire, woman both threatens his undoing and is the only possible source of remedy for that condition, and this ambivalence towards woman is one which Yeats projects onto the Easter Rising, a projection enabled by Yeats's association of radical nationalism with Maude Gonne for whom he harboured an unrequited love. Hence that ambivalence towards the event embodied in the phrase 'terrible beauty' (which, as David Lloyd has noted, yokes together the frightening masculine power of the sublime and the feminine, domesticated appeal of the beautiful [Lloyd, 1993, 73]). The tension, which relates both to the Rising and to woman, remains irreconcilable.

Woman, then, represents both form and content, that which imparts order and that which needs harnessing. Insofar as she is associated with form, though, she is also – in another shift in perspective – that which threatens Yeats's aggressive characteristics by appearing as subduer or castrator, the dual personified features of that order as symbolised by Lady Gregory rather than Maude Gonne. Moreover, and by extension, that naturalised version of the social which is symbolised by Lady Gregory's Coole Park – the organic ideal, that is, – also, in its serenity appears to be on the side of death. Yet it is death which Yeats compulsively attempts to defeat, and even in its idealisation of a state of transcendence his poetry betrays its attachment to that which has apparently been transcended. Death, then – ultimately in contrast to Freud, for whom it is the negation of social relations – is associated with form for Yeats, though as with some of the symbols of life-in-death – such as Byzantium – or of determinate energy – such as the dancer and the dance – which appear in his poetry, content imparts life to form. The big house of the Ascendancy is one symbol of this relationship, one which 'ideally combines its impersonal (and so deathlike) rituals with a boisterous energy which never quite spills over their limits' (Eagleton, 1998, 293). Crucially, 'These binary oppositions [of content and form, life and death] break apart all the time in the substance of the poetry, but the structure of the poetic utterance is meant to gesture to their reconciliation' (Eagleton, 1998, 294). Hence the resolution of the two can never be satisfactorily achieved (how, for instance, can life and death truly be said to co-exist in the same moment?). Brilliantly at this point, Eagleton touches on Yeats's brief flirtation with fascism and the appeal that this held for him, since fascism offers but cannot deliver a kind of reconciliation of these oppositions. Its authoritarian form governs a violently energetic content, but its proposed society 'is a shoddy artefact, its form too tight and its content too unstable' (Eagleton, 1998, 294). Its brief appeal lay for Yeats in the formal rigidity it offered in contrast to the undisciplined and undisciplinable content of democracy, but this 'artificial' resolution fell short of any organicist ideal.

Yeats, then, inverts the Freudian association of form with *Eros* and the death drive with *Thanatos*, and can only accommodate that inversion by regarding 'destructiveness as a kind of ecstatic creation' (Eagleton, 1998, 294), leading us to register another reversal: even though at times in Yeats form (death) is animated by content (life), there is also a sense in which he transforms death into a kind of life. But since this involves 'wilfully abnegating the self', 'the detached *hauteur* which this involves is itself a kind of living death, [and] it is hard to know whether you have outwitted death or obediently done its work for it' (Eagleton, 1998, 294–5).

We need to pause a moment at this point to render explicit what is largely implicit in Eagleton's argument, since this aporetic relation between life and death, content and form which he detects in Yeats is not merely, of course, a philosophical irresolution. The influence of deconstruction is certainly discernible in this essay, but, whatever the vertiginous permutations of these undecidable relations, they must be grounded in a material social context and the ideological phenomena to which they give rise. We have noted before, of course, Eagleton's important argument that the organicist ideology which has been so potent a force in English culture was untenable in Ireland because social divisions there were so stark and unmediated. It is, then, Yeats's desire for such an organicist ideal to take root set against the social fact of its failure that generates the characteristic tensions of his poetry.

Since Eagleton is dealing with Yeats's work in its diversity, highlighting tendencies which characterise his output and which often pit one aspect of it against another, it is difficult to find embodied in one poem all of those features outlined above, but as a means of illustrating Eagleton's argument I want to make some brief, concluding comments on 'Under Ben Bulben', the poem which ends with Yeats's own epitaph – *'Cast a cold eye/ On life, on death./ Horseman pass by!'* – and which, claims Eagleton, represents an attempt 'to pre-empt death itself, turn history into a shadowing of his own utterance' (Eagleton, 1998, 292). The poem invokes a sense of the relations between man's 'two eternities' which it claims authentic Irish culture understood. Indeed, the poem represents an attempt to assert mastery over death, not through mere resignation or secure confidence in the afterlife, but through a contemptuous dismissal of its significance. Hence Yeats's striking image of interment:

> Though grave diggers' toil is long,
> Sharp their spades, their muscles strong,
> They but thrust their buried men
> Back in the human mind again. (ll. 21–4)

There are various forms of conversion and inversion going on here. Initially the gravediggers' labour is presented in its monotony as a kind of death, and is of course the physical act of laying to rest over which the soul triumphs, but it also, through the word 'thrust', imparts some of its energy to that very triumphant soul. Not only does this illustrate some of the contradictory relations between life and death to be found in Yeats, but it might also be said to be indicative of the social contradictions at the heart of his aristocratic vision: the toil of the peasants – if we can assume that is what they are – is disdained by the poet, placing the two radically at odds, and yet they are conjoined to the extent that the soul appropriates the peasants' labour.

Life, though, if it is to be fulfilling, must also embrace a destructive impulse, albeit in the form of a heroic aggression or intoxicating irrationality which again is the source of contact with the spiritual, the means by which the individual completes his 'partial mind' (l. 30). This is a necessary prelude to those domesticating, and therefore castrating, life-denying forces of work and marriage. Such claims lead us into an overt concern with questions of form, with those art works of the past whose formal perfection communicated to humanity something of the divine in contrast to the confusion or amorphousness manifest in the present. Unsurprisingly, then, Yeats's defiance of death is just as much a defiance of the degenerate present, and he exhorts Ireland's unacknowledged legislators to look backwards:

> Irish poets, learn your trade,
> Sing whatever is well made,
> Scorn the sort now growing up
> All out of shape from toe to top,
> Their unremembering hearts and heads
> Base-born products of base beds.
> Sing the peasantry, and then

> Hard-riding country gentlemen,
> The holiness of monks, and after
> Porter-drinkers' randy laughter;
> Sing the lords and ladies gay
> That were beaten into clay
> Through seven heroic centuries;
> Cast your mind on other days
> That we in coming days may be
> Still the indomitable Irishry. (ll. 68–83)

Both in form and content, Yeats's simply constructed but nonetheless 'well made' verse lauding the feudal past disdains the democratic formlessness of the present as represented by the low-born and symbolically disfigured individuals who dominate it. That past, embodied in those beaten into shape – animated works of art themselves – was not so formal and life-denying as to rule out the licentiousness of drunkards. But the sense of control which this verse generates is somewhat at odds with its tone, with the anger of Yeats's disdain for the contemporary middle class and especially its fixation on the sexual act (which, to echo another of Eagleton's points, carries arguably eugenicist implications). In the context of the verse as a whole, this appears as a distraction to be got out of the way before returning to the main theme, but since it so demonstrably supplies the motive for that main theme it is the rest of the poem which might be read as merely symptomatic. Moreover, there is a solipsistic quality to this verse, since we might legitimately wonder to whom it is addressed. Ostensibly to other poets, of course, but the sentiments and expression of them are so characteristically Yeatsian that it's difficult to know who, other than himself, Yeats actually had in mind: the effect is of Yeats supplying the remedy to his own problems. Isolated and aloof, Yeats resorts to inventing his others – if that is the appropriate term – in his own image. Projecting himself as Ireland's futurity, it is no surprise perhaps that he can then claim to snub death so completely as he does in writing his own epitaph. But this, of course, is an empty gesture, and Yeats's poetry remains unique.

4 A Picture of Oscar Wilde?

The Picture of Dorian Gray is a crucial text in Oscar Wilde's output, not simply because it is his best known work after *The Importance of Being Earnest*, but because of the role it has played in our understanding of Wilde himself. Far from there being any sign of the death of the author in critical studies of Wilde, one of their distinguishing features has been a tendency constantly to treat life and work as commentaries on each other, sometimes in rather crude ways. In the case of *Dorian Gray*, the temptation has been to discuss the narrative as almost allegorical, and therefore as remarkably prescient of Wilde's own eventual fate: Dorian's defiance of his portrait's increasingly degenerate and reproachful physiognomy is made to parallel Wilde's own apparently outrageous willingness to court his own doom, a doom which may even be regarded as having been brought about by his own hand when he decided to take the Marquess of Queensberry to court for the libellous card he left at Wilde's club. That kind of treatment of text and life has a lengthy history, but its most influential incarnation must surely be Richard Ellmann's biography, which from Wilde's early days at Portora Royal School discerns in him a masochistic desire for punishment. At Portora, Wilde apparently became fascinated with the trial of Rev. W. J. E. Bennett for publishing a book defending the real presence of Christ. Ellmann quotes uncritically from the dubious source of Frank Harris's biography that Wilde claimed he wanted 'to go down to posterity in such a case as "Regina versus Wilde" ' (Ellmann, 1987, 23). Such anticipatory moments litter the biography, and there are even suggestions that Wilde's contemporaries saw parallels between his fiction and his demise. It's not clear where Ellmann gets the information for the following incident which apparently occurred during exercise in prison one day:

> Wilde was walking the round when he heard somebody mutter, 'What are you doing in this place, Dorian Gray?' 'Not Dorian Gray, but Lord

Henry Wotton,' said Wilde. The man whispered 'I was at all your first nights, and at all your trials,' as if they were comparable dramatic performances. (Ellmann, 1987, 487)

Indeed, Ellmann speculates on another and more intimate connection between Wilde's and Dorian's fate in his claim, based on a story since convincingly rejected (see Holland, 1997, 12–15), that Wilde contracted the syphilis which was ultimately to bring about his death from a sex worker whilst at Oxford: 'Perhaps now the parable of Dorian's secret decay began to form in [Wilde's] mind, as the spirochete began its journey up his spine towards the meninges' (Ellmann, 1987, 91). Whilst Ellmann is more cautious than some in recognising the distinctions between Wilde and the principle figures in *Dorian Gray* – in humanist vein, he claims that 'Wilde is larger than his three characters together; they represent distortions or narrowing of his personality' (Ellmann, 1997, 302) – there is nonetheless an insistence on Wilde's trials, prison life and death in exile as the doomed telos of his existence. This is less a case of life imitating art – not least since the determining relations between life and text are not so much reversed as deconstructed in such an account – than of biography imposing the formal coherence and moral structure of tragedy on its diverse and often problematic sources (though admittedly there are certain coincidences which encourage such treatment: even Wilde's fall came at the moment of his greatest success).

It appears difficult to contemplate Wilde and his works without some reflections on the significance of his tragedy, then, in whatever sense that tragedy is grasped as a form of necessity. This is one element of Eagleton's own writings on Wilde which have taken different forms, critical and dramatic. His play, *St Oscar*, in its very title invokes Wilde's apparent fascination with Guido Reni's portrait of St Sebastian, and in the original stage version ended with Wilde adopting a Sebastian-like pose. This sense of Wilde as martyr again suggests a wilfulness to his demise, and Eagleton appears to accept the Ellmann line about Wilde often recklessly pursuing his own persecution (he also accepts Ellmann's claims about syphilis [Eagleton, 1997, 61]). But in what cause exactly might he be said to have been a martyr?

Wilde's explicit offence of 'gross indecency' would appear to render him a martyr in the cause of sexual freedom. But the danger Wilde was perceived as posing to Victorian society was not reducible to his sexual dissidence, though it became indissociably linked to that. Wilde had a disconcerting influence on his contemporaries, even before most of them had any knowledge of his sexuality. At their most radical, Wilde's writings inverted contemporary bourgeois utilitarian wisdom and privileged surface over depth, fictionality over sincerity. Indeed, Eagleton finds in Wilde – in a way which confounds any simple periodisation of literary and philosophical trends, but for reasons which are nonetheless properly historical – 'a postmodernist *avant la lettre*, with his belief that interpretation is endless, criticism a form of creative writing, truth more aesthetic than cognitive, the human subject an ephemeral construct, the world a product of the sign, the body and its pleasures a subversive undoing of a pharisaical ideology' (Eagleton, 1995, 335). Hence Eagleton's engagement with Wilde is in many, if not all, respects a continuation of his engagement with postmodernism.

This characterisation of Wilde as proleptically postmodern, though, is not a straightforward one, since Eagleton perceives Wilde as being in some respects bound up with certain apparently contradictory, but actually related trends within Victorian *fin de siecle* culture: the 'flight to the real' on the one hand, and the search for some metaphysical certainties or spiritual experience on the other. Each is, in its own way, representative of the Romantic dissatisfaction with middle-class normality – its business ethics and puritanical morality, its sheer mundaneness – which results in a desire for transcendence, either by contact with some unmediated authenticity (the 'real') or through some contact with cosmic forces (Eagleton, 1995a, 11–21). And indeed there are to be found some distinctive and, at times, apparently contradictory combinations of the two, as with Wilde's own elitist commitment to socialism, the achievement of which would generate conditions in which the ethic of living for others would become redundant. Socialism would be the means of achieving a universalised individualism of the sort that Wilde enjoyed in the present. As we shall see, Wilde was sceptical of the possibility of acting in ways which would bring about determinate consequences, and so would never have lifted a finger to attempt to realise any such utopian future. Rather, he preferred to 'lie on the couch all day and be one's own communist society' (Eagleton, 1995, 339). Indeed, Wilde's advocacy of socialism – unlike that of another kind of aesthete, William Morris – is an exceptional and highly derivative part of his total output (Guy and Small, 2000, 275–80).

But to the extent that Wilde's writing does advocate forms of indeterminacy this is paradoxically also for Eagleton the product of determinate kinds of 'doubleness': that of an Irishman and sometime republican who deliberately suppressed the signs of his origins in order to pass as English – and therefore someone whose relationship to Society was inevitably rendered ambivalent – of a family man who ended up in prison convicted of 'gross indecency' with male sex workers, and of a socialist who was lionised by elements of Society. For such a figure selfhood was inevitably unstable, fictionality a way of life and pleasure subversive of bourgeois norms. In this lies much of Wilde's radicalism, whether it was conscious or not, and a sense of this informs much recent critical work on him. Often itself informed by postmodern theory at some level, such work inevitably tends to discover in him a kind of dissidence which is congenial. Before considering in more detail Eagleton's reflections of Wilde's politics – and as a prelude to these considerations – I want to look briefly at what seem to me the different limitations of two contrasting treatments of him, one which celebrates his postmodern political potential and the other claiming to find in the details of Wilde's literary production evidence which effectively undermines the political motives attributed to him.

The first of these is Vicki Mahaffey's sophisticated and not entirely uncritical treatment of Wilde, in which she discovers in his use of language and theories of representation a desire to destabilise the fixed meanings necessary to social and political authority. Her own elaborately punning style of argument, with its attention to linguistic complexity, can be read as sympathetically pursuing Wilde's subversive agenda which she perceives as residing in a

> verbal and conceptual play which is micronational and multinational in its disregard for national borders. Its ethic is to remember at all times the insufficiency of the individual, the inadequacy of a single performance, and the creative (as well as criminal) potential of dissatisfaction. In short, individual morality and social justice cannot be assured by a universally applicable principle, but are instead – like wordplay – the results of insightful and self-aware readings of discrete texts, contexts, and subtexts as they inform a range of situations. (Mahaffey, 1998, 65–6)

('Borders' is used here somewhat figuratively, and Wilde's 'micronational' ethic appears to be a consequence in part of his Irish background and the fact that Ireland had never been a united, independent territory.) As with much recent criticism, the radical potential of Wilde is counterposed with those forces which destroyed him, and here Mahaffey outlines further the significance of the plural meanings which she believes he deployed against the oppressiveness of the law:

> Wilde appealed to the law for protection against Queensberry's representation of him, forgetting, perhaps, that the law is structured around mutually exclusive characterisations of guilt and innocence; in a trial, the goal is to label a defendant, to pronounce a verdict and, if necessary, to 'sentence' (or textualise) the offender, and as Wilde writes in *De Profundis*, 'all sentences are sentences of death'. The law brings the authoritarian power of language to bear on a more chaotic human reality, using language to distinguish black from white; this, in a much more primitive sense, was also Queensberry's method – but it was not Wilde's. ... What makes Wilde a strangely moving object lesson in the politics of representation is largely the divergence between his own writing – which is a prescription for joyous self-production, an acutely intelligent celebration of diversity and change that refuses to be framed or unnaturally stabilised – and the social plot which wrote him in, first as trivial jester (nothing Wilde) and finally as transgressive villain, a 'scary Wildman.' (Mahaffey, 1998, 43)

Well, the law brings to bear more authoritarian powers than language, of course, but this apart, there are at least two objections to be made to Mahaffey's advocacy of what she sees as the proper basis of Wildean subversiveness. First, what was wrong with the law as it applied to Wilde was not that it failed to grasp the messiness of existence (in itself, a claim about the nature of reality), but that it criminalised a specific kind of offence of which Wilde was unquestionably guilty. Second, formulating the case in this way suggests that all law is a means of imposing a crude authority, and therefore something to be in itself resisted, whereas, whilst it may indeed be compromised by its defence of certain class and other interests according to the determinate power structures of a society, there are – as we have already seen – dangers in privatising justice in the way that is implicit in Mahaffey's arguments (should there be different forms of justice for different groups or even for different individuals?). In its claim to uphold certain universal principles the law may also be the means by which socially disadvantaged groups can claim justice, and it is, indeed, the partial nature of the law and its failure adequately to realise genuinely universal human rights that may be the basis of critique and political mobilisation. Moreover, it is not clear that in all respects Wilde's elaborately punning style or the opacity of his writing, which emphasises mystery, secrecy and impenetrability, are grounded in the kind of pluralistic ethic Mahaffey elaborates. It may in part have been rendered necessary precisely because of legal proscriptions.

Mahaffey's treatment of Wilde contrasts with the ways in which he has been discussed in the past, and in many respects is a welcome relief from such discussions. A more recent, determinedly revisionist account of Wilde, though, downplays both Wilde's political significance and his literary 'merit' on the grounds that it consists solely in his 'wit', a term whose significance is merely taken for granted. Josephine Guy and Ian Small's *Oscar Wilde Profession* deploys a 'materialist' approach which claims to analyse him in relation to the 'culture industry' of his time. Both terms are divorced from the Marxist cultural criticism with which they are most frequently associated, as the authors discuss Wilde's sense of himself as a writer, and emphasise his desire to be financially successful and the necessary awareness of the market and the need for self-promotion which this entailed. This, they point out, contributed significantly to the generic range of his work and, indeed, to its tone, as he marketed himself as the producer of literary works which, right down to their very material forms, advertised themselves to a cultural elite. This approach leads them into a self-confessed 'cynicism' about Wilde, not least in relation to claims about his political significance. Declan Kiberd, for instance, claims that Wilde's defence of lying may be related to a well-established Irish cultural 'ratification of the lie' which, under colonial rule, constituted a form of resistance to the law (Kiberd, 1997, 279). Implicitly in response to this, Guy and Small argue that Wilde deliberately played on his Irish Republican background as part of his self-promotional tour of America. Hence, his political stance was, at least substantially, a pose, and that pose in turn contributed to his advocacy of inauthenticity. Hence, in America, Wilde was

> commodifying a form (or brand) of Irishness as Aestheticism that he knew would sell to his American audience. This view of the North American tour may seem unsympathetic and is certainly unromantic; but it is in accord with Wilde's willingness on his return to Britain to commit himself to a profession already renowned for its lack of integrity and to advertise himself by explicitly promoting a cult of insincerity. Put another way, the inconsistency and cultivated insouciance that came to characterise Wilde's journalistic voice, and that was later elevated in his critical essays to a defence of lying, may initially have been commercially rather than politically motivated. (Guy and Small, 2000, 35–6)

Commodification, on this account, merely renders Wilde's convictions somewhat hollow and is in turn the basis of his advocacy of depthlessness. There is some degree of insight in this recognition that the material context of cultural production impacted on Wilde's aesthetics, but, on the whole, it is symptomatic of Guy and Small's approach throughout their book which consistently treats him as a more or less astute businessman. Despite the occasional recognition that, for instance, Wilde was 'a writer for whom aesthetic and financial imperatives could often pull in opposing directions' (Guy and Small, 2000, 237), the tendency throughout is to smooth out contradictions and to downplay the manifest ideological significance of Wilde's symbolic relations to his age. The materialist part of their discussion consists in an account of Wilde's adaptation to the literary market conditions of the time rather than any discussion of the determining force of complex social relations such as Eagleton attempted to outline in *Criticism and Ideology*. One of the consequences of this is largely to neglect the striking contradiction between Wilde's petty bourgeois practice as a writer and his ideological disdain for bourgeois values, integral to which was precisely his own Romantic conceptualisation of the artist. Wilde's 'aesthetic' lifestyle outstripped his ability to pay for it, and the two were thus both increasingly at odds and interdependent, his lifestyle making greater and greater demands on his ability to profit from his writing.

By contrast, Eagleton aims neither merely to celebrate nor to down-play Wilde's political importance. Rather he attempts to grasp both the value and the limitations of his dissidence. Wilde's speech in *St Oscar* is one which mimics aspects of the epigrammatic style which pervades his work, but it also conveys something of Eagleton's ambivalent attitude towards Wilde:

> ... you may be wondering why I'm so unpleasantly fat. It's mainly to compensate for the starvation of the Irish race. I eat, so to speak, vicari-ously, on their behalf. It's nothing personal. I take hardly any pleasure in it. What you can't see is that inside this obese body an even fatter man is struggling to get out. Just as outside every slim man there's a fat man struggling to get in. Epitaph 56. Or do I mean epigram? Strange how I always confuse those words .... No, that's not true. There's nothing *inside* a man at all. Always judge by appearances, they're far more reli-able than reality. The English think that's hypocrisy. Do you ever wonder they distrust appearances when you see what they've done to half the world? They escape to an inner place called the truth. It's very deep – like a sewer. Whereas I'm superficial: profoundly so. There's nothing skin-deep about *my* superficiality. (Eagleton, 1997a, 17)

Wilde's opening claim is a 'witty' way of claiming to live for others which simultaneously inverts the logic of that morality. Its irony, though, draws attention to the separation between 'the Irish race' and himself, one determined by Wilde's own class difference from the majority of the Irish people as well as his privileged position in England. In making this comment, he draws attention to the body which stands as a metaphor here for aestheticism itself, for the surplus which is culture and on which the aesthete feasts. The pointed distinction drawn here between Wilde and the Irish majority contrasts both positively and negatively with his mother's earnest nationalism in the ensuing dialogue in which she upbraids him for his refusal of his Irishness and of authenticity in general. That refusal partly took the form of a parody of a certain kind of Englishness, and the dissident pleasure in signifying practices which Wilde embodied for the English was one of the things that made him threatening to them, not least since he drew attention to their own superficiality, to the hollowness of their convictions and appearances, in much of his work. There is also an intimation in this speech of Eagleton's grasp of Wilde's particular kind of tragedy in that confusion of 'epitaph' and 'epigraph', as if the reverse side of his delight in aphoristic inversion was a masochistic commitment to his own downfall. But Eagleton's pun also draws attention to the physical limits that were forced on Wilde's cultural self-inventions: later, we find Wilde in prison, asserting another 'pose', humility, before the mask slips and he is compelled to register the claims of the body: 'What a fucking awful place prison is. Since I've been here I've had ulcers, abscesses, and gumboils; now I've got the shits' (Eagleton, 1997a, 50).

According to Edna Longley, in *St Oscar* Eagleton 'used Wilde to present a timeless thesis about imperialist oppression' (Longley, 1994, 183). Since she doesn't specify what that thesis is, it's difficult to contradict her, but since there is no straightforwardly endorsed spokesperson for Irish nationalism in the play, nor is it easy to see her point. Wilde was the son of a famous Republican and was prosecuted by Edward Carson, the barrister who later founded the Ulster Volunteer Force to oppose Westminster's commitment to Home Rule, and Eagleton at least partly seeks to examine Wilde's relations to both. Perhaps Eagleton's generally negative treatment of the Unionist icon Carson is at issue. But Wilde's final engagement with him is hardly reducible to Unionist v. Republican positions: rather it highlights the populist vulgarity of the Orangeism to which the Trinity-educated Carson *ironically* committed himself. The dialogue suggests that this is a creed in whose metaphysical justifications he could hardly be said to believe, yet the irony of his position cannot be publicly acknowledged since it is necessary that the masses believe something if order is to be maintained. 'There's no meaning without order', claims Carson, for whom the postmodern Wilde is a representative of 'chaos' who had to be stopped (Eagleton, 1997a, 60–1). At least as much scrutinised in this play are the philosophical underpinnings of the various figures' ideological commitments as the specific politics they espouse. Wilde's scepticism towards all of their commitments highlights their contradictions, but his refusal of politics per se is rendered naïve in the face of the social power which brings about his downfall. To Lady Wilde's claim that 'Myths are what ordinary people have to live by', Oscar responds: 'Myths are fictions that have forgotten they're such; whereas I never forget for a moment how ludicrously unreal I am' (Eagleton, 1997a, 24). If Carson recommends two years hard labour for Wilde in court on the grounds that 'it is time that Mr Wilde had a little more seriousness introduced into his futile existence' (Eagleton, 1997a, 45), it is clear that the play both sympathises to some degree with the sentiment whilst abhorring both the sentence and the social order which it helps to underwrite. That order may rely on fictions, but it is nonetheless a reality, as is the body whose sufferings help to maintain it.

Even if the thesis underpinning *St Oscar* is commonly enough misunderstood, the play is nonetheless vulnerable to the criticism that it feels as if a position is being argued too closely. Not that taking positions is inadmissible in good drama – a liberal assumption – but that position is insufficiently *dramatised* (though admittedly Wilde's elevation of speech over action presents challenges in this respect). What the play stages, then, is Eagleton's ambivalence towards the figure of Wilde who is himself presented as something of an indeterminate figure, 'A cock and a cunt together' as Wilde is made to say (Eagleton, 1997a, 16), and therefore someone who resists the fixed meanings of the symbolic order. But Eagleton's perception of Wilde's gender indeterminacy is linked to his homosexuality as if the reasons for this were self-evident. '*Saint Oscar* occasionally portrays his sexuality as a kind of doubleness, not of course because homosexuals are actually "half man and half woman", but because this provided me with a way of linking that dimension of him to his other contradictions', writes Eagleton (Eagleton, 1997a, 5). In fact, as much recent work has demonstrated, Wilde's effeminacy – and its relationship to his homosexuality – is a complex phenomenon, grounded at least as much in class distinctions as in the reification of gender differences.

Class, gender and sexuality

The perception that Wilde's work is pervasively, if guardedly, concerned with homosexuality – that this is the 'truth' which is concealed there – may be said to represent an extension of the sexologists' conviction as outlined by foucault that sexuality constituted the truth of the individual. But there are other reasons for expressing scepticism towards such a truth, the most important being those advanced by Alan Sinfield who argues that the trials' revelations of Wilde's sexual relations with men fixed an influential version of the queer in the public mind. Thanks to the New Journalism of the period, the Wilde trials were the most sensational of the nineteenth century, and the figure of the queer which was produced in the representations of Wilde generated the connection between homosexuality and effeminacy – as well as with a further connotatively related term, that of the artist – which has persisted down to the present. The social meaning of 'effeminacy', though, is complex and bound up with class relations just as surely as it is with gender. Of course, it designates an 'inappropriate' femininity in a man, but equally the ideal condition of manliness in the nineteenth century was not simply a simile for – indeed, should be carefully distinguished from – 'masculinity': it designated the virtuous condition which is necessary to citizenship and which therefore related gender to national, and by extension patriotic, ideologies. Those ideals of citizenship were themselves bound up with historic ideologies of class legitimation. J. G. A. Pocock describes the emergence in post-Restoration Britain of a non-feudal, but nonetheless gentry ideology of manliness as bound up with a disinterestedness which middle-class men were less capable of achieving because of their specific commercial interests: 'The ideal of the patriot or citizen entailed the image of a personality free and virtuous because unspecialised. The function of his property was to give him independence and autonomy as well as the leisure and liberty to engage in public affairs; but his capacity to bear arms in the public cause was an end of his property in goods and the test of his virtue' (Pocock, 1985, 109). By contrast, commercial wealth tended to feminise a man, since he was someone 'still wrestling with his own passions and hysterias and with interior and exterior forces let loose by his fantasies and appetites, and symbolised by such archetypically female goddesses of disorder as Fortune, Luxury, and most recently Credit herself' and it took industrialisation to generate a convincing image of the bourgeois as a heroic figure (Pocock, 1985, 114). Indeed, bourgeois self-legitimation entailed an inversion of the prior wisdom, as its own version of civic virtue – in which the bourgeois 'displayed in frugality and reinvestment his willingness to subordinate private satisfaction to public good, of which he would be rewarded with a further share' (Pocock, 1975, 446) – increasingly convicted the old elite of a devotion to 'luxury', to the same feminised pleasures of appetitive indulgence to which the middle classes had been considered prone. The puritanism and work ethic of the middle classes thus rendered them morally superior to their decadent social 'superiors', even though the decadence of that class manifested itself in a devotion to a conspicuous consumption of commodities which the bourgeois order was particularly successful in providing. What becomes increasingly pronounced in the nineteenth century, then, is a tension between the moral superiority which the middle classes claimed for themselves and the 'luxury' which commodification made possible, not least as a consequence of imperial expansion.[1]

The aesthete, too, was implicated in these conflicts. Enabled by his leisure class lifestyle, he (usually) was immersed in sensuous elements of culture and thus exhibited contempt for the utilitarian conviction that if art had any value it lay in its ability to dispense morality. The genealogy of the aesthete is a complex one, and though aestheticism embodies a critique of bourgeois civilisation, that critique is not necessarily a progressive one. One of aestheticism's most influential figures is the French writer, Gautier, for whom middle-class utilitarianism was anathema, an attitude bound up with his fervently royalist anti-republicanism. In British culture, meanwhile, the aesthete's self-absorption was derided for his refusal of social and moral responsibilities. In popular culture, this type of the aesthete is Frederick Fairlie from Wilkie Collins' novel, *The Woman in White* – an oversensitive, nervous creature who consequently neglects the patriarchal authority invested in him. But whereas Fairlie is principally devoted to art, absorbed in his private pleasures, Wilde's aestheticised *lifestyle* evinced an absorption in commodities at the same time as his pronouncements explicitly devalued frugality and the work ethic. Hence, at a time in the late nineteenth century when debates around gender and sexuality were intensely debated as contradictions in the ideologies governing them were beginning to open up, 'the entire, vaguely disconcerting nexus of effeminacy, leisured idleness, immorality, luxury, insouciance, decadence and aestheticism, which Wilde was perceived as instantiating, was transformed into a brilliantly precise image', the queer stereotype (Sinfield, 1994, 118). One of the abiding consequences of this history is that attitudes towards sexuality have been significantly determined by the history of class antagonisms. For most of the twentieth century, the majority of the left regarded homosexuality as a bourgeois and/or aristocratic perversion.

This is not to say, though, that the perception that male homosexuality was tacitly integral to elite culture is merely an illusion based on a post-Wildean reading of certain of that culture's codes. The public schools which trained British males to be class and national leaders witnessed increasing anxiety about same-sex desire as they grew in both size and number in the later part of the nineteenth century. As they expanded, these schools increasingly recruited their students from middle-class families who sought the status of a 'traditional' education for their children. Nonetheless, the old distinctions remained and traditional wealth remained snooty about 'trade' as well as the utilitarian ethos of the middle classes, even though the reformed public schools of the second half of the nineteenth century had attempted to suppress the dissolute and arrogantly snobbish behaviour of their pupils so evident in the earlier part of the century. Such class tensions persisted well into the twentieth century, influencing perceptions of male homosexuality. Alan Hollinghurst's *The Swimming Pool Library*, published in 1986, is profoundly sensitive to class relations over the course of the twentieth century. It features the diaries of Lord Nantwich, a valued colonial administrator – valued as such, indeed, because of his idealistic homosexuality – who became the victim of a State pogrom against gay men in the 1950s instituted by the Director of Public Prosecutions, a bourgeois self-made man. After the 'success' of this pogrom, Nantwich notes from his prison cell how the DPP has been given a peerage: 'Oddly typical of the British way of getting rid of troublemakers by moving them up – implying as it does too some reward for the appalling things he has done' (Hollinghurst, 1988, 260). There was, though, no absolute division between classes in terms of their attitude to homosexuality. Both Wilde and the Establishment acted to keep Lord Alfred Douglas out of the dock, whereas Wilde's disgrace could only serve to shore up the moral order without causing serious damage to social authority. Indeed, that authority was consolidated as the deranged Marquess of Queensberry became a middle-class hero.

A great deal of critical close reading has been devoted to making explicit the male homosexual subtext of *Dorian Gray*, much of it assuming that homosexuality can be read off the codes which were in the process of being constituted at the time of the novel, and which only became fully visible after the trials (Sinfield, 1994, 98–105). Wilde presents us with an intensely homosocial milieu in which male beauty is freely admired. Basil worries that the portrait will reveal something of his own soul and for this reason initially refuses to exhibit it. Women, on the other hand, are represented as placing limits on male freedoms, inconsequential, or themselves New Women who are conveniently indifferent to men. Lord Henry's wife is one of the latter, and there are the usual Wildean hints that marriage is merely a formal arrangement, as when Lord Henry states that ' "the one charm of marriage is that it makes a life of deception absolutely necessary for both parties. I never know what my wife is doing, and my wife never knows what I am doing" ' (Wilde, 1981, 4). Dorian ruins the reputations of men and women alike. It is not coincidental that all of this occurs within a leisure class: the whole ethos of the novel is at odds with bourgeois norms. *Dorian Gray*'s contradictory reception in middle-class journals can be explained in terms of the apparently contradictory nature of the book itself: to the extent that the novel is located inside that leisure class world, permitting no other evaluative stance outside of it than that of the Vanes, it appears to collude with that world's values; but since Dorian is judged and finally condemned, it appears to endorse conventional morality.

There is, then, an apparent contradiction here, since the novel's rejection of familial claims on the individual appears to be at odds with its ultimate moralism, an implicitly sexual moralism which is pervasive in Wilde's work. Vicki Mahaffey demonstrates in considerable detail that 'The inexorable "truth" that Wilde represents again and again in his works is that sin brings its own punishment, and that sexual activity is sinful' (Mahaffy, 1998, 64). This is compatible with that long-established account of Wilde's life, endorsed by Ellmann and, following him, Eagleton. There is, though, a way of reading the novel and grasping its central contradiction which does not comply with this ideological narrative of Wilde's life.

Sexuality, history and determinism

Despite the static quality of much of *Dorian Gray* – a quality only dispelled towards the end of the novel, as Dorian becomes increasingly aware of time and the possibility of judgement pressing on him – it is a book informed by a particular understanding of history, one evident in Wilde's own complex identification with the novel: 'Basil is what I think I am; Lord Henry is what the world thinks me; Dorian what I would like to be – in other ages, perhaps' (Wilde, 1962, 352). Wilde's 'self', on this account, was strung out between personal and public perceptions and across history. This non-identity of selfhood is related to another feature of the novel: its focus on the body, not so much as a site of erotic interest beyond the first couple of chapters – and even there the interest is more on the part of Basil and Lord Henry than the reader – but in its reproachful degeneration in contrast to Dorian's own (temporary) defiance of time and the Old Testament logic that the wages of sin is death. It becomes Dorian's conscience, or as Wilde preferred to describe it, his 'soul'.

The finally determining division of the novel, then, is that between bodily sin and the soul, a division which corresponds to that between art and reality. However, if Dorian's death has any inevitability about it, it is not the consequence of any Faustian pact he makes with Lord Henry – who, in any case, becomes less and less of a sinister mephistophelean character as the novel progresses – since Dorian might presumably have carried on his life in defiance of the portrait's apparent recriminations. It is only because he decides to destroy the portrait that he ends up killing himself, suggesting that his death is less the consequence of external judgement than of some internal principle which has become alienated from him. Indeed, the relationship between Dorian and his portrait is a remarkably private, even intimate one, confined to the attic room which used to be his school room. The only other witness to the relationship is Basil, and he becomes a victim of it.

Dorian is as much fascinated as horrified by his own portrait and exults in his defiance of it: 'there would be real pleasure in watching it', he reflects. 'He would be able to follow his mind into its secret places. This portrait would be to him the most magical of mirrors. As it had revealed to him his own body, so it would reveal to him his own soul. ... Like the gods of the Greeks, he would be strong, and fleet, and joyous' (Wilde, 1981, 106). Indeed, the portrait is less a passive reflection of his soul, than an active agent in his conduct, galvanising Dorian to commit his most terrible crime: 'Dorian glanced at the portrait, and suddenly an uncontrollable feeling of hatred for Basil Hallward came over him, as though it had been suggested to him by the image on the canvas, whispered into his ear by those grinning lips' (Wilde, 1981, 158). The reference to the Greeks in the first of these quotations is significant, and only one of many in the text which points up another of its divisions: that between Christian and Greek – that is, *pre-*Christian – forms of morality. The Christian narrative is obvious enough. Dorian is tempted in Basil's garden by the devilish Lord Henry. Basil's offer of redemption to the earnestly sinful Dorian results in Basil's Christ-like sacrifice, registered as blood on the hand of the figure of the portrait. The significance of Dorian's murder of Basil is not 'realised' (to use the terms of the novel) by Dorian, who instead has any trace of Basil's physical presence chemically dissolved and who attempts to forget the murder through three days immersion in sensuality in an opium den (the further refusal of redemption is signified here through the negative parallel between Dorian's sojourns in the deathlike, mechanical world of sin populated by 'monstrous marionettes' [Wilde, 1981, 186] and the three days between Christ's crucifixion and his resurrection).

Nonetheless, when Lord Henry seduces Dorian with his talk, it is with reference to a 'New Hedonism', rather than the 'New Hellenism' which elsewhere Wilde commended. The distinction is significant, implicitly relating to the distinction Wilde draws in the letter quoted above between himself and Lord Henry. Basil, with whom he more closely identified, seeks a reconciliation of that division in his culture between ' "a realism that is vulgar, an ideality that is void" ' (Wilde, 1981, 10), and the Hellenism which Wilde advocated was one which aspired to reconcile the Christian division of body and soul in a way which connects him with a particular tradition of thought prominent amongst those who attempted to defend male same-sex love in late Victorian Britain. Figures such as Pater and – at greater length and with more of an awareness of its importance for matters of sexuality – John Addington Symonds expounded the view that Christianity's spread had been necessitated by the excesses of the decadent Roman Empire, but that this had set body and soul against each other in an antagonistic relation in which the latter demanded sacrifices of the former. It was left to the Renaissance period to begin the process of overcoming this ethic which was most influential in England in the medieval period. The pre-Christian aesthetic morality of the Greeks – at its most admirable in the Dorian period, according to Symonds – did not proscribe *acts*, but rather advocated a principle of temperance on the basis that excessive indulgence was unseemly. For Symonds, this Greek ethic prefigured a natural morality – one which the science of the time was also rendering possible – grounded in the body itself. Something of Symonds's grasp of this ethic is perhaps best conveyed by an extract from his *Memoirs*:

> The violated organ, whether stomach, brain, heart, lungs or reproductive apparatus, is equally a deity offended by the youthful sinner.
>
> The Greek virtue of temperance ... was a recognition of the equilibrium which man should aim at in the maintenance of his chief glands through sober use of them.
>
> In a large measure it was a virtue based on physical foundations. (Symonds, 1984, 250)

Such ideas permeate the writings on Greece that Symonds published during his lifetime. A strong sense of evolutionary determinism also informs Symonds' work, though its appropriation of Darwin is one which 'carefully read out of Darwin (or perhaps never read in him) the rejection of teleology and with it the longstanding providential view of history as an inevitable progress towards human perfection' (Dale, 1988, 127). His view of history, then, despite its claims to be scientific, evinced a belief in a traditional, English sense of the benevolent, yet inevitable, unfolding of history, however much that historical process may demonstrate an indifference to individuals along the way.

It has become increasingly clear how steeped in Symonds's work Wilde was,[2] and Wilde's writings, too, evince a strong belief in determinism, to the extent that he was sceptical about the efficacy of any form of agency. His most witty short story, 'Lord Arthur Saville's Crime', may be read as a satire on purposive action (Alderson, 1998, 150–3) and in *Dorian Gray* James Vanes's actions in the pursuit of justice merely lead to his absurd accidental death. Art, for Wilde, was the means of achieving some relief from necessity: it possesses formal organisation, whereas life is unpredictable and, individually, we can exert no control over it (Wilde, 1970, 359). Rather, Wilde's evolutionary sensibility stresses that individualism of an aesthetic rather than heroic sort contributes towards the diversity of 'the race' by expanding its range of experiences. Such advocacy of 'sin' represents Wilde in a decadent mood, whereas *Dorian Gray* – written around the same time as 'The Critic as Artist' – can be read as a corrective to that mood, a reassertion of the necessary limits to sin, and it is this which brings us back to a consideration of the body.

According to the novel, we are all selfish. There is no escaping our narcissistic condition, since even our most apparently altruistic gestures are determined by the sastisfactions with which they reward us. When Dorian – unaware that Sybil Vane has killed herself – writes his letter asking her to forgive him, we learn that 'It is the confession, not the priest, that gives us absolution. When Dorian had finished the letter, he felt that he had been forgiven' (Wilde, 1981, 96). The sentiments here are clearly the narrator's rather than Dorian's, who has yet to realise the truth that all one's actions are self-regarding. The formalist aesthetics entailed by the individualist ethics which inform this passage are akin to the value Wilde places on art in *The Critic as Artist*: the determinate forms of art permit the individual some control over life and his emotions in contrast to the chaos of life. In this sense, the moralism of the age which at this point, after being reproached by the portrait, Dorian accepts, was itself merely a form of egotism. Indeed, for Lord Henry, 'Conscience makes egotists of us all' (Wilde, 1981, 102). Virtue, too, is a pose whose appeal resides in the effects it has on the individual. When Dorian 'spares' the rural innocence of Hetty Merton, he is dismayed that the only impact on his portrait is a negative one:

> He could see no change, save that in the eyes there was a look of cunning, and in the mouth the curved wrinkle of the hypocrite. ... it was an unjust mirror, this mirror of his soul that he was looking at. Vanity? Curiosity? Hypocrisy? Had there been nothing more in his renunciation than that? There had been something more. At least he thought so. But who could tell? ... No. There had been nothing more. Through vanity he had spared her. In hypocrisy he had worn the mask of goodness. For curiosity's sake he had tried the denial of self. He recognised that now. (Wilde, 1981, 221–2)

The portrait thus places Dorian in an impossible position, damned if he's 'virtuous', damned if he's not, and it is his inability to live with *that* knowledge that leads him to attempt its destruction.

Of course, this makes a nonsense of the whole principle of damnation (and therefore of redemption, at least in the Christian terms offered by Basil). But it is not only the sincerity of Dorian's virtuous acts which is called into question. Take for instance Lord Henry's wife:

> She laughed nervously as she spoke, and watched [Dorian] with her vague forget-me-not eyes. She was a curious woman, whose dresses

always looked as if they had been designed in a rage and put on in a tempest. She was usually in love with somebody, and, as her passion was never returned, she had kept all her illusions. She tried to look picturesque, but only succeeded in being untidy. Her name was Victoria, and she had a perfect mania for going to church. (Wilde, 1981, 45)

As with all the other characters in the novel, Victoria Wotton is very much a victim of her senses, though her nervousness distinguishes her from the male characters, and the description here is characteristic of Victorian representations of the New Woman. Moreover, this nervous condition undermines what might otherwise be taken to be earnest behaviour, since if going to church is a 'mania' it verges on the pathological. This is consistent with representations of moral behaviour in general in the novel, governed as they are entirely by self- or instinctual satisfaction. Even James Vane is predisposed to hate Dorian as the consequence of 'some obscure race-instinct for which he could not account, and which for that reason was all the more dominant within him' (Wilde, 1981, 66). Lord Henry reflects that crime is to the lower classes 'simply a method of procuring extraordinary sensations' (Wilde, 1981, 213). Moreover, it is not only Dorian for whom life and art are transposed: the depiction of the Vanes, for instance, presents us with another instance of life imitating (low) art, since they live their lives by what are to them the satisfying conventions of melodrama. They differ from Dorian only in being unable to recognise the fact and by the relative vulgarity of those conventions.

Other-regarding behaviour, then, is simply impossible, and the crude materialist and 'consumerist' discourse of the nerves which pervades both the novel and that of Victorian aestheticism more generally[3] reinforces, and quite possibly ideologically determines, the narcissistic individualism displayed in the novel. The novel's real concern with morality, therefore, is not so much with ensuring that Dorian is suitably punished for his transgressions as with the question of whether morality is possible at all. The implicit answer, since Dorian's soul and body are ultimately revealed to be united rather than distinct entities, lies in the kind of natural morality which for Wilde and others had its precedent in ancient Greece. There is no final demonstration of what exactly this morality might consist in, not least given Dorian's peremptory refusal ever to dwell on or 'realise' situations, but this is nonetheless the reconciliation to which the novel gestures.

The world of the aesthete to which we are introduced in the novel is itself the opulently material one of commodities. Indeed, as Rachel

Bowlby argues, the figure of the insatiable aesthete, 'far from being different from the new consumer of the period, turns out to be none other than his or her "perfect type" ' (Bowlby, 1993, 7). Dorian as consumer not only takes pleasure in commodities but raids both the past and other cultures for the sensations they yield rather than for any insights they may possess for him in another striking prefiguration of the depthless parodic qualities of the postmodern. Even in terms of its genre, Bowlby argues, the novel represents a kind of pick 'n' mix of styles and forms which offer the reader no privileged moral vantage point from which to judge Dorian (Bowlby, 1993, 21–2). It does offer, though, in that Greek principle at which the novel at least hints, an external principle of judgement. This principle, however, relies on an ideological mystification: on an evolutionary determinism which might finally resolve the divisions between body and culture, sin and the soul, and establish a natural ethics. As so many commentators have recognised, though, *Dorian Gray* possesses such relevance for us because it depicts a narcissism which material historical forces – specifically the increasingly pervasive commodity fetishism which is evident in the novel – have ensured have only become more pervasive with time. If such commodification has been particularly associated with the growth of a contemporary gay subculture – therefore perpetuating certain associations with 'effeminacy' to the extent that such associations maintain their currency – this has been because a commercialised scene was the only space available for the growth of such a subculture in the years after the partial decriminalisation of male homosexuality in 1967, given that legal reform did not constitute moral reform and hence usher in, of itself, transformations in civil society beyond the market (Evans, 1993, 89–113).

As we have seen, then, Eagleton's sense of Wilde's tragedy is partly indebted to the conventional narrative embodied principally in Ellmann's biography, and to this extent is complicit with a certain ideological apprehension of Wilde. But Wilde's tragedy is also, for Eagleton, something more than the culmination of his desire: if we find ourselves able to identify with Wilde, it constitutes a critique of his own times and, to the extent that the significance of his tragedy continues to resonate in the present, our own. It is not merely in its persecution of male homosexuals that that society is critiqued, but in its suppression of Wilde's scandalous affront to utilitarian reason, his attempt to promote 'a different order of truth altogether'. When Richard Wallace happens across the Wilde of *St Oscar* in Paris, physically broken, financially destitute and in exile under a pseudonym, we have the following exchange:

> WALLACE: You don't look to me much like the image of the future, Oscar.
> WILDE: I'm an image of the failure of the present. That's the only image of the future worth having. (Eagleton, 1997a, 57)

We need, though, to grasp Wilde's suffering in historical terms rather than to fetishise him as victim or hero. If 'the future' – our postmodern present – has to a significant extent enabled the individualism which was suppressed in Wilde, it has done so not only as 'a strained, fictive parodic travesty of the real thing' (Eagleton, 1990, 31), but also for a minority of the world's population and therefore at the expense of other tragic figures whose significance needs to inform our critical relations to our culture and our practical interventions in society.

Notes

Introduction

1. See Maley (1994). For a far more sophisticated and appreciative account of Eagleton's style, see Connor (1994).

1 Marxism, Culture and English Studies

1. The best brief introduction to Marx is Eagleton's own (Eagleton, 1997), an elaboration of Marx which has one eye on the poststructuralists. Contrast it, for instance, with the rather different emphases in his still invaluable account of Marxist literary criticism (Eagleton, 1976). See also, in this series, Moyra Haslett's *Marxist Literary and Cultural Theories*, which provides an account of debates in the past quarter of a century since Eagleton's was first published. For discussions of Marxist economics, Fine (1989) is probably still the best starting point, but Harvey (1999) must be regarded as the definitive version for our times.

2. England's lack of a thoroughgoing bourgeois revolution has produced important debates between Marxists about the significance of this. For Perry Anderson, for instance, the absence of such a revolution has meant that the values of England's hegemonic bloc have been characterised by a 'comprehensive conservatism ... covering society with a pall of simultaneous philistinism (towards ideas) and mystagogy (towards institutions), for which [it] has justly won an international reputation' (Anderson, 1992, 31). Ellen Meiksins Wood (1991), however, considers that England has been more thoroughly marked by the logic of capitalism than any other country.

3. See John Saville's magnificent study, *1848: The British State and the Chartist Movement* (1987), which revises the long-standing, manifestly ideological view that Chartism was a victim of its own incompetence and of the indifference of working class people towards it.

4. On this, see Sinfield, 39–42.

5. See, for instance, Bennett, 1979, 106–10.

6. Whilst it is clear that Eagleton's later work departs from the approach outlined in *Criticism and Ideology*, I disagree with Warren Montag's view that Eagleton simply turned his back on an Althusser whom he had misread (Montag, 2003, 6–8). Montag attributes a structuralism to the book which is absent from it in order to convict Eagleton of a reductively structuralist reading of Althusser. This suits Montag's own purposes, but *Criticism and Ideology* is not in any meaningful sense structuralist: the

categories for materialist analysis Eagleton provides are not essentialist and demand an attention to historical change, as well as to the historically contingent relations between them, whilst the ultimately determining force of the GMP merely bears witness to Eagleton's Marxist orthodoxy. Eagleton was always more judiciously critical of Althusser than many others who were influenced by him.

7. One instance of such a reading is Geoffrey Bennington's 'Demanding History' in Attridge *et al.*, 1987.

2 Culture and Postmodernism

1. It should be noted however that Lacan himself makes a comparison between the imaginary/symbolic relation and the nature/culture one, at least as the latter is articulated by Lévi-Strauss (Lacan, 1992, 274).

3 Marxism, Culture and Irish Studies

1. For a fairly brief account of this, see Alderson, 1998, 112–19. Discussion of the racialisation of the Irish, though, has been a feature of Irish Studies since at least Curtis (1968). Sheridan Gilley (1978) rejects Curtis's claims in a thoroughly unconvincing fashion which has nonetheless managed to persuade some. Gilley does not take account of the increasing influence of polygenism detailed in Nancy Steppan (1980) and, more recently, by Robert J. C. Young (1995).

2. Howe's observation is polemical, without registering the complexity of the situation. I quote it here merely as an example of the ways in which politico-philosophical conceptions of history are complicated by reference to Ireland.

3. Though there have been other accounts of the revisionist controversy, the most complete record of the origins of revisionism and of the debates to which it has given rise is provided in Brady, 1994.

4. I am drawing on what I think are the most valuable aspects of Ahmad's arguments here. However, *In Theory* has received some of its most highly – certainly its most perceptively – critical reviews from other Marxists on account of its historical errors and egregious treatment of Edward Said in particular. The general sense was that the book's polemic misfired, not least because its targets were badly chosen. See, in particular, Brennan (1994), Lazarus (1993), Parry (1993) and Sprinker (1993). Later comments by some of these writers have been more sympathetic to his general purpose, and Brennan notes crucially that, in contrast to many of Ahmad's academicist critics, 'no one reading his work can miss that he breathes the air of men and women who planned strikes, went to prison, risked their lives, and studied not simply Marxist theory but the history of the labour movement' (Brennan, 1997, 86). The irony is that one might say similar things about Said.

5. A similar point has been made in analogous terms – that Eagleton effectively 'colonises' forms of dissent – by Showalter (Showalter, 1989) in relation to feminism. For some, where it is not simply regarded as arrogance on Eagleton's part, this is no

doubt symptomatic of the inattentiveness of dialectical engagement to the particulars of those movements/academic fields of study with which it engages. The problem with such an objection is that its logic tends to disarm any critical relation to such movements, as I suggest in the rest of this discussion of Lloyd.

4   A Picture of Oscar Wilde?

1. My account of the discourse of luxury here, as well as of the influence of Hellenistic ideals on Wilde below, differs in emphasis in significant respects from Linda Dowling's more detailed *Hellenism and Homosexuality in Victorian Oxford*, which nonetheless suffers, in my view, from its almost exclusive focus on – and, at times, idealisation of – Oxford University. Such are some of the problems attendant on micropolitical analyses.

2. Numerous quotations from symonds in Wilde's *Oxford Notebooks* (1989) have been identified both by the editors and by Horst Schroeder (Schroeder, 1993, 52–3 and 53–4), and Wilde reviewed Symonds's work extensively (Wellens, 1994, 364). The editors of the *Notebooks* also emphasise the Hellenistic perspective of the novel, but suggest in contrast to the interpretation here that Wilde privileges an Hegelian idealism over Paterian materialism.

3. For an account of the influence of psychological and biological science on aesthetics via figures such as Grant Allen and Walter Pater, see Small (1991, 64–88).

Annotated Bibliography

Shakespeare and Society: Critical Studies in Shakespearean Drama. London: Chatto & Windus, 1967

Even stylistically this early text is indebted to Raymond Williams, and this represents Eagleton in pre-Marxist mode. The humanist emphasis of the book focuses on the relationship between individual and society in Shakespeare as a means of reflecting on that relationship today. The final chapter treats this theme, and the role of art, in relation to industrial society, but appears to be tagged on to the discussion of Shakespeare and, ending with Lawrence, hardly appears to bridge the gap between Elizabethan and post-war England. Perhaps that, though, is a reflection of the Oxbridge syllabus at that time.

The Body as Language. London: Sheed & Ward, 1970

This is an important early work. Though concerned principally with Marxism and theology – a product of Eagleton's involvement in the Catholic left – it establishes his interest in both the body and tragedy and pre-empts the later, Lacan-inflected perspective of *Sweet Violence*. The final chapters – including a Leninist revision of the role of the priesthood – may sound faintly absurd, though given the politicised role which the Catholic clergy have played at certain times in certain parts of the world, such an impression perhaps represents a rather parochial perspective.

Exiles and Émigrés: Studies in Modern Literature. London: Chatto & Windus, 1970

Still very much under the humanist socialist influence of Raymond Williams – the introduction even refers to 'the shape of a complete culture' (12) – and committed to a notion of 'great art', these are nonetheless insightful discussions of the established canon of modernist authors, all of whom, though subsumed under the rubric 'English literature', were from outside England. The central thesis is that English culture was so impoverished as to be unable to produce serious literature, but one oversight which may be said to be constitutive of this pre-feminist work is its non-consideration of women writers of the period (Woolf is discussed, but doesn't merit a chapter of her own, grouped as she is straightforwardly in class terms along with Forster, Huxley and Waugh).

Myths of Power: A Marxist Study of the Brontës. London: Macmillan, 1975

Eagleton's first explicitly Marxist study, one which points towards but does not fully realise the analysis he pioneers in *Criticism and Ideology*. I have rehearsed above much of the detail of the argument, though mostly as it relates to *Wuthering Heights*, and it is important to note that the 2nd edition includes an introduction (1988) in which Eagleton subjects to criticism the limitations of the original.

Criticism and Ideology: A Study in Marxist Literary Theory. London: Verso, 1976

I have rehearsed at great length in Chapter 1 the details of the argument in this work. Despite its qualified tendencies to take for granted the category of 'literature', and to assume that criticism itself can rise to the status of a science which transcends history, this remains an important book in its grasp of what a materialist criticism of the 'relatively autonomous' sphere of literature needs to engage with. It would be pointless however to make a start on this without some prior knowledge of Marxist criticism, and the best place to start would be with the book which was conceived as the counterpart to this, *Marxism and Literary Criticism.*

Marxism and Literary Criticism. London: Methuen, 1976

An introduction to some of the problems of attempting to elaborate a marxist literary criticism, this is also a valuable introduction to Marxism itself. It suffers, though, from the limitations of *Criticism and Ideology,* and will probably seem something of a blast from the past to students acquainted with poststructuralism.

Walter Benjamin, or Towards a Revolutionary Criticism. London: Verso, 1981

A book which is impossible to summarise, but which marks a crucial transformation in Eagleton's approach, marking as it does a rejection of his earlier 'scientific' Marxism and a commitment to a more engaged style of criticism which entails a greater awareness of the ideological features of critical practice as well as those of the text. Whereas scientific Marxism took for granted, indeed reproduced, the technocratic ideology of capitalism as well as its characteristic intellectual division of labour, this book began to take seriously the material relations which determine critical practice and exhibits a scepti-cal attitude towards academia – one which many of us feel, but typically tend only to express privately, thus colluding with the ideology of 'professionalisation'. Eagleton initially notes for instance the process by which Benjamin is being assimilated by an academia which has little sympathy for his Marxism. This is not an introduction to Benjamin's thought, but a reflection on key Benjaminian themes which attempts to profit from his example. It is also a major critical engagement with poststructuralist theory.

The Rape of Clarissa. Oxford: Blackwell, 1982

This is Eagleton's most extended engagement with a single text. Beginning with an account of Richardson himself – his class background, ideological perspective (including his relation to the ideology of femininity) and, bound up with both, the complex processes of textual production which culminated in *Clarissa* – the book goes on to pro-vide a detailed reading of the text informed by feminism, deconstruction and psycho-analysis as well as Marxism. Rather than merely bringing those theoretical perspectives to bear on the text, though, it also uses the novel's history to interrogate the theory. In a way characteristic of his later criticism, it treats dialectically the values embodied in Clarissa and Lovelace: if there are aporias in the text, then, they result from historically unresolved ideological conflicts. The book received a hostile response from some feminists. Elaine Showalter claims that it represents another instance of 'the appropriation of the tide of feminist feeling in the interests of patriarchy, the production of a new kind of (critical) hero' (Showalter, 1989, 129), not least in its lack of engagement with previous feminist criticism of *Clarissa* by women and in Eagleton's own apparent lack of self-reflexiveness. It seems to me that she somewhat misses the point of Engleton's response – in many ways a concession of her criticisms – contained in the same volume.

Literary Theory: An Introduction. Oxford: Blackwell, 1983

Literary Theory is most students' first encounter with Eagleton. It does contain valuable syntheses of major trends in literary theory, but it is far from being a disinterested account (and for this reason, some academics are unhappy with its 'slanted' exegeses). The conclusion, with its call for the death of literature, makes the agenda explicit.

The Function of Criticism: From The Spectator *to Poststructuralism.* London and New York: Verso, 1984

This is in many ways Eagleton's most engaging discussion of the evolution of literary criticism and an unaccountably neglected book, more accessible and less idiosyncratic than *Walter Benjamin* and more sophisticated than *Literary Theory* (though it might be read in conjunction with the latter). Taking up Jürgen Habermas's notion of the 'public sphere' – that ideal space in which debate between equals should be free and unconstrained – Eagleton traces the disintegration of that sphere from its partial realisation in the eighteenth century, under pressures exerted by industrialisation, 'democratisation', the professionalisation of criticism and the emergence of 'mass culture'. It ends by noting – and implicitly partially identifying with – the situation of Raymond Williams, from a working class background at Cambridge and with no access to a counter-public sphere such as was available to, say, Brecht, and by reasserting the need for socialist and feminist criticism to engage critically with that parody of the public sphere which is the culture industry.

Against the Grain: Selected Essays. London and New York: Verso, 1986

This collection of important essays, many from *New Left Review,* in many ways also provides an overview of Eagleton's transition from scientific Marxism – evident in the dense account of the ways in which Conrad's *The Secret Agent* produces its ideological determinants – to a more self-reflexive critical exercise (and, indeed, the Preface charts this change). Many of the chapters are therefore more or less polemical forms of engagement, whereas others, including 'Marxism, Structuralism and Poststructuralism' and the often quoted 'Capitalism, Modernism and Postmodernism', provide penetrating analyses of the relations between cultural and theoretical movements. Eagleton himself notes in the final sections 'a gradual abandonment of theoretical seriousness'. And why not?

William Shakespeare. Oxford: Blackwell, 1986a

This short book considers a variety, though not all, of the plays, grouping them under the headings 'Language', 'Desire', 'Law', ' "Nothing" ', 'Value' and 'Nature' rather than genres. In this way, Eagleton foregrounds his engagement with the plays in terms of current theoretical concerns, though the instabilities he discerns in the plays are ultimately related to the instabilities of the period in which they were written. It is possibly the best and most compelling of Eagleton's more philosophical criticism.

The Ideology of the Aesthetic. Oxford and Cambridge, MA: Blackwell, 1990

Many regard this as Eagleton's finest work, the one which explicitly re-establishes his interest in the relations between body, subjectivity and ideology, and explores these in relation to the philosophical category of the aesthetic. It is, as we have seen, a theme which is present in Eagleton's work in his early theological writings, through his critical engagement with Althusser and down to the present. Each of the essays represents a dialectical engagement with a particular thinker and can be read discretely, though it would be best to read them in conjunction with the first and final chapters.

The Significance of Theory. Oxford and Cambridge, MA: Blackwell, 1990a

Includes two lectures given by Eagleton at Bucknell University, an immensely valuable introduction to his work by M. A. R. Habib and an interesting interview with him in which he reflects on both theoretical and sytlistic shifts in his work (and which contains a line which will no doubt serve as his epitaph: 'I've spent several years trying to stop writing books, but it seems to be unavailing' (86)). The first of the lectures is a reflection on 'theory' itself which ends with a familiar claim by Eagleton that its value is that of 'keeping (radical) energies warm' in the absence of any revolutionary political practice. The second is an account of Adorno's aesthetics pretty much the same as that to be found in *The Ideology of the Aesthetic,* cheekily published the same year.

Ideology: An Introduction. London and New York: Verso, 1991

Ideology is one of the trickiest concepts in Marxist thought, and is considered by some non-, ex- or post-Marxists to be incoherent. Partly this is because of its complex history and the various ways in which it has been defined. This book is both a defence of the term and a critical account of the history of it, alert to the implications and problems of certain theorisations of it. Ultimately, Eagleton argues for a non-essentialist understanding, recognising that ideology is best understood in terms of its function rather than in any specific forms it takes since the latter are likely to vary historically. The book is still the most readable introduction to the concept. Some have found the conclusion rather thin, but it is in keeping with Eagleton's shift away from theoreticism after his earlier Althusserianism.

Heathcliff and the Great Hunger. London and New York: Verso, 1995

The first volume in the trilogy of works on Irish culture, *Heathcliff* is a fairly eclectic collection, though there are overlapping themes. The book was controversial partly for reasons considered in some detail in Chapter 3 above. The title chapter is as far from the 'scientific' Eagleton as you can get, and has been taken both far too seriously and not seriously enough: its gambit is self-consciously provocative, but its reflections on the different significance of 'culture' in England and Ireland and on narrative and history are the important matters. 'Homage to Francis Hutcheson' both seeks to rescue Hutcheson from relative obscurity and is an instance of that increasing concern with ethics evident principally in both *The Ideology of the Aesthetic* and *Sweet Violence.* 'Ascendancy and Hegemony', which (re-)introduces Gramsci to Lacan via Edmund Burke, and 'Changing the Question', on the status of Ireland as colony and member of the Union, are the book's most important politico-historical essays.

The Illusions of Postmodernism. Oxford and Malden, MA: Blackwell, 1996

It is arguable that this book relies too heavily on generalisations about postmodernism rather than the kinds of specific engagement we find in, say, *Ideology: An Introduction.* It succeeds, though, in being one of the most lucid critiques of the main philosophical features of postmodernism available, bringing together many of the arguments on this topic Eagleton has rehearsed elsewhere.

Marx and Freedom. London: Phoenix, 1997

One of the best short introductions to Marx, more philosophical in orientation than *Marxism and Literary Criticism,* and clearly written to address postmodern objections to Marxism.

Crazy John and the Bishop and Other Essays on Irish Culture. Cork: Cork University Press, 1998b.

This is arguably Eagleton's most consistently impressive set of essays on Irish culture. Its contents are diverse, including the essay on Yeats and another which attempts to rescue a positive value from Beckett's apparently relentless negativity (implicitly this is directed at Adorno). Other essays focus on neglected Irish figures such as the eighteenth-century poet William Dunkin and the republican socialist Frank Ryan, whom Eagleton upholds as a figure whose criticisms of liberal pluralism, apologists for imperialism and cultural nationalists retain their relevance down to the present. 'The Good Natured Gael' extends Eagleton's concern with the relations between body, subjectivity and ideology through an extended discussion of the eighteenth-century discourse of sentiment and why this discourse was especially prominent in the writings of influential Irish and Scottish writers. The collection as a whole evinces a more rigorous engagement with the detail of Irish culture and history than the earlier *Heathcliff* without sacrificing a sense of larger historical processes.

The Eagleton Reader. Ed. Stephen Regan, Oxford and Malden, MA: Blackwell, 1998

This is a valuable collection of material which fully recognises that Eagleton's important writings are not limited to his book-length work. It includes not only judiciously selected excerpts from his major writings, but lectures, essays and reviews not reproduced in the other collections of his work listed here, providing both a valuable record and an ideal overview of his career.

Scholars and Rebels in Nineteenth-Century Ireland. Oxford and Malden, MA: Blackwell, 1999

To my mind, Eagleton's most disappointing work. Analysing the Irish 'national' intellectuals of the mid-late nineteenth century in terms of Gramsci's distinction between organic and traditional intellectuals – those, that is, who emerge from and represent their own class as distinguished from those who regard themselves as a class apart – it fails to come to any particularly arresting conclusions and tends too much towards summary and anecdote. The whole thing feels more rushed (and forced) than any of Eagleton's other work and its sporadic insights are undeveloped.

The Idea of Culture. Oxford and Malden, MA: Blackwell, 2000

The concept of culture overlaps significantly with that of ideology: it may be ideological in its attribution of value to a set of practices, but may also be invoked sociologically or anthropologically to describe the values and practices of given societies. In postmodern times, any notion of a universal culture tends to be challenged by a valorisation of cultural pluralism. Like 'ideology', then, 'culture' also has a complex history and this book attempts to disentangle the different meanings of the term as well as to argue against both culturalist and naturalist reductionism in explaining human societies. The book pre-empts many of the concerns of *Sweet Violence*. It is also more generous to Raymond Williams than previous work and significantly revises the harsh criticisms of him made in *Criticism and Ideology*.

The Gatekeeper: A Memoir. London: Allen Lane, 2001

Those expecting a confessional biography from Eagleton will be disappointed by this series of reflections on the kinds of figures and doctrines which have dominated his life, all grouped under disparate chapter headings. Despite its humour, it provides some sense of the overlap between theoretical interests and personal experience, and in particular it traces his ambivalence towards most of the institutions with which he has been associated, from the Catholic Church to Oxbridge and the rest of academia. That ambivalence is determined by both his political convictions and class background, and we discover that his theoretical concern with the relations between subjectivity and authority are grounded in lived contradictions. Writing of his tutor and supervisor at Cambridge, Eagleton comments that 'His world was the Law which had brought my father to his ruin, but it was a Law which my father asked me to love' (177).

Figures of Descent: Critical Essays on Fish, Spivak, Zizek and Others. London and New York: Verso, 2003

It is sometimes complained of Eagleton that his academic writing does not engage closely enough with the details of individuals' arguments, but many of his best reviews – and he is an excellent reviewer – are meticulously argued, careful and serious engagements with the work of individual writers. This is a collection of some of his best writings – mostly substantial pieces for the *London Review of Books* which he describes as a kind of remnant of the public sphere – which are by turns witty, polemical and highly informative (there is no finer brief introduction to the Frankfurt School, for instance, than his essay in this collection, and in that respect the collection might act as a partisan dictionary of contemporary thought). Here we are offered the more detailed engagements which inform the larger arguments to be found in his book-length studies.

Sweet Violence: The Idea of the Tragic. Oxford and Malden, MA: Blackwell, 2003a

Represents the culmination of a long-standing interest in tragedy which is bound up with Eagleton's theological concerns, as well as his engagements with Benjamin, Lacan and Raymond Williams, all of whom have written importantly on tragedy. The book traces the development of the idea of the tragic and the ideological values it has upheld through some of its defining features or influential theorists. It ends with an important attempt to retrieve for socialism a certain value to be found in tragedy. There are problems with the argument at times: an unspecified but nonetheless a priori understanding of tragedy is occasionally invoked to highlight the ideological or inadequate nature of certain versions of it (a problem shared too by his book on ideology itself), but the book stands alongside *The Ideology of the Aesthetic* as one of his most important. One doesn't need to be a Christian to find the final chapter compelling.

References

Adorno, Theodor, and Max Horkheimer. *Dialectic of Enlightenment.* Trans. John Cumming. London and New York: Verso, 1976.

Ahmad, Aijaz. *In Theory: Classes, Nations, Literatures.* London: Verso, 1992.

Alderson, David. *Mansex Fine: Religion, Manliness and Imperialism in Nineteenth Century British Culture.* Manchester and New York: Manchester University Press, 1998.

Althusser, Louis. *Essays on Ideology.* London and New York: Verso, 1984.

Anderson, Perry. *Considerations on Western Marxism.* London and New York: Verso, 1979.

——. *English Questions.* London and New York: Verso, 1992.

Armstrong, Isobel. *Radical Aesthetic.* Oxford: Blackwell, 2000.

Arnold, Matthew. *Complete Prose Works, vol. 5: Culture and Anarchy.* Ed. R. H. Super. Ann Arbor: University of Michigan Press, 1965.

Attridge, Derek. 'Introduction: Derrida and the Questioning of Literature'. Jacques Derrida. *Acts of Literature.* New York and London: Routledge, 1992.

Balibar, Etienne and Pierre Macherey. 'On Literature as an Ideological Form,' *Oxford Literary Review,* 3:1, 1978, 4–12.

Bartolovich, Crystal and Neil Lazarus (eds). *Marxism, Modernity and Postcolonial Studies.* Cambridge: Cambridge University Press, 2002.

Baudrillard, Jean. 'The Precessions of the Simulacra'. Trans. Paul Foss, Paul Patton and Philip Bleitchman. *Simulations.* New York: Semiotext(e), 1983.

Belsey, Catherine. *Critical Practice.* London: Methuen, 1980.

Benjamin, Walter. *Illuminations.* Trans. Harry Zohn. London: Fontana, 1973.

Bennett, Tony. *Formalism and Marxism.* London: Methuen, 1979.

Bennington, Geoffrey. 'Demanding History'. Eds Derek Attridge, Geoffrey Bennington and Robert Young. *Post-structuralism and the Question of History.* Cambridge: Cambridge University Press, 1987.

——. 'Inter'. Eds Martin McQuillan, Graeme MacDonald, Robin Purves and Stephen Thomson. *Post – Theory: New Directions in Criticism.* Edinburgh: Edinburgh University Press, 1999, 103–19.

—— and Jacques Derrida. *Jacques Derrida.* Trans. Geoffrey Bennington. Chicago: University of Chicago Press, 1993.

Bowie, Malcolm. *Lacan.* London: Fontana, 1991.

Bowlby, Rachel. *Shopping with Freud.* London and New York: Routledge, 1993.

Bradshaw, Brendan. 'Nationalism and Historical Scholarship in Modern Ireland'. Ed. Ciaran Brady. *Interpreting Irish History: The Debate on Irish Historical Revisionism. 1938–94.* Dublin: Irish Academic Press, 1994, 191–216.

Brady, Ciaran. *Interpreting Irish History: The Debate on Irish Historical Revisionism, 1938–94.* Dublin: Irish Academic Press, 1994.

Brennan, Timothy. *At Home in the World: Cosmopolitanism Now*. Cambridge, MA and London: Harvard University Press, 1997.

——. 'Review of Aijaz Ahmad'. *In Theory: Classes, Nations, Literatures* in *Textual Practice*, 8:2, 1994, 127–35.

Brontë, Emily. *Wuthering Heights*. Oxford: Oxford University Press, 1995.

Burke, Edmund. *Reflections on the Revolution in France*. Harmondsworth: Penguin, 1986.

Butler, Judith. *Gender Trouble: Feminism and the Subversion of Identity*. London and New York: Routledge, 1990.

——. Letter, *London Review of Books*, 1 July 1999, 4.

Callinicos, Alex. *Against Postmodernism: A Marxist Critique*. Cambridge: Polity, 1989.

Cecil, David. *Early Victorian Novelists: Essays in Revaluation*. 2nd edition. London: Hutchinson, 1967.

Coleridge, Samuel Taylor, *On the Constitution of the Church and State. Works, Volume 10*. Ed. John Colmer. Princeton: Princeton University Press, 1976.

Collins, Wilkie. *The Woman in White*. Oxford: Oxford University Press, 1980.

Connor, Steven. *Postmodernist Culture: An Introduction to Theories of the Contemporary*. Oxford: Blackwell, 1989.

——. 'The Poetry of the Meantime: Terry Eagleton and the Politics of Style'. *The Year's Work in Critical and Cultural Theory*, 1994, 243–64.

Curtis, L. P. *Anglo-Saxons and Celts: A Study of Anti-Irish Prejudice in Victorian England*. Bridgeport: University of Bridgeport, 1968.

Dale, Peter Allen. 'Beyond Humanism: J. A. Symonds and the Replotting of the Renaissance'. *CLIO*, 17:2, 1988, 109–37.

Davidoff, Leonore and Catherine Hall. *Family Fortunes: Men and Women of the English Middle Class, 1780–1850*. London: Hutchinson, 1987.

Deane, Seamus. 'Wherever Green is Read'. Ed. Ciaran Brady. *Interpreting Irish History: The Debate on Irish Historical Revisionism, 1938–94*. Dublin: Irish Academic Press, 1994, 234–45.

Debord, Guy. *The Society of the Spectacle*. Trans. Donald Nicholson-Smith. New York: Zone Books, 1995.

Derrida, Jacques. *Positions*. Trans. Alan Bass. Chicago: University of Chicago Press, 1981.

——. *Acts of Literature*. Ed. Derek Attridge. New York and London: Routledge, 1992.

——. *Specters of Marx*. London and New York: Routledge, 1994.

Dews, Peter. *Logics of Disintegration: Poststructuralist Thought and the Claims of Critical Theory*. London and New York: Verso, 1987.

Dickens, Charles. *Barnaby Rudge*. Harmondsworth: Penguin, 1986.

Dowling, Linda. *Hellenism and Homosexuality in Victorian Oxford*. Ithaca and London: Cornell University Press, 1994.

Eagleton, Terry. *The New Left Church: Studies in Literature, Politics and Theology*. London and Melbourne: Sheed and Ward, 1966.

——. *Saints and Scholars*. London and New York: Verso, 1987.

——. *Nationalism: Irony and Commitment*. Derry: Field Day, 1988.

——. 'The Flight to the Real'. Eds Sally Ledger and Scott McCracken. *Cultural Politics at the Fin de Siècle*. Cambridge: Cambridge University Press, 1995a, 11–21.

——. 'Ireland's Obdurate Nationalisms', *New Left Review*, 213, 1995b, 130–6.

——. *Saint Oscar and Other Plays*. Oxford and Cambridge, MA: Blackwell, 1997a.

——. 'Postcolonialism: The Case of Ireland'. Ed. David Bennett. *Multicultural States: Rethinking Difference and Identity*. London and New York: Routledge, 1998a, 123–34.

Easthope, Antony. *British Post-Structuralism since 1968.* London and New York: Routledge, 1988.

Ellmann, Richard. *Oscar Wilde.* London: Hamish Hamilton, 1987.

Evans, David T. *Sexual Citizenship: The Material Construction of Sexualities.* London and New York: Routledge, 1993.

Fine, Ben. *Marx's Capital,* 3rd edition. Basingstoke: Macmillan, 1989.

Foster, R. F. *Modern Ireland.* London: Allen Lane, 1988.

——. *Paddy and Mr Punch: Connections in Irish and English History,* London: Allen Lane, 1993.

——. *The Irish Story: Telling Tales and Making It Up in Ireland.* Harmondsworth: Allen Lane, 2001.

Foucault, Michel. *The History of Sexuality,* vol. 1. Trans. Robert Hurley. Harmondsworth: Penguin, 1981a.

——. 'The Order of Discourse'. Ed. Robert Young. *Untying the Text: A Poststructuralist Reader.* London and New York: Routledge & Kegan Paul, 1981b, 48–78.

Freud, Sigmund. *Civilisation and Its Discontents* (1930). *Civilisation, Religion and Society.* Harmondsworth: Penguin, 1991.

Fukuyama, Francis. *The End of History and the Last Man.* Harmondsworth: Penguin, 1992.

Geras, Norman. 'Post-Marxism?', *New Left Review,* 163, 1987, 40–82.

Gilley, Sheridan. 'English Attitudes to the Irish in England, 1780–1900'. *Immigrants and Minorities in British Society.* Ed. Colin Holmes. London: Allen & Unwin, 1978.

Graham, Colin. *Deconstructing Ireland: Identity, Theory, Culture.* Edinburgh: Edinburgh University Press, 2001.

Guy, Josephine and Ian Small. *Oscar Wilde's Profession: Writing and the Culture Industry in the Late Nineteenth Century.* Oxford: Oxford University Press, 2000.

Hall, Catherine and Leonore Davidoff. *Family Fortunes: Men and Women of the English Middle Class, 1780–1850.* London: Hutchinson, 1987.

Harvey, David. *The Condition of Postmodernity.* Oxford: Blackwell, 1990.

——. *The Limits to Capital,* 2nd edition. London and New York: Verso, 1999.

Haslett, Moyra, *Marxist Literary and Cultural Theories.* Houndmills: Macmillan, 2000.

Hilton, Boyd. *The Age of Atonement: The Influence of Evangelicalism on Social and Economic Thought, 1785–1865.* Oxford: Clarendon Press, 1988.

Holland, Merlin. 'Biography and the Art of Lying'. *The Cambridge Companion to Oscar Wilde.* Ed. Peter Raby. Cambridge: Cambridge University Press, 1997, 3–17.

Hollinghurst, Alan. *The Swimming Pool Library.* London: Chatto & Windus, 1988.

Howe, Stephen. *Ireland and Empire.* Oxford: Oxford University Press, 2000.

Jameson, Fredric. *Postmodernism, or, the Cultural Logic of Late Capitalism.* London and New York: Verso, 1991.

Jardine, Alice and Paul Smith (eds) *Men in Feminism.* London and New York: Routledge, 1989.

Kettle, Arnold. *An Introduction to the English Novel, vol. 1.* 2nd edition. London: Hutchinson, 1967.

Kiberd, Declan. 'Oscar Wilde: the Resurgence of Lying'. *The Cambridge Companion to Oscar Wilde.* Ed. Peter Raby. Cambridge: Cambridge University Press, 1997, 276–94.

Lacan, Jacques. *Ecrits: A Selection.* London: Routledge, 2001.

——. *The Ethics of Psychoanalysis, 1959–1960: The Seminars of Jacques Lacan*. Ed. Jacques-Alain Miller. Trans. Dennis Porter. London: Routledge, 1992.

Laclau, Ernesto and Chantal Mouffe. *Hegemony and Socialist Strategy: Towards a Radical Democratic Politics*. London: Verso, 1985.

Lazarus, Neil. 'Postcolonialism and the Dilemma of Nationalism: Aijaz Ahmad's Critique of Third-Worldism'. *Diaspora*, 9:3, 1993, 373–400.

——. *Nationalism and Cultural Practice in the Postcolonial World*. Cambridge: Cambridge University Press, 1999.

——. 'The Fetish of "the West" in Postcolonial Theory'. *Marxism, Modernity and Postcolonial Studies*. Eds Bartolovich and Lazarus. Cambridge: Cambridge University Press, 2002, 43–64.

Ledger, Sally and Scott McCracken (eds). *Cultural Politics at the* Fin de Siècle. Cambridge: Cambridge University Press, 1995.

Lentricchia, Frank. *After the New Criticism*. London: Methuen, 1983.

Lloyd, David. *Anomalous States: Irish Writing and the Postcolonial Moment*. Dublin: Lilliput, 1993.

——. Review of *Heathcliff and the Great Hunger Bullán*, 3:1, 1997, 87–92.

——. *Ireland After History*. Cork: Cork University Press, 1999.

—— and Lisa Lowe (eds) *The Politics of Culture in the Shadow of Capital*. Durham, N.C: Duke University Press, 1997.

Longley, Edna. *The Living Stream: Literature and Revisionism in Ireland*. Newcastle upon Tyne: Bloodaxe, 1994.

Lovell, Terry, 'Jane Austen and the Gentry: A Study in Literature and Ideology. *The Sociology of Literature: Applied Studies*. Ed. Diana Laurenson. Keele: Sociological Monograph Review, 1978, 15–35.

Lukács, George. *History and Class Consciousness: Studies in Marxist Dialectics*. London: Merlin, 1971.

Lyotard, Jean-Francois. *The Postmodern Condition: A Report on Knowledge*. Trans. Geoff Bennington and Brian Massumi. Manchester: Manchester University Press, 1984.

Macherey, Pierre. *A Theory of Literary Production*. Trans. Geoff Wall. London and New York: Routledge, 1989.

Mahaffey, Vicki, *States of Desire: Wilde, Yeats, Joyce and the Irish Experiment*. Oxford: Oxford University Press, 1998.

Maley, Willy. 'Brother Tel: The Politics of Eagletonism'. *The Year's Work in Critical and Cultural Theory*. 1994, 273–87.

Marx, Karl. *Surveys From Exile*. Harmondsworth: Penguin/New Left Review, 1973.

——. *Early Writings*. Harmondsworth: Penguin/New Left Review, 1975.

——. *Capital*, vol. 1. Trans Ben Fowkes. Harmondsworth: Penguin/New Left Review, 1976.

——. *Selected Writings*. Ed. David McLellan. Oxford: Oxford University Press, 1977.

——. *Capital*, vols 2 and 3. Trans. David Fernbach. Harmondsworth: Penguin/New Left Review, 1978/1981.

McQuillan, Martin. 'Irish Eagleton: Of Ontological Imperialism and Colonial Mimicry'. *Irish Studies Review*, 10:1, 2002, 29–38.

—— and Graeme MacDonald, Robin Purves and Steven Thomson, eds. *Post-Theory: New Directions in Criticism*. Edinburgh: Edinburgh University Press, 1999.

Merleau-Ponty, Maurice. *Phenomenology of Perception*. Trans. Colin Smith. London: Routledge & Kegan Paul, 1962.

Montag, Warren. *Louis Althusser*. Houndmills: Palgrave Macmillan, 2003.

Morton, Donald. 'Pataphysics of the Closet: Queer Theory as the Art of Imaginary Solutions for Unimaginary Problems'. *Transformations*, 2, 2001, 1–70.

Mulhern, Francis. *The Future Lasts a Long Time: Essays in Cultural Politics*. Cork: Cork University Press, 1998.

Parry, Benita. 'A Critique Mishandled'. *Social Text*, 35, 1993, 121–33.

——. 'Liberation Theory: Variations on Themes of Marxism and Modernity'. *Marxism, Modernity and Postcolonial Studies*. Eds Crystal Bartolovich and Neil Lazarus. Cambridge: Cambridge University Press, 2002, 125–49.

Pocock, J. G. A. *The Machiavellian Moment: Florentine Political Thought and the Atlantic Republican Tradition*. Princeton: Princeton University Press, 1975.

——. *Virtue, Commerce and History*. Cambridge: Cambridge University Press, 1985.

Raby, Peter (ed.). *Cambridge Companion to Oscar Wilde*. Cambridge: Cambridge University Press, 1997.

Regan, Stephen. 'W. B. Yeats and Irish Cultural Politics in the 1890s'. Eds Sally Ledger and Scott McCracken. *Cultural Politics at the Find de Siècle*. Cambridge: Cambridge University Press, 1995, 66–84.

Repton, Humphrey. 'A Letter to Uvedale Price' (1795). *The Picturesque: Literary Sources and Documents. Vol. II: Debating the Theory and Practice of the Picturesque*. Ed. Malcolm Andrews. Mountfield: Helm, 1994, 199–204.

Ryan, Michael. *Marxism and Deconstruction: A Critical Articulation*. Baltimore: Johns Hopkins University Press, 1984.

Said, Edward. *Orientalism*. London: Routledge and Kegan Paul, 1978.

——. *Culture and Empire*. London: Chatto & Windus, 1993.

Saville, John. *1848: The British State and the Chartist Movement*. Cambridge: Cambridge University Press, 1987.

Schroeder, Horst. 'A Graeco-French Collocation in *The Critic as Artist*' and 'Wilde's Commonplace Book and Symonds's *Studies of the Greek Poets*' in *Notes and Queries*, 238, 1993, 52–4.

Shakespeare, William. *The Merchant of Venice*. Ed. John Russell Brown. London: Methuen, 2001.

Showalter, Elaine. 'Critical Cross-Dressing; Male Feminists and the Woman of the Year'. Eds Alice Jardine and Paul Smith. *Men in Feminism*. London and New York: Routledge, 1989.

Sinfield, Alan. *Literature, Politics and Culture in Postwar Britain*. Oxford: Blackwell, 1989.

——. *The Wilde Century: Effeminacy, Oscar Wilde and the Queer Moment*. London: Cassell, 1994.

Small, Ian. *Conditions for Criticism: Authority, Knowledge and Literature in the Late Nineteenth Century*. Oxford: Clarendon Press, 1991.

Sprinker, Michael. 'The National Question: Said, Ahmad, Jameson'. *Public Culture*, 6:1, 1993, 3–29.

Steppan, Nancy. *The Idea of Race in Science: Great Britain, 1800–1960*. London: Macmillan, 1982.

Symonds, John Addington. *The Memoirs of John Addington Symonds*. Ed. Phyllis Grosskurth, London: Hutchinson, 1984.

Timpanaro, Sebastiano. *On Materialism* (1970). Trans. Lawrence Garner. London: New Left Books, 1975.

Unsigned Review of *Wuthering Heights. Britannia* [15 January, 1848]. *The Brontës: Critical Heritage.* Ed. Miriam Allott. London and Boston: Routledge & Kegan Paul, 1974, 223–6.

Wade, Geoff. 'Changes: A Critical Survey of Terry Eagleton's Work'. The Year's Work in Critical and Cultural Theory, 1994, 219–29.

Walsh, Nick Paton. 'Hell on Earth', *The Guardian: G2*, 18/4/03, 4–5.

Watt, Ian. *The Rise of the Novel.* London: Chatto & Windus, 1957.

Wellens, Oskar. 'A Hitherto Unnoticed Review by Wilde'. *Notes and Queries*, 239, 1994, 364.

Wilde, Oscar. *The Letters of Oscar Wilde.* Ed. Rupert Hart Davis. London: Rupert Hart Davis, 1962.

——. 'The Critic as Artist'. *The Artist as Critic.* Ed. Richard Ellmann. London: W. H. Allen, 1970.

——. *The Picture of Dorian Gray.* Oxford: Oxford University Press, 1981.

——. *Oscar Wilde's Oxford Notebooks.* Ed. Philip E. Smith II and Michael S. Helfand. Oxford and New York: Oxford University Press, 1989.

Williams, Raymond. *Culture and Society, 1780–1950.* London: Chatto & Windus, 1958.

——. *The English Novel From Dickens to Lawrence.* London: Chatto & Windus, 1970.

——. 'Base and Superstructure in Marxist Cultural Theory'. *Problems in Materialism and Culture.* London and New York: Verso, 1980, 31–49.

Wolfreys, Julian. *Deconstruction·Derrida.* Houndmills: Macmillan, 1998.

Wood, Ellen Meiksins. *The Pristine Culture of Capitalism: An Historical Essay on Old Regimes and Modern States.* London and New York: Verso, 1991.

——. *Empire of Capital.* London and New York: Verso, 2003.

Yeats, W. B. *Yeats's Poems.* Ed. A. Norman Jeffares. London: Papermac, 1989.

——. *Autobiographies: Memories and Reflections.* London: Bracken Books, 1995.

Young, Robert J. C. *Colonial Desire: Hybridity in Theory, Culture and Race.* London and New York: Routledge, 1995.

——. *Torn Halves: Political Conflict in Literary and Cultural Theory.* Manchester and New York: Manchester University Press, 1996.

Index